The Mediators

Deborah M. Kolb

The MIT Press
Cambridge, Massachusetts
London, England

This book was set in Melior
by The MIT Press Computergraphics Department
and printed and bound by Halliday Lithograph
in the United States of America.

Library of Congress Cataloging in Publication Data

Kolb, Deborah M.
 The mediators.

 (MIT Press series on organization studies; 6)
 Bibliography: p.
 Includes index.
 1. Mediation and conciliation, Industrial—United States. I. Title. II. Series.
HD5504.A3K64 1983   331.89′142′0973   83–11395
ISBN 0–262–11088–1

The Mediators

MIT Press Series on Organization Studies
John Van Maanen, general editor

1. *Competition and Control at Work: A New Industrial Sociology*, Stephen Hill, 1982

2. *Strategies for Change: The Future of French Society*, Michel Crozier, translated by William R. Beer, 1982

3. *Control in the Police Organization*, edited by Maurice Punch, 1983

4. *Disorganized Crime: The Economics of the Visible Hand*, by Peter Reuter, 1983

5. *Industrial Democracy at Sea*, edited by Robert Schrank, 1983

6. *The Mediators*, Deborah M. Kolb, 1983

For Jonathan, Sam, and Elizabeth

Contents

Preface   ix

**1
The Second-Oldest Profession**   1

**2
Roles Mediators Play: Orchestrators and Dealmakers**   23

**3
Arranging the Mediation Forum: Intervention and Negotiating
Patterns**   46

**4
Mediator Strategies: Building and Narrowing**   72

**5
Mediators and Spokesmen: Complementary Strategic
Roles**   113

**6
Mistakes and the Evaluation of Strategic Approaches**   134

**7
Conclusions: The Roots of Orchestrating and Dealmaking and
Their Implications**   150

Appendix: Methodology   175
Notes   197
Bibliography   217
Index   225

Preface

Nine years ago a friend of mine casually asked me whether I cared to accompany him on a mediation case. Curious, and with no other plans for the evening, I went along. This was my first experience with a process that has occupied and intrigued me ever since. My expectations of what would occur were meager. There were two groups, the local school committee and the teachers, who shouted accusations at each other whenever they got the chance. Each group had a room of its own, the teachers in the library and the school committee in the principal's office. From time to time the two groups would meet in the cafeteria to drink sodas and to do battle with each other. The mediator kept a loose-leaf notebook in which each of the fifty or so issues was recorded, altered, or deleted as time wore on. With me in tow, the mediator shuttled between the library and the principal's office, occasionally meeting in the hall with an attorney. After two sessions of talking, walking, and deleting, it ended one May morning at 4:00 A.M., when the parties seemed to stop their shouting long enough to shake hands in agreement. This observer was astounded. I had no idea that a settlement was even possible, no less imminent, nor could I begin to reconstruct how all the talking and walking translated into a settlement. Now I think I understand.

The major contributors to the process by which I came to understand were a group of mediators who allowed me to watch them at their work. With patience and good humor, they explained to me what was patently obvious to them. I know they have a basic distrust of generalizations made about their work and could undoubtedly describe their cases with all their intricacies and nuances far better than I, if only they cared to. But they are people of deeds, not words. I only hope that my words are fair to their deeds.

For the words themselves, I am indebted to John Van Maanen and Lotte Bailyn, first as thesis advisers and then as colleagues. This book bears their imprint even more than they realize. Without Abraham Siegel and Charles Myers, who helped arrange the introductions, this study would have been impossible. Some of my teachers and colleagues made special contributions to the substantive development of this work, while others enhanced the milieu in which it was produced. I am grateful to Edgar Schein, Michael Piore, Thomas Kochan, Ralph Katz, Robert McKersie, Gideon Kunda, Priscilla Glidden, Paul McKinnon, Steven Barley, and Jeanne Lindholm. Arnold Zack merits a special note of mention. How could he have known that a casual invitation would lead to this book?

Funds from the President's Office at Simmons College and the able typing of Marcia Stanzcyk, Pam Baud, and Barbara Noe brought the manuscript into final form.

Nine years have elapsed since I observed that first mediation. Through it all—graduate school, cases that went all night, and the ups and downs of writing—my husband, Jonathan, was there to support me, to give me the benefits of his analytic insights, his incisive editorial pen, and the delight of his humor and wit. My children, Sam and Elizabeth, although unclear about what I studied, gave me plenty of opportunity to practice what mediation skills I possess. I dedicate this book to all of them.

The Mediators

1

The Second-Oldest Profession

Brutus.
We'll hear no more.
Pursue him to his house and pluck him thence,
Lest his infection, being of catching nature,
Spread further.

Menenius.
One word more, one word.
This tiger-footed rage, when it shall find
The harm of unscanned swiftness, will too late
Tie leaden pounds to's heels. Proceed by process,
Lest parties, as he is beloved, break out
And sack great Rome with Romans.

Sicinius.
Noble Menenius,
Be Thou then as the people's officer.
Masters, lay down your weapons.

Coriolanus (act 3, scene 1, lines 315–324, 328–330)

Mediation may not be the oldest profession, but it surely must be close. As long as people have had disputes with each other, mediators have emerged to counsel the use of reason over arms. Shakespeare cast Menenius in such a role to seek a compromise between the tribunals of Rome and Coriolanus, the general and would-be consul. The failure of a similar effort later in the play presaged the tragedy of Coriolanus and the sacking of Rome by the Volscians.

In other times and places, distinguished persons have undertaken to mediate conflicts between states and nations. Through mediation Pope Leo the Great forestalled Attila's invasion of Italy and Leo XIII resolved the Carolina Islands land dispute between Germany and Spain. Secular leaders have also established reputations for themselves as mediators: Bismarck in the creation of the New German Empire, Theodore Roosevelt in the formulation of the peace accords that ended the 1905 war between Japan and Russia, and the modern efforts of Henry Kissinger, Jimmy Carter, and Philip Habib to contain the persistent conflagrations in the Middle East.

Indeed, an enduring feature of social organization seems to be the institution of mediation. The *mangi-ugual* of Kalinga, the Ifugoa *monkalun*, the Nuer leopard-skin chief, and the *kong-chhing* in Singapore act as mediators in the settlement of disputes that arise over property, death, and dowries. These mediators derive their authority and prestige from their social position, wealth, or demonstrated prowess. Their conciliatory efforts in resolving particular disputes serve to reinforce the norms and structure of the local society that unresolved conflict threatens to disrupt.[1]

Mediation has also been a formal part of the institutional framework of labor relations from the time that national unions came to prominence in the late nineteenth century. At that time several states enacted legislation that provided for the appointment of ad hoc tribunals whose members would traverse the state offering their "good services" to parties engaged in strikes or other job actions. The Erdman Act of 1898 marked the first time that the federal government recognized mediation as a distinct mode of dealing with industrial disputes. Since that time the provision of mediation services by the government has been a cornerstone of U.S. public policy on collective bargaining.

In the United States the pluralistic interests of labor and management are for the most part channeled into the convention of localized collective bargaining. At regularly scheduled intervals local representatives of labor and management convene in order to negotiate the contractual terms and conditions of a collective-bargaining agreement that will govern their working relationship for a specified period of time. Mediation is generally carried out in this context. If the parties are unable to reach a bilateral accommodation of their contractual interests, they are required by law to involve a mediator in their deliberations, although they are not bound to reach a settlement in his[2] presence. Presumably neutral with regard to the interests of labor and management, mediators seek, without recourse to formal sanctions, to facilitate the settlement of labor contracts short of strikes or other overt work actions.

In short, mediation is a policy instrument intended to further the cause of industrial peace, a goal to which it undoubtedly contributes. But like the efforts of Menenius, the *mangi-ugual*, and the leopard-skin chief, those of labor mediators serve as well to channel the form of disputes, to restrain the power of competing interests, and so to preserve the institutional fabric of the system. These efforts are therefore worthy of close scrutiny.

The Art and Science of Mediation

A certain aura of mystery shrouds the practice of labor mediation. Practitioners claim that mediation is an art with as many theories, philosophies, and approaches as there are mediators. Through their choice of metaphors, mediators emphasize particular features of their work: the intuitive over the systematic and the unexpected over the planned. To their way of thinking, the process of mediation is shaped simultaneously by the unique characteristics of individual disputes and the special skills and insights of the mediators handling these cases.[3] Arthur Meyer, a noted practitioner, captures the essence of this view: "The task of the mediator is not an easy one. The sea that he sails is only roughly charted and its changing contours are not clearly discernible. Worse still, he has no science of navigation, no fund inherited from the experience of others. He is a solitary artist recognizing, at most, a few guiding stars and depending on his personal powers of divination" (1960, p. 160).

The bases for this claim of artistry are many. Foremost among them is the ever changing circumstances of the disputes mediators attempt to resolve. Each contract dispute that comes to mediation has something of its own unique character, stemming from such factors as the personalities and backgrounds of the participants, the nature of the issues over which they disagree, and the political and economic backgrounds of the negotiators. This open-ended potential for diversity, mediators argue, means that, beyond the most rudimentary procedural principles, no book of rules can prepare the mediator. The artistry of mediation stems, then, from the mediator's ability to analyze and then smoothly to handle unique circumstances as they arise.

The way in which mediation is conducted contributes additionally to the practitioners' belief that mediation is an art practiced on an individual basis. Mediators receive minimal, if any, formal schooling in the process of mediation. Then, for the most part, they work by themselves as third parties in disputes and have few opportunities to observe the work of others. They learn and refine their techniques through subjective analyses of their own performances in real cases. Given the uniqueness of the case situations that they must analyze and remedy, it is evident that no two mediators can compare their approaches on the basis of the same set of facts. Consequently, the development of each mediator's approach or style is always shaped by experiences that are highly personalized and differ from those of his colleagues.

From the perspective of the practitioner, mediation does look like an art. But the claim to artistry may serve other purposes as well. It serves to close the profession to outsiders, even though the knowledge and skills required for admission are hardly more than common sense (Hughes, 1958; Wilensky, 1964). Further, by labeling their work as art practiced on an individual basis and with ever changing contours, mediators insulate themselves from public scrutiny and absolve themselves of responsibility for policy outcomes (Douglas, 1962). One side effect of this insulation from public scrutiny has been a persistent sense that understanding of mediation as a social process has remained rudimentary.

It is the perception of many that the scientific study of mediation lags behind its use. Yet mediation is hardly a field of study that has been ignored by the research community. Social scientists from an assortment of disciplines have surveyed, interviewed, and observed mediators.[4] Mediator behavior has been the subject of theory, models, and laboratory simulations.[5] Why then does this perception persist? In part, the answer lies in the ways that science has been applied to the art of mediation.

The scientific study of mediation assumes a set of characteristics at odds with the artistic claims of practitioners. Despite their different theoretical and methodological approaches, all social scientists seek to develop a set of principles that will descriptively or prescriptively apply to all mediators. But when only the character of the dispute context is permitted to vary,[6] a significant component of the mediators' claim to be practicing an art is ignored. For if mediators learn on their own and develop unique approaches, then it is necessary to investigate their varied modes of practice within the case settings in order to discover if and why mediators differ in (1) what they intend and (2) how they behave. To accomplish this requires a theoretical and methodological approach that captures both the mediator's perspective (intent) and a more objective analysis of his performance (behavior). This application of science may be more suitable to the study of the practical dimensions of the mediation art.

Interpretive Theory and the Study of Mediation

Interpretive theory is more a lens through which understanding human activities may be acquired by informed observation than it is a tightly specified causal model of behavior.[7] Central to the theory is a view of individuals as self-conscious, creative, and active. From this view arises a particular conception of social interaction. People enter social situations with certain goals in mind and develop lines of action in response to these situations based on the meanings they apply to them. In other words, action, meaning, and purpose are intertwined. Based on this conception of individual activity comes a view of the social world as the ongoing creation of people interacting with each other in particular social situations. Thus the theory assumes that the society has no inherent structure apart from what people give it.[8]

When translated to mediation, interpretive theory highlights the mediator as the creative force in the mediation process. Part of a social network composed of members of bargaining committees and their spokesmen, the mediator interacts in case contexts with these people in varied ways. The contribution of interpretive theory is that it emphasizes the considerable discretion the mediator has in determining how he will interact with these people and arrange the major case elements.[9] The differences in the pratical ways that mediators choose to conduct their cases vis-à-vis the other actors is captured in the concept of role.[10] The mediator's role is based on his analysis of the case as well as his own definition of personal aims and objectives. The specifics of a role may be observed in the actions the mediator takes in the fulfillment of these ends. For the mediator the major areas of practical concern are the disputing parties and their issues, assessments that once arrived at enable him to gauge what the parties anticipate and require in the way of assistance.[11] The specific actions taken by the mediator will be based on these assessments and indeed cannot be understood without attending to them.

This interpretive view of mediation is one that is perfectly consistent with the practitioners' public claims about the art of mediation. But there is a difference. Although it emphasizes what is artful, it leaves open the possibility, again based on the theory, that there is pattern to the art. This is not surprising. The more a mediator mediates cases, the more likely it is that he will develop some consistency in practice that will render his work more structured and hence more manageable. Thus it may be that what mediators claim to be doing in the way of assessment and interpretation may be creating, or to use Weick's (1979) term, "enacting," the very reality to which, they believe, they are reacting. That is to say that if a mediator enacts a case, it means simply that he imposes an order on the dynamics of the case rather than discovers one.[12]

Upon what bases will enactment occur? They stem from social "perspectives" that mediators develop from practice. According to Becker et al. (1961), perspective is a "coordinated set of ideas a person uses in dealing with some problematic situation and refers to a person's ordinary way of thinking and feeling about acting in such a situation" (p. 35). Not all contingencies will be covered by perspective, nor will all situations be experienced in precisely the same way. But when persistent problems are encountered, and when a group of mediators faced with similar situations has occasion to interact with reference to these situations, shared perspectives that transcend the individual mediator may be observed. These shared perspectives may serve to distinguish different varieties of mediation practice.

With these concepts in mind, the claims of practitioners about their work can be reexamined. When a perspective underlies the enactment of a role, the causal connections between analysis and action become problematic. For if one accepts the practitioner's claim to art, then analysis precedes and indeed drives strategic choices. Role, then, as a summary of these behaviors would be emergent:

Analysis $\longrightarrow$ Strategy $\longrightarrow$ Role

The principle of enactment suggests, however, that the causal relation may be reversed, that a particular role perspective guides various strategic choices in a more or less routine way. In this view, analysis is more retrospective than prospective and may be seen more as an attempt to justify strategy rather than to guide it:[13]

Role $\longrightarrow$ Strategy $\longrightarrow$ Analysis

Such a causal relation challenges some cherished mediator beliefs about what it is they do and how they do it. For it suggests that there is more science to mediation than they would have us believe. But it is not formal science in the sense that it can be reduced to general laws. Rather, it is scientific in the social and practical every-day sense and traceable to the intentional efforts of the mediators (Garfinkel, 1967).

The purpose of this book is to assess which of these conceptions— the artistic or the enacted—best describes what occurs in the daily practice of mediation. The evidence is drawn from a close, com- parative study of mediators who work for two government agencies. These agencies differ in their histories, structures, the clientele they serve, and the training and background of the mediators who work there. These contextual characteristics are the background features against which the practice of mediation takes place.

Sites of Study

Labor mediation in the United States is practiced by a wide variety of individuals, among them lawyers, professors, clergy, and arbi- trators. Although theoretically anybody can call himself a mediator and offer his services to labor and management, the full-time prac- tice of mediation is primarily the province of governmental agencies that make it their major function.[14] The Federal Mediation and Conciliation Service (FMCS), an independent federal agency, has jurisdiction over disputes in industries engaged in interstate com- merce, private nonprofit health facilities, and agencies of the federal government. State agencies or boards of conciliation are empowered in some twenty-five states to provide mediation services to state, county, and municipal parties within the jursidiction of the re- spective states and to small companies not covered by FMCS. This study was conducted in a field office of FMCS and a state board of conciliation.

The Federal Mediation and Conciliation Service

The FMCS traces its roots to the U.S. Conciliation Service, which was established in 1913 under the enabling legislation for the De- partment of Labor. One provision of the act follows: "The Secretary of Labor shall have the power to act as mediator and to appoint commissioners of conciliation in labor disputes whenever in his judgment the interests of industrial peace may require it to be done" (37 Stat. 738 #8.29, USCA #51). In selective instances, mediation services were proffered by staff members of the Department of Labor, but it was not until 1917 that the U.S. Conciliation Service was formally organized with a staff of thirteen and a budget of $50,000. Although the service had no statutory authority, during World Wars I and II it came to play a major role along with the War Labor Boards in resolving industrial disputes. During World War II, the service established regional offices in chief industrial centers and employed 250 mediators at the peak of the war (Shaw, 1969).

When Congress passed the Taft-Hartley Amendments to the National Labor Relations Act in 1947, it created the FMCS as an independent agency responsible to the president. The existing administration and the field structure of the agency remained unaltered, but the act established, for the first time, the role of federally sponsored mediation in collective bargaining: "The settlement of issues between employees and employers through collective bargaining may be advanced by making available full and adequate governmental facilities for conciliation, mediation and voluntary arbitration to aid and encourage employers and representatives of their employees to reach and maintain agreements . . . " (NLRA, Amended, 1947, Title II, Sec. 101). Title I of the act requires that in order to terminate or modify an existing labor contract, the party seeking such action must notify FMCS thirty days prior to the expiration of the existing agreement. The National Labor Relations Act was further amended in 1974 to bring private, nonprofit health facilities under the coverage of the act and, therefore, within the jurisdiction of FMCS. By Executive Order 11491, labor disputes in the federal sector were brought under FMCS auspices as well.

Structure and Procedures

FMCS is the largest federal mediation agency.[15] Its 300 full-time mediators are located across the country in seventy-two field offices, seven regional offices, and at central headquarters in Washington, D.C.[16] The staff in the national office administers the agency and provides training and technical support for the regional and field mediators across the country. The daily administration of field mediation activity is delegated to the seven regional offices, in particular, to the regional director and his staff.[17] The staff in the regional office not only mediates in its geographical locale but also oversees the workload and reporting for the region. Mediators located in the seventy-two field offices are charged with the line responsibility for mediation.

Field offices, which may range in size from one to six mediators, have no administrative staff of their own. All administrative procedures, including case assignment, reporting, travel, and vacation policy, are handled from the regional office. Case assignment is one of the major functions of the region. The regional offices receive both thirty-day notices filed by the parties in advance of a contract expiration and new unit certifications from the National Labor Relations Board. The assistant regional director and his staff screen these notifications to determine whether FMCS has jurisdiction and then assign them as cases directly to field mediators. In making these assignment decisions, regional staff aim for continuity and seek to assign a dispute to a mediator who has worked with the parties previously, unless requested by the mediator or the parties to do otherwise. This objective is tempered by the mediator's workload and/or the diagnosed need for a particular kind of industry expertise. Actual assignments are made via an internal activity form, and indeed, from the time of assignment, regional control over the field mediator's activity is primarily through formal reports. The average field mediator has a workload of fifty to sixty cases annually.

Upon receipt of the case assignment, the field mediator will typically contact both parties twenty days before the contract expiration to learn of negotiating progress and to inform them of his availability if they require it. If the mediator is not contacted again by the parties, he will typically make a followup call five to seven days before the contract expiration to determine whether the parties need a mediator in the final stages of their negotiations. In cases with regional or national impact, telephone contact is more frequent.

About 50 percent of the assigned cases are settled without mediator involvement or by an informal meeting with the chief spokesmen to review the status of the contract. If this occurs, the mediator receives from the parties a brief report of the settlement, which is filed with the regional office, thereby officially closing the case. For the other half of the cases, the mediator becomes "active" and meets directly with the parties to the mediation. Typically, the mediator stays with the case until it is resolved with or without a strike.[18]

Field mediators become involved in disputes in two other ways: requests for assistance on public-sector cases and last-minute calls from parties who are at impasse, but who failed to file a thirty-day notice. Typically, requests for FMCS to participate in public-sector cases are cleared through the regional office. If a state agency also has jurisdiction, an FMCS mediator and one from the state agency will work in tandem. Responses to calls for assistance may or may not be cleared through the region, depending upon the nature of the request. Those handled on the phone or by an informal meeting are often not reported, whereas those requiring "active" assistance usually will be.

Sites

The field office in which this study was conducted had six mediators working in it at the time. Four of the six had been with the Service for over twenty years. Consistent with FMCS recruitment policy, all had backgrounds in labor relations on either the union or management side. This particular field office, because of the longevity of some of its members, has the reputation in FMCS for being among the most professional. Several of the mediators have "distinguished-service" plaques adorning their walls.

The field office occupies part of a floor in a modern office building overlooking the city's harbor. Each mediator has his own spacious office with a desk and conference table. There are four large conference rooms and access to others as needed elsewhere on the floor. One secretary oversees the workings of the office—typing reports, answering telephones, greeting the parties, getting coffee.[19] Whenever possible, the mediators prefer to convene meetings at their offices. When they are not engaged in "active" mediating, this practice allows them to attend to their record keeping, make status checks on newly assigned cases, and gives them time to peruse the the extensive reports and journals provided them by the national office.

The field office is involved in about 350 cases annually, although some if its work is seasonal. Typically, January and February and the summer months are slow times for contract expirations. So, too, weeks early in the month tend to be slow. When the caseload picks up, the mediator will often convene cases daily and sometimes into the evening and night. When the mediators work past their normal hours, they take compensatory time off at the nearest opportunity. At month's end, it is not uncommon to find the office deserted during the morning hours. At really busy times, cases may be piggy-backed—two a day.

State Agency

The state agency had its beginnings in the late nineteenth century. In response to an increasing amount of strike activity, particularly in the boot and shoe industry, legislation was enacted to create a board of conciliation and arbitration. The thrust of the mandate instructed board members to investigate the causes of the dispute and to provide aid in the form of mediation and/or arbitration, whatever it took to resolve the dispute (Moran, 1968). The act, still carried in the general laws, provides that "when the board has knowledge that a strike or lockout which involves an employer and his present or former employees, is seriously threatened or has actually occurred, the board shall as soon as may be, communicate with such employer and employees and endeavor by mediation to obtain an amicable settlement." The three-member board, with no other staff, would travel to the site of labor strife. The board members were empowered both to mediate and to arbitrate, but typically they would attempt a mediated resolution of the dispute, and if those efforts failed, arbitration would be used.

In 1919 a state reorganization act placed the independent conciliation and arbitration board under the auspices of the newly created department of labor. The department commissioner was given the authority to hire staff to aid in the investigative and resolution functions. Early staff appointments were based on political allegiance rather than experience in dispute resolution (Moran, 1968). In 1938 the arbitration and conciliation functions were separated. Board members, with the titles of associate commissioners of labor, confined their activities to arbitration, and three staff mediators, called industrial relations adjusters, were hired to carry out the mediation functions. The labor commissioner had (and still has) the power to hire and fire mediators, while case assignment was made by the board chairman.

The Taft-Hartley Amendments prescribe that at the same time that parties give a thirty-day notice to FMCS, they are to notify "any State or Territorial Agency established to mediate and conciliate disputes within the State or Territory where the dispute occurred." Thus state mediators (about five in number during the

1940s and 1950s) often worked in tandem with FMCS mediators on private-sector disputes within the state.

With the extension of the state collective-bargaining laws, first to municipal employees in 1965 and then to all public employees in 1973, the state agency came to emphasize public-sector-dispute resolution for workers not covered under federal laws. The new laws placed mediation as the first step in a multiphase dispute-resolution procedure that includes factfinding and final-offer arbitration for police and firemen.

Whereas the nineteenth-century mediators were expected to "hear of" disputes, today's mediators are notified. The public-sector statute allows either party, after a reasonable period of negotiations, to petition the board for a determination of impasse. The board is then required to conduct, within ten days, an investigation to determine whether the parties are indeed at impasse and whether they have negotiated prior to their petition. Within five days after a determination of impasse, a mediator is to be appointed, and from the time of appointment, the mediator has twenty days to resolve the dispute. In contrast to the Taft-Hartley mandate, which gives considerable latitude to FMCS in terms of timing the entrance into a dispute, the state agency offers its mediation services only after an impasse exists, as determined by the mediator. Further, the state legislation prescribes certain time limits for the use of mediation as a substitute for the contract expiration/strike deadline in the private sector.

Structure and Procedures

The Board of Conciliation and Arbitration is a division of the Department of Labor and Industry, which is itself part of the Office of Manpower Affairs, a secretariat that reports to the governor. A cross section of other manpower-related divisions, among them employment security and various training programs, are also part of this office.

The board itself is composed, as the history suggests, of two distinct components. A tripartite board, appointed by the governor, handles grievance arbitrations. The board is written into contracts much in the way provision for private arbitration might be. The neutral member of the board is the director of both the mediation and arbitration wings of the board, though in practice the mediation wing has tended to function independently.

Currently, almost all of the state mediation cases are disputes in the public sector, where the right to strike is proscribed. Under the law, parties may petition the board for a determination of impasse. The petition may be initiated either jointly or by one of the parties. A formal petition is filed with the board, which presumably initiates an investigative procedure to determine whether an impasse exists. Such investigations are rarely held. The mediators tend to assume that if a petition is filed, an impasse exists. Since the law makes failure to notify the parties regarding the existence of an impasse within ten days equivalent to finding that an impasse exists, this is the tactic used. Often the mediators get involved early in the negotiations, before much bargaining has taken place, in order to have a tentative agreement before the relevant legislative bodies make their final budget decisions.

When petitions are received, they are entered into a log that identifies the case by number, the parties, and the date of petition receipt. About 90 percent of the petitions are filed by the union. The local convention in assigning cases is to give this responsibility to the most recently hired mediator. Assignments are typically made geographically, and as mediators attain seniority in the agency, they can select the geographical locale of their choice. There are also some exceptions to the geographical assignment. When a petition is filed jointly and both parties request a particular mediator, that request will be honored if the chosen mediator has time and if travel costs are not prohibitive. The field mediator, at the time of the study, also tried to match the skills of the mediator to the issues in the case, to the extent that he was aware of them. For example, a mediator with a degree in law might be assigned a case in which the parties have an issue pending before the State Labor Relations Commission.

Upon receipt of a case assignment, the mediator contacts the representatives of both parties to arrange a meeting. In the state agency, therefore, there is no distinction made between monitoring the progress of a case and "active" mediation. Under the law, the mediators have twenty days to assist the parties in the resolution of their dispute. The mediators do not consider the twenty-day limit binding, however, and tend to keep the parties in mediation as long as the parties and/or the mediator deem that progress can be made. This may be as long as a year. If the case is resolved in mediation, it is recorded in the log and on the petition and the case is closed.

If mediation fails to yield a resolution, the mediator certifies the case to factfinding, where it will be heard, and a factfinder will render a nonbinding recommendation for settlement. The single petition filed by the parties for third-party assistance covers both processes. The state agency does not do factfinding, but does provide lists from which the parties can choose a private factfinder.

The state agency becomes involved in cases in three other ways as well. The State Labor Relations Commission often refers cases that appear before it to the agency for a mediated resolution. These requests are typically made directly to a particular mediator and do not go through the normal case-assignment system. The state agency receives copies of the thirty-day notices submitted to FMCS, but limited secretarial help precludes follow-up. However, when large employers that are important economically to the state are at impasse, those notices are picked up by the few mediators who usually work in tandem with the federal mediators. A few, less than 1 percent of the state cases, involve small companies in the private sector. These cases are initiated by client calls directly to a particular mediator. Although jurisdictional lines between the FMCS field office and the state agency may be crossed, the preferences of the parties are respected. In essence, the state mediators handle the bulk of public-sector cases, except when the parties explicitly request assistance from FMCS. FMCS covers most of the private industrial and health-care institutions, except when small firms request a state mediator. Finally, when labor disputes involve a major employer in the state, both a state and a federal mediator are likely to be present. In total, the state agency mediates some 450 cases annually.

Site

Nine mediators are employed by the state agency. Six work out of the central city office and serve the urban and suburban communities within an eighty-mile radius. The other three mediators are stationed by themselves and serve segments of the state outside the geographical reach of the urban office. The six mediators in the central office come from diverse backgrounds. Three entered the agency over twenty years ago under the civil-service provisions and at that time had no prior experience in labor relations. Of the four most recently hired by the Secretary of Labor and Industry, three came from union organizing backgrounds and one entered the agency first as a staff member of the board of arbitration.

The agency occupies offices in a downtown state office building, on a floor devoted to agencies housed under the Department of Labor and Industries. The mediation office shares its quarters with the Apprenticeship Training Division of the Secretariat, and office-space and secretarial distinctions between the two agencies are blurred. The mediators share small offices in twos and threes. There is one small conference room, shared with other agencies of the Department of Labor and Industries. Secretarial and clerical staff sit with staff from the other agencies.

The obvious space limitations preclude convening mediation sessions on a regular basis at the agency's headquarters. Further, the type of caseload, namely, public-sector disputes, militates against daytime mediation during working hours. School-committee members and city councillors typically work at other occupations and are free for contract negotiations only after working hours. Much of the state mediator's work, therefore, is done in the late afternoons or evenings, when meetings are convened in local mayoral offices, town halls, schools, and libraries. Given their evening workload, the state mediators are not often in their offices during the work day. They may stop in to pick up messages, case assignments, and petitions, or they may get this information over the telephone.

The state mediator's caseload is steady and not subject to as much seasonal fluctuation as the federal mediator's. The close of a fiscal year and the approach of a new school season, however, tend to be busier than other times. As deadlines for budget submissions approach, the mediators may piggyback cases, but more typically they have four or five mediation meetings per week held in the late afternoon and evening. As with the federal mediators, they too take compensatory time off during the days.

The organizations in which the state and federal mediators work and the character of the dispute environments they serve are the background features against which mediation is enacted. These features differ in certain respects between the two agencies and serve to shape their contrasting perspectives on mediation that form the substance of succeeding chapters. Mediators in the two agencies work with parties that often differ markedly from each other. The federal mediators deal with parties in the private sector, in particular, chief negotiators who are typically experienced in the ways of negotiation and mediation. Since private employees have the legally protected right to strike, an action that is costly for both sides, the always present threat to exercise this option seems to highlight the interdependent relationship between the parties and, thus, creates an impetus for them to compromise and to resolve their differences. The state mediators operate in a different bargaining environment. Public-sector collective bargaining is relatively recent, and parties are still learning about its limits and potential. A coterie of experienced professional negotiators such as exist in the private sector is still forming in the public sector. Public unions are denied the right to strike, and it is often suggested that it is encumbent upon third parties in this domain to create pressures for compromise and conciliation as a substitute for the strike (Liebowitz, 1972; Robins, 1972).

The agencies differ organizationally as well. The policies and procedures of FMCS foster the impression that mediation is but another phase of the negotiations process. Through the monitoring procedures, federal mediators follow negotiations and may or may not become involved in the process. In contrast, state law requires that the parties attest to the existence of an impasse before the mediator becomes involved, making the mediation follow a formal acknowledgment that the parties are unable to resolve their own differences. Recruitment and training practices at the agencies differ as well. Federal mediators have acquired significant negotiating experience before they enter the service, and they undergo considerable classroom and apprenticeship training prior to becoming independent field mediators. Until quite recently, the state mediators had no selection or training policy, and therefore these mediators are less well prepared and considerably more heterogeneous in their backgrounds and level of expertise.

Differences in the work environments create different social milieus. The federal mediators are able to exercise their preference for convening cases in their own offices, a practice that offers them ample time to interact with and solicit assistance from their colleagues. The state mediators are more often on their own, mediating at night in towns or cities with people who are strangers to them. Opportunities for collegial interaction, feedback, and support are fewer for the state mediators. From these contrasts in environment and structure emerge the different perspectives on mediation that these practitioners bring to the disputes they seek to resolve.

Methodology

The research reported in this book is based on the systematic observation of mediators in these two agencies and on a comparative analysis of mediation practices. The study began with a round of interviews with mediators from both offices (Kolb, 1977) and continued with the observation of the office settings and, in the company of mediators from both offices, of their cases. Most of the findings reported here are based on observations of mediators at work on their cases and interviews held with them in the context of their casework. (A more complete treatment of methodology is contained in the appendix.)

I attended a total of sixteen cases in the company of the mediators, comprising over 400 hours of meeting time. Of the sixteen cases, ten were conducted by state mediators and six by those from the federal field office. Those cases selected for observation were ones that had just been referred to mediation, and observations of the entire case were made whenever possible. Four federal mediators conducted the six cases I observed. These cases constitute a total of eighteen separate sessions, and I was present at fifteen (see table 1.1). Each of the cases resulted in a settlement without a strike, although a strike threat was a serious possibility in the Albion Broadcasting and the Alfred Corporation cases (fictional names).[20] This high rate of settlement is consistent with the experience of mediators in FMCS. Without other avenues of dispute resolution to pursue, the parties, given enough time, will eventually resolve their differences.

Five state mediators conducted the ten state cases I observed, covering the range of occupation groups typically encountered by these mediators. Twenty-four sessions were convened in the context of these impasses and I observed twenty sessions, and seven cases in their entirety. In five of the cases, a tentative agreement was reached at the conclusion of mediation, one of which was rejected by the Sheridan firefighters. In three of the cases, the parties continued to negotiate after their sessions with the mediator, and they reached agreement in the bilateral forum. Two of the cases were referred to factfinding by the mediator after his efforts failed to yield a settlement. The settlement rate here of 70 percent is in the range the state agency reports for its caseload. Typically, 75–85 percent of those cases where petitions are filed settle in mediation.

Table 1.1
Summary of cases observed: duration, occupation, disposition

Mediator	Case name	Occupation of union members	Number of case sessions	Number of sessions observed	Disposition
FMCS					
Mediator Allen	Albion Broadcasting	Broadcast, clerical staff	4	4	Ratified settlement
Mediator Allen	Alfred Corporation	Industrial workers	1	1	Ratified settlement
Mediator Baker	Bates, Inc.	Industrial workers	4	4	Ratified settlement
Mediator Baker	Bard Manufacturing	Industrial Workers	3	3	Ratified settlement
Mediator Carr	Carroll University[a]	Nonprofessional workers	2	2	Return to negotiations
Mediator Dixon	Duke Hospital	Nurses	4	1	Ratified settlement

State agency

State agency					
Mediator Richards	Rutgers School Committee	Teachers	3	1	Ratified settlement
Mediator Richards	Regis School Committee	Teachers	5	3	Ratified settlement
Mediator Richards	Reed School Committee[a]	Teachers' aides	1	1	Return to negotiations
Mediator Shaw	Scripps School Committee[a]	Teachers	4	4	Return to negotiations
Mediator Shaw	Sheridan Firefighters[b]	Firefighters	1	1	Rejected, factfinding
Mediator Thomas	Taft School Committee	Teachers	1	1	Ratified settlement
Mediator Thomas	Tulane Firefighters	Firefighters	3	3	Ratified settlement
Mediator Unger	Ulster School Committee[a]	Teachers	2	2	Return to negotiations
Mediator Unger	Urbana Housing Authority	Maintenance workers	1	1	Referred to factfinding
Mediator Vance	Vanderbilt School Committee	Cafeteria workers	3	1	Referred to factfinding

a. After mediation, these parties continued to negotiate and reached a settlement in the bilateral forum.
b. A tentative agreement was reached in mediation, but the union rejected it and it was then referred to factfinding, where it was settled and ratified.

In sum, the cases that I observed may be considered typical of
the state and federal mediators' practice. The six federal cases covered several different industries and unions, including industrial
settings as well as a health-care facility. The ten state cases were
likewise reasonably representative of the kinds of cases these mediators have. The observed cases taken as a whole were also typical,
in that they reflect the variety of factors mediators and their observers allude to when they describe the diversity of mediation
practice. In the Duke Hospital, Tulane Firefighters, and Vanderbilt
School Committee cases, the parties were negotiating their first
contracts. In some of the cases the issues in dispute were considered
by the mediators to be particularly difficult. For example, in the
Carroll University case, management planned to subcontract the
union's work and was engaged in negotiating the terms and conditions of this transfer; and in the Ulster School Committee case,
the parties were negotiating a reduction-in-force clause that would
immediately go into effect. In two cases, Alfred Corporation and
Urbana Housing Authority, the parties were in mediation after the
union membership had rejected a tentative settlement agreed to in
negotiations. Relationships between the parties were strained in
the Albion Broadcasting case, where the parties refused to meet in
the same room with each other. In certain cases, for example, Bard
Manufacturing, Taft School Committee, and the Rutgers School
Committee, the mediator knew the parties well and had worked
with them before, whereas in the Alfred Corporation and Reed
School Committee cases, among others, the mediators and the chief
negotiators were strangers to each other. None of the cases involved
a major employer in the state or the press, nor was there a case in
which the union was on active strike (although a strike was a distinct
possibility in two cases). Yet the cases do seem to be a representative
sampling of the kinds of disputes these mediators normally
encounter.

As an observer, I witnessed all phases of these cases. Although
the mediators and parties knew the broad outlines of my research
purpose, we agreed that I could best learn their approach to the
practice of mediation if I were treated as a trainee. In the office of
the FMCS mediators, and driving to cases with state mediators, I
reviewed the historical records, learned all the mediator knew about
a case prior to its start, and discussed proposed strategy with him.

During the case sessions, I sat at the table with the mediator and was permitted by most, though not all, to take detailed notes on the proceedings. I was present at all the meetings and caucuses when the mediator was present, including many that took place "off the record." When lulls occurred, the mediator and I discussed his view of the case, the "readings" he took of the issues, positions, and people, his plans for the next move, and his analysis of the one just past. Data from these observations and interviews comprised well over 1,000 pages. These data were analyzed along several dimensions:

1. *Roles* All the presentations each mediator made to the parties and to me about his perceived role were compared. These presentations included introductory speeches the mediator gave to the parties as well as the discussions with me about each mediator's approach and perspective on the process. These verbal accounts were compared across mediators, cases, and agencies.

2. *Meeting sequences* Sequencing and ordering meetings is a tactic mediators use to control the proceedings. Timing and tabulations of meeting types were used to compare these tactics across mediators and agencies.

3. *Strategies and tactics* To study this crucial facet of mediation, the data were analyzed according to the ways each mediator seemed to experience a case and to make decisions about what techniques to use. In comparative format, I arrayed each mediator's assessment of the parties, their issues, his methods for learning priorities, and the ways he encouraged the parties to move from their positions.

4. *Mistakes and accounts* In his use of various strategies and tactics, a mediator was observed sometimes committing errors. At times, he acknowledged this, or the parties pointed it out to him. These instances were recorded, along with the justifications provided by the mediator for his behavior and the explanations for failure. These comparisons highlight the risks that attend the use of particular strategies and tactics.

These four empirical dimensions developed from the increased knowledge and familiarity I gained with each passing case, facets of the process that seemed most salient when compared across mediators, and the tenets of interpretive theory.

Mediation is a confusing and complicated interactive process influenced by the environment in which it occurs. This work does not intend to describe or analyze all its facets, but rather to focus on the mediators' perspectives on its enactment. Nor do I mean to suggest that the perspectives delineated here would necessarily describe the practice of all other state and federal mediators. How well the analysis captures practice elsewhere would depend upon similarities in organizational and environmental contexts that are seen to shape the definition of the mediator's role. Nor do the modes of practice necessarily describe the roles played by the "myth-makers," those nationally or locally renowned mediators who are sought for their knowledge and expertise "to clean up the town," as one such luminary has described it. These mediators, because of their reputations and skill, can undoubtedly exploit the potential of the process in ways that are, for the most part, unavailable to institutional mediators, except, perhaps, at the highest agency levels. But these renowned mediators mediate only a few cases annually, leaving the bulk of the routine work to mediators like the nine studied here. Thus it is from the close and systematic analysis of the normal cases of these institutional mediators that insight will come on how art is daily translated into practice.

2

Roles Mediators Play: Orchestrators and Dealmakers

When practitioners claim that mediation is an art with as many approaches as there are mediators, they are making a statement about roles. For an approach to mediation will be based on the particular mediator's perspective on his own part in the process and those of the other players—the chief spokesmen and bargaining committees. These perspectives will inform the mediator's choices about which tactics to use and when to employ them in order to aid the settlement process. The state and federal mediators seem to have differing perspectives on the roles of the mediator, and these color the specific approaches they take to resolving disputes, even when cases appear on the surface to be quite similar.

According to both state and federal mediators, they frequently work with union bargaining committees that have come to mediation with long lists of demands that are unscreened, or "raw," from the membership meeting. Although mediators from the two agencies describe this situation similarly, their interpretations of what it means and how it is to be handled seem to differ. To the federal mediator, "unweeded" lists demonstrate lack of preparation, a sure sign of inexperience. Parties who come to mediation with such a list must first "bring their issues into focus," reduce the number of demands, and narrow the differences on those remaining. Only then, the federal mediators say, can "real" mediation commence. To accomplish this, the federal mediator will typically instruct the "unprepared" committee to meet in caucus with its chief negotiator and develop a proposal that "narrows the issues."

The state mediator similarly "reads" the long list of demands as evidence of a committee's inexperience. In contrast to the federal mediator, however, the state mediator feels that committees typically lack the sophistication, knowledge, and experience to drop demands themselves without substantial prodding and pushing from the mediator. Bargaining committees need his assistance, the state mediator reasons, to decide what should legitimately go into subsequent proposals and what should be dropped along the way. To that end, in separate meetings between the mediator and the committee, proposals are evaluated item by item. State mediators try to determine by direct questioning the rationale, commitment, and degree of flexibility each committee attaches to each demand. If a demand is thought by the mediator to be "unrealizable or lacking in merit," he tries to convince the committee to drop it. One mediator described the tactic as "hammering."

This brief example suggests that to understand why a mediator takes the action he does, one must look beyond the unique features of the case to the underlying perspective that shapes how the mediator interprets these features. This is because the divergent responses of mediators are based not on the proposals per se, but rather on a definition of how they should act toward the parties in specific situations. This definition is summarized in the concept of role.

When mediators are queried about their roles, they tend to respond by making a normative distinction between passive and active mediator roles. The image of the passive mediator is the silent observer, someone who confines his activities to providing coffee and sharpening pencils. The active mediator is one who, through his efforts, makes a major contribution to the achievement of a settlement. The forms this major contribution may take vary. Descriptions of them include applying pressure, channeling communications, allowing the parties to save face, persuading and leading the group in its task accomplishment and social relationships. The conditions under which certain roles become more prominent are thought to reside in the specifics of a dispute and the stage in its resolution.[1]

As the concept is used here, role is meant to be a summary label that covers both cognition and action. The mediator's thoughts, values, and assumptions about his work are revealed in the perspective or point of view through which the process is seen and interpreted. A given perspective, developed from experience, guides the choices mediators make about what tactics to use and the meaning of these actions for the achievement of a settlement. Roles also refer to the actions themselves, for it is in the actual playing that the themes of a role are created and maintained. The cognitive and active elements of the state and federal mediation roles are important in that they yield different patterns of mediation.

Two Examples

Based on case observation and the associated explanations mediators provide for their actions, it appears that each agency, whether state or FMCS, has its own distinctive brand or pattern of mediation. State mediators act and describe themselves as "dealmakers," while their federal counterparts see themselves as "orchestrators." These differing conceptions of role seem to reflect the contrasting perspectives that the two groups of mediators have on resolving disputes, and these differences in turn color the tactics and techniques they employ as mediators. To make these distinctions concrete, consider the following cases.

Reed School Committee: State Mediator as Dealmaker

In the Reed case, the school committee had been negotiating with the local unit of teachers' aides for almost a year prior to mediation. The union, in particular, was anxious to reach an agreement on some of its issues before the fiscal year elapsed and the possibility for retroactivity was lost. On the union committee sat three aides from the unit, the local union president, and a regional union representative with previous private-sector experience. The town was represented by one member of the school committee who was responsible for the negotiations with all the units in the school system. Also on the committee were the superintendent of schools, the town's business agent, and a labor-relations attorney who worked with the school committee on these matters. The attorney left the mediation midway through the proceedings.

Mediator Richards started the mediation with the union, which was meeting in a school library. He introduced himself and passed around a yellow sheet of paper for all committee members to sign. The union president described the situation. "These people have been making $2.36 for the last few years. Other groups received raises, but they did not. They currently have ten days of sick leave, which is non-accumulative, the same snow-days policy as the teachers, no vacations, and no retirement system. These people have nothing but their wages. And now the school committee wants to take away their snow days." The mediator questioned the union president on several items: history of negotiations, the salary increases offered, benefits the teachers receive, and a description of the aide job. The mediator ended by saying, "I'll see what I can get for you."

Richards joined the school bargaining committee in the principal's office, passed around the sign-up sheet, and then read from the petition for mediation: "The petition I have says that you have had three–four meetings and that the open issues are wages, hours, and working conditions." John Smith, the school committee member, described the committee's position on the aide's job: "This is a simple part-time job for mothers who want to earn some extra money. Our proposal reflects that philosophy of the job."

The mediator stated his disagreement with the school committee's philosophy of the job. He then took out the contract given him by the union and worked through it, provision by provision, to identify and discuss the "open" issues. He introduced the aides' position that the union members be considered permanent employees with full retirement rights, to which the school committee responded that said petition had been rejected by the town meeting. The mediator persevered. He distinguished between two parts of the petition as he saw it: the request to be permanent employees and the eligibility for retirement. Though he was clear that he had not discussed the matter with the union committee, he knew the members wanted to be considered permanent because it gave them protection in the event of layoffs.

The next item was fringe benefits. He asked whether the aides had medical insurance. When the school committee said no, he asked whether clerical workers and/or teachers had the coverage. The same procedure was followed for vacations and snow days—he listed the other units and asked whether they had the provision in their contracts. He learned that some units had the coverage while others did not. Richards then suggested that the school committee revert to past practice on snow days. When the committee vetoed his suggestion, he argued that, even with a wage increase, the deletion of snow days would result, overall, in a monetary loss for the aides.

The school committee bolstered its position with a presentation of the concessions it had already made. It reiterated the status of the budget, whose deadline was approaching. It argued that the union would forfeit the entire budget if it failed to accept the school-committee offer. Richards made light of the deadline constraint. Based on his experience, he was well aware that school committees could always extract more money from town meetings. Again, he returned to the discussion of other fringe benefits. Each time the committee said "No movement," he asked about the practices in other units. "If the cafeteria workers get snow days, it is only just that the aides get it. They are all your employees."

The committee still refused. The mediator gave, then, what he called his "speech" on mediation. "I make this speech every time. Now is an okay time. I come in, I want to make a deal. I need something to work with. I think we can get a settlement today. All I need from you is some flexibility, contingent, of course, on my getting the union to accept. But I don't know what you want—one, two, or three years with a reopener? I can work with you. Tell me what you want, and I'll try to bring it home. I lectured them [the union]—when the mediator is here there are no more negotiations."

The school committee reiterated its position. "We've gone the limit, there is nothing else." Richards responded, "With wages this low, you are only talking pennies." He looked for another area to explore. Could it do something on "sub days," the time the aides fill in as substitute teachers. "As I bounce over it, little things might do it." He left the committee to consider what he had said.

En route to the union committee meeting, he commented, "I really love mediation. I like to go in and bang heads. I can be a real SOB." To the union, the mediator reported the positions of the school committee and described his efforts to persuade it to change its positions. As part of this presentation, he mentioned the wage increase he thought it deserved and should be able to get. The union president interrupted to ask whether the figure he quoted was that of the school committee. The mediator demurred. He acknowledged that the school committee was three cents away from his figure. He concluded, "Tell me what it will take to wrap it up." The union requested a caucus.

In the hallway, while the union caucused, the mediator discussed what he was trying to accomplish—a deal to bail out the union. "I want to bail them out. I'm not often in the role of an impartial mediator. There are times when one side needs my help more than another. . . . I come on like a gentleman. I use all the logic and argument. Then I convince them by persuasion, and then I take them and bang their heads. Today, if I'm not persuasive enough to get a settlement, there isn't one there."

The union spokesman called the mediator into the meeting room. There the president presented the union's revised proposal and posed a question for the mediator to ask the school committee. The union was unsure whether the aides, if discharged, were covered under the grievance procedure. The mediator was sure that they were but agreed to ask. "I'll ask very naively. 'If a person is fired, does she have the right to grieve?' "

The mediator initiated his meeting with the school committee by asking whether discharge was subject to the grievance procedure. The school committee was quite clear that the right to discharge was reserved to management. Richards argued vehemently for the principle of just cause, and when it still disagreed, made a bet with it that even if it refused to put just cause in the contract, the management right to discharge was illusory because the State Labor Relations Board (SLRB) could order such a discharge arbitrated. The school committee still refused to budge. The issue of "just cause" for discharge was reintroduced by the mediator at several junctures during his meeting with the school committee.

Frustrated on this issue, Richards asked again what it was "willing to give." It informed him that as a result of its caucus it had changed its position on the sub days and modestly on wages. The school-committee proposal on substitute pay was different from what he had understood it to be, based on the discussion with the school committee in the earlier meeting. He had conveyed his mistaken impression to the union just previously and accused the school committee, therefore, of changing its mind. "I may have misled the union. I thought the provision applied when a teacher went home sick. I thought the compromise was for the part day and after that you would pay them for the first full day, not the second. What's the difference? Give it to them, it's just a few bucks. You're getting the services and the work of a substitute, and you can control it."

The school committee refused. Richards continued to press for changes on the other fringe benefits—holidays, snow days, and sick leave—with the argument that since the other units get these benefits, the aides are entitled as well. When he returned to the issue of grievance over discharge for the last time, the school-committee member interrupted him. "I have a question about mediation. We are still where we were when we started. I am not pleased with the whole proceeding."

At that point, the mediator presented the union's revised proposal. He tried and in his words begged the school committee to increase its wage offer. "Let me go back. You know it will cost more to figure that extra penny. You don't care. Where can you find another penny? I hope we settle it right away. If not, when? We can wrap it up in fifteen minutes."

The school committee refused. En route to the union committee meeting, Richards summarized by saying that he had tried as hard as he could. He felt he had obtained from the school committee as much as he possibly could. He presented the school committee's proposal to the union, laced with descriptions of his efforts to get the school committee to move, that is, that he had begged for an extra penny. "I've gotten as much from the school committee as possible and at least what's here will be forthcoming." His advice to the union was to accept the package and to think about negotiations for the next contract. He then left to attend the second mediation of the three he would conduct that day.

The school committee refused to meet again with the union committee before the budget deadline. The union subsequently accepted the school committee's package, which included a 10 percent wage increase, five additional sick days, deletion of snow-day pay, and compensation at the teacher rate if an aide substituted for more than one day.

Albion Broadcasting: Federal Mediator as Orchestrator

Mediator Allen convened the Albion Broadcasting case in a conference room at the FMCS field office. The station manager and his labor-relations attorney constituted the management bargaining committee. The membership of the union committee fluctuated somewhat over the course of the four mediation sessions. Present at all the meetings were two representatives from the union's regional office and the shop steward from the local. Between three and five members of the unit were present at each session, though they were not always the same.

Before the introductory joint meeting, the management attorney drifted into the mediator's office and confided that the crucial issue in dispute was the work shifts for the announcers, a fact the mediator already knew from his telephone conversations with one of the union representatives. Allen then convened a joint meeting with management on one side of the long table and the union on the other, with the mediator at its head. He passed around a sign-in sheet and then introduced himself. "My role is to help the parties reach a settlement and minimize the disputes between you. I have no authority to settle—settlement is in your hands. I want to develop a dialogue on these open issues and, if necessary, offer my ideas. You obviously disagree. You wouldn't have come unless there was some dispute over the issues. I hope we can narrow the issues and reach an agreement, but the burden of reaching an agreement rests with union and management."

The mediator turned to the union representative and asked him to present the union's most recent position. Six issues were raised in its proposal: work schedule and pay for the broadcasting staff, pay for promotional spots, salary for the news and music directors, pension contribution, wages for clerical workers and part-time new staff, and compensation for preparation time. After the union presented each demand, Allen turned to management to get its position on that issue. Any time one side or the other attempted to present an argument or justification for its position, the mediator cut the discussion and announced that, for the moment, he wanted them only to present the issues.

The mediator then separated the parties. Management moved to another conference room, and the mediator remained with the union. He asked the union reps to review for him the history of negotiations to the present. After a question to the committee about its expectations—"What's going to happen here today?"—and its response, he summarized his own perceptions. "I know there are six areas of disagreement between you, but the scheduling of air time seems to be the crunch issue. Is that a fair statement?" The committee agreed. The mediator ended by instructing it to develop a proposal on just the scheduling issue.

En route to the management conference room, the mediator commented on his perceptions of the situation. "There are some real disagreements here between the parties, and a few of the union members are really fired up about this issue. But the union reps here are real pros. I've worked with them before. They'll be the steadying force with the committee and move the union to compromise when the time is right." He described his own role at this juncture: "To know the issues and understand the positions."

The management committee presented the mediator with the history of the station management, the nature of its competition, and its justification for the proposed on-air schedule change. The mediator tried to clarify what the schedule change would mean to on-air hours and posed some of the questions the union had asked him to clarify with management. As he had done with the union, Allen summarized his sense of the dispute, that since the schedule was the crunch issue, it should consider and negotiate it separately from the others. To do this, he proposed an "airing-out" session on just the scheduling issue to generate a "dialogue."

After lunch he convened a joint meeting to discuss the schedule. During the meeting, the mediator was silent while the parties discussed, sometimes quite vehemently, their respective positions. After a noticeably long break in the dialogue, Allen proposed that each side caucus separately. While the parties met, he explained his reason for calling a joint meeting on the schedule. "As a mediator, you don't go in and argue positions. You have to find out the story; you put the burden on the parties. The management wanted to blast the union. That's not my job. I also wanted to hear what the union rep had to say. I wanted to let management hear it from the horse's mouth."

After a short caucus, the mediator met with the union people and asked them for their ideas on resolving the scheduling issue. He instructed them to "come up with a proposal that satisfies you and management too." His reasoning, he confided later, was to get a "concrete proposal from the union to put the monkey on the back of management so they would have to make a move."

The union caucused and called Allen back in to present its proposal on scheduling. The mediator recorded it and read it back to the committee from his notes to make sure it was correct. Management rejected the union's proposal and began to justify its reasons for doing so. The mediator interrupted the station manager. "You don't have to convince me." Allen suggested a joint meeting so that management could give its response. He commented to me afterward, "Every time the parties throw something at me, I throw it back at them. I'm trying to orchestrate the case so each side faces up to its responsibility."

A joint meeting was convened, and the mediator immediately turned the floor over to the station manager for his response to the proposal. As he had done in the previous joint meeting, the mediator did not participate except to break into an argument in order to allow a person who was trying to speak to do so. When the parties started to make accusations of bad faith, the mediator adjourned the session for the day.

At the start of the second session, the mediator met first with management, which expressed a desire to meet separately in order to avoid the overt hostility that marked the conclusion of the last session. The mediator acceded to this desire and asked the company whether it had a proposal to make. It did. The mediator copied the management proposal and duplicated it to pass out to the union committee. While doing this, he commented on his precautions: "You notice I double checked the language. You have to be very careful about language. Of course, management should be delivering its own proposal."

The mediator gave copies of management's proposal to the union. In response, the union reps posed some questions about the proposal that they wanted clarified. The mediator wrote down the questions and read them back to the union for verification. The mediator met with management, dictated the union's questions, and left management to caucus. Soon after, management recalled the mediator and gave its response to the questions. Again, Allen copied them, read them back, delivered them to the union, and left the union to caucus.

While the union caucused, the mediator commented on how the parties were using him as a go-between: "You can be a conduit or an agent. I won't be an agent. I won't argue their positions. They want the mediator to do everything. I hope they'll meet together to get the information directly. I hope they'll get mad enough to do it."

After lunch, the union rep asked the mediator to join the union, where it presented its counterproposal. Once again the mediator read back his notes to it before taking it to management. He reiterated, on the way to management, his view on carrying messages: "That's why I like the parties to tell each other directly, so I don't mess up."

Allen presented the proposal to management and left it to caucus. After a considerable time, the management attorney recalled him to announce that management rejected the union's proposal. It claimed that it had nothing more to offer, that it had gone as far as it could. Since the contract had already expired and negotiations appeared stalled, it asked the mediator's advice on how to handle retroactivity to create a new deadline after which retroactivity would no longer apply. The mediator described the "usual" methods for such situations, but emphasized that it had to decide how to do it and, further, that once it had decided, he would encourage it to meet jointly with the union and present its response to the union proposal and its position on retroactivity. He left it to caucus. Later, the station manager and his attorney came into the mediator's office and reiterated their stand on separate meetings. They asked him to tell the union that they rejected the proposal and had set the deadline after which retroactivity would no longer apply as five days hence.

The mediator met with the union and presented management's statement. The shop steward asked whether the mediator would consider recommending a mediator's settlement. The mediator said no, that "it might not do it." Later he elaborated. "Suggestions for settling should come from the reps. The committee wants to use me as an arbitrator, which I am not."

At the start of the third session, the union rep spoke to the mediator in his office and reported that in the interim, the union reps and the station manager had met and agreed to negotiate seriously. But they preferred to do it off the record, away from the volatile union committee. The mediator proposed separately to each committee an off-the-record meeting of the station manager and his attorney, one of the union reps, and the shop steward as a way to move negotiations forward. He presented this as his proposal. He left both sides to caucus on this plan, and they agreed.

The mediator convened the joint off-the-record meeting in a third conference room. The meeting was marked by active participation of all the members of the subcommittee, except the mediator, who sat silent throughout. During the lunch break he commented on his posture at this meeting: "One of the functions of the mediator is to change the conditions and environment of the negotiations. My silence wasn't that unusual. Sometimes mediators extricate themselves entirely from this type of meeting."

For the remainder of the third session, the reps from each side met in the joint off-the-record meetings, interspersed with caucuses held with their respective sides. After the session was concluded, the mediator described his role: "I'm a gatekeeper. They're, in Simkin's terms, in the area of settlement. You watch developments like a parent. If one balks, you start persuading—something like you have a deal here, is it worth threatening to do X. This is where I am effective. At the next session I'll play the same role I did all day, which is to let them handle it."

At the start of the fourth session, the mediator met with the full union committee, at which time the rep suggested that it wanted to present its proposal in a full joint meeting. The mediator convened it. The union presented its proposal; management caucused and then called the mediator in to give him its final offer to take to the union. The mediator suggested that it do so directly: "If this is it, then I shouldn't carry the ball. If I carry it, they'll think I am waiting for a counterproposal. You've got to do it."

At the joint meeting, management presented its offer, the revised on-air schedule with the premium for work over and above five days, contribution to the pension, a modest salary increase for the news and music directors, and an increase in the fee for promotional spots. The union caucused, returned to the joint meeting, and accepted the offer. All present shook hands and congratulated the mediator.

Orchestrating and Dealmaking: An Analysis

Many differences strike the reader between the Reed and Albion cases. Reed School Committee, a public-sector dispute concerning a union with minimal bargaining leverage, lasted only one session, working against a budget deadline. The issues may be considered typical, in that salary was the central issue, while fringe benefits and the grievance procedure, although of concern, were secondary. Albion took longer, against a deadline that changed midway through the process. Although salary and fringes were issues, the major one was a working condition that had economic implications for the station and its broadcast staff. The conclusions of the cases differed. Mediator Richards and the aides were disappointed at the minimal progress made on the issues, in particular, the salary offer, snow days, and discharge. The conclusion of the Albion case was more amicable, though neither side completely achieved what it had sought, a situation obviously inherent in the accommodation process of mediation.

Beyond these obvious differences in the cases, the mediators acted quite differently. Mediator Richards was frenetic, always with one side or the other trying to get an agreement. He and I grabbed minutes for conversation as we shuttled from room to room. In contrast, mediator Allen was seemingly more relaxed—caucuses were held without him, he was akin to a silent observer in many of the meetings, and he and I had many lulls during which he could, in his office, leisurely discuss and account for his actions. These different levels of activity are a part of what distinguished the dealmaking and orchestrating approaches taken by these two mediators.

More specifically, the differences between dealmaking and orchestrating may be detected in the verbal accounts the mediators gave and the deliberate actions they took in the service of a settlement. In their assessments of the status of negotiations at the time the mediations commenced, in their definitions of the mediator's contribution to the resolution process, and in their explanations for why the parties made concessions, the mediators revealed the cognitive assumptions upon which their roles were based. Behaviorally, differences in role may be observed in the formal descriptions the mediators gave to the parties of their roles, their positioning and control of communication channels, and the changes in tactics that occurred during the case.

Cognitive Perspectives

Mediators Richards and Allen had distinctive perspectives on their respective cases that shaped the forms of their participation. Mediator Richards, in possession of a petition that declared that the parties were at impasse, considered mediation a wholly new process, distinct from the negotiations that had preceded it. The fact that the parties had negotiated for a year without reaching a settlement only served to reinforce his perception that the previous negotiations had been fruitless. From his perspective he saw ample evidence that might explain why the parties needed a mediator to help them make a deal. The union was weak, not only because it was new and inexpert in negotiations, but also because its labor market skills had little value to the school committee. Aides could easily be replaced. The members of the school committee, he felt, were also novices at collective bargaining. According to Richards, the spokesman for the school committee was "inflexible and inexperienced." The negotiator demonstrated this in the "intractable and unreasonable" positions he took and in his unwillingness to defer to the experienced attorney, who left the session, Richards suggested, because the spokesman would not heed his advice. Based on this interpretation, Richards believed that unless he adopted a deal-making role, the parties would be unable to settle. Indeed, he believed that the settlement (as disappointing as it may have been) was achieved as a result of his persuasive efforts, efforts that had as their intent persuading the school committee to make concessions and then prodding the union to accept them as the most it could hope to achieve.

Mediator Allen articulated a different perspective on the process. He described mediation as a continuation of the previous negotiations, but in a new forum. He had maintained telephone contact with both parties during their premediation negotiations. During the mediation itself, the actions he took rarely touched on the substance of the dispute. Indeed, he seemed uninterested in the specific issues. Rather, he orchestrated the process in order for the parties continually to confront their issues and each other. Allen's actions can be understood in the context of his perception of the parties. He looked to the union representatives, men he had worked with before, to stabilize their committees, to come up with ideas for compromise, and to push for a settlement at the appropriate time. Likewise, he believed that the management attorney would, given the time, be able to convince the station manager to modify his scheduling objectives consistent with a plan the union could accept. The mediator viewed the station manager as "inflexible and irrational" in his conviction that he could hope to extract more work from the broadcast staff without more pay. But rather than make any of these arguments himself, Allen structured the proceedings so that the parties could make them to each other. In the accounts of the roles they played, the state mediator emphasized his contributions to the substantive development of a deal, whereas the federal mediator attended more to the process by which the parties were able to reach agreement.

Observable Actions

Mediators Allen and Richards gave to the parties official presentations of their respective conceptions of the mediator's role. Federal mediator Allen did so at the start of the first session: "My role is to help the parties reach a settlement and minimize the dispute between you. I have no authority to settle—settlement is in your hands. I want to develop a dialogue on these open issues and if necessary, offer my ideas. You obviously disagree. You wouldn't have come unless there was some dispute over the issues. I hope we can narrow the issues and reach an agreement, but the burden of reaching an agreement rests with union and management." State Mediator Richards described his role to the school committee as part of an effort to encourage concessions: "I come in. I want to make a deal. I need something to work with. I think we can get a settlement today. All I need from you is some flexibility, contingent, of course, on my getting the union to accept it. . . . I can work with you. Tell me what you want, and I'll try to bring it home. I lectured them [the union committee]—when the mediator is here, there are no more negotiations."

The official presentations were reiterated to me in our private conversations. Mediator Allen said that as a mediator his role was not to argue positions, but to put the burden on the parties, to let them argue their own positions face to face. Mediator Richards characterized such an approach as too passive: "I refuse to play a passive role and just let the parties talk. I will not be a messenger either. First they have to convince me and then we'll see what I can do about it." Beyond the formal presentations to the parties and private accounts of these public presentations, the observable actions taken by these two mediators define and serve to clarify further the differences between orchestrating and dealmaking.

The communications functions a mediator performs are an integral part of the service he provides to the settlement of disputes (Simkin, 1971). Mediators Richards and Allen channeled communications in several ways—conveying proposals and positions, posing questions and gaining responses—yet they accomplished these functions in differing ways. Richards was the proposal carrier throughout the case. He conveyed two formal proposals given him, one from the union and one from the town. He carried positions, apart from proposals, as well. In the early stages of the mediation, before the union positions were solidified into a proposal, Richards reported tentative questions and positions on the issues of sub days, the recognition clause, and snow days to the school committee. Positions, proposals, and questions, for example, whether discharge was subject to the grievance procedure, were opportunities for him to present the union's positions and justifications, bolstered considerably by his own arguments.

Mediator Allen, too, conveyed positions, proposals, and questions, but *only when explicitly requested to do so*. During the early and later stages of the case, he had the parties communicating directly across the table. Only in the middle stages, when management felt the verbal punishment it received in the joint meetings precluded further participation in this forum, did the mediator accede to its request. And even then he continued to press it to meet jointly in order to announce its rejection of the union proposal and the five-day retroactivity deadline. Like Richards, Allen eschewed a message-carrying role, but not because it constrained him; rather, it was from the conviction that the parties should communicate their messages directly and from a fear that mistakes might be made in transit. When he did convey questions and proposals, he did only that. He wrote them down and dictated or duplicated them. He refused, as he said, to be an agent, but would reluctantly be a conduit.

In summary, almost all of the communication between the committees was channeled through state mediator Richards, where he, as a dealmaker, acted as a surrogate for the opposing side—presenting positions, arguments, and justifications. He also embellished on the messages he carried. In contrast, as an orchestrator, federal mediator Allen favored direct communication between the committees and only channeled questions and proposals when explicitly requested to do so.[2] Further, the messages Allen conveyed were limited in their contents to what he had been given (or to part of what he had been given) by the committees. He explicitly omitted the justification and arguments that stood behind the messages, hoping that the parties would get "mad enough" about the limited amount of information he conveyed to revert to communicating across the table rather than through an intermediary.

Earlier studies of mediation identify stages through which mediations pass and the kinds of behaviors associated with particular phases (Douglas, 1962; Kressel, 1972). Mediators Allen and Richards also described themselves as taking on (or "progressing through") different roles over the courses of the cases. Richards spoke of his progression through a series of persuasive roles—logical persuader, argumentative persuader, and banger of heads. His attempts to persuade the school committee to concede on grievance for discharge, an issue he was committed to, bears out this role characterization. He first asked whether such a clause existed, and when informed that it was a right reserved to management, he calmly asked, "What if you are wrong?" From there, he argued its centrality to the whole philosophy of industrial relations, that allowing employees to grieve discharge is the "civilized way to see if you are wrong." He argued that the other units have it, that he personally believed in it. After continuing in that vein, he bet them that the State Labor Relations Commission would nullify the right through arbitration. When the school committee still refused to concede, he ended the long discussion by saying "I give up. I tried to shed some light. You would rather choose being arbitrary and forceful to an orderly method. I'll just tell them to take it to the Labor Relations Commission, and I hope you get burned."

Similarly, Allen described his role as changing over the course of the case, although the specific actions he took appeared similar throughout. He saw himself learning the issues and understanding the position at the outset. During the middle phases, he was a conduit between the parties, and during the subcommittee joint meetings, he characterized himself as a gatekeeper. In that role, he watched over the proceedings and planned to intervene only if discussions broke off. And when he spoke of persuading, he never mentioned that he would do so over the substance of the dispute. Rather, he planned (but never felt pressed) to use his persuasive reservoir to encourage the parties to continue their dialogue and not risk the heavy costs that a strike would incur.

These observable elements of role behavior derive directly from the cognitive perspectives the mediators had about the needs of the parties. Generally, in the public sector, where the pressure from a strike is missing, the parties are inexperienced, and, in the Reed case particularly, the aides had minimal bargaining power, mediator Richards believed that settlement could only be achieved through his dealmaking efforts. In contrast, working with experienced negotiators who well understood the interdependence of the parties and the costs of a strike, mediator Allen believed that the parties themselves would be the source of substantive suggestions to resolve the dispute. He saw himself as instrumental because he had created the forum or framework for the parties to explore these possibilities. These distinctions are summarized in table 2.1.

Orchestrators and Dealmakers: The Other Cases

In the accounts mediators Allen and Richards gave of their roles in these two cases, selected characteristics of the parties and the bargaining environments figured prominently. These differences in case character are undeniable—private versus public sector; a small, low-paid bargaining unit as opposed to broadcasters critical of their station; parties that were new to collective bargaining versus seasoned professionals; a brief one-session case contrasted with one that comprised four day-long sessions. Do these contrasting case features provide sufficient explanation for the articulated and observed differences in roles? Such a finding would be uniquely consistent with the artistic myth of mediation. If that were true, then the roles of orchestrator and dealmaker would not be expected to transcend the unique character of individual cases.

To address this issue, consider comments made by mediators Allen and Richards in the contexts of other observed cases. First, state mediator Richards's description of the Regis School Committee case: "I put together a deal here. It was beautiful, but it fell apart because the school committee couldn't deliver." And on the Rutgers School Committee case: "I'm trying to make a deal here. I'm pretty sure I know what the union will take, but I have to go in and work on the school committee." On the same case: "I refuse to be a messenger. I told them if they want me to tell the other side something, they have to convince me first."

Table 2.1
Summary of the distinctions between orchestrating and dealmaking drawn from the Reed School Committee and Albion Broadcasting cases

	Dealmaking	Orchestrating
Cognitive perspective		
1. How mediators view the status of negotiations	Over	Continued in a new forum
2. Assessment of the parties' needs	Help, power equalization	A forum to explore differences
3. Accounts for why the parties make concessions	Pressure from the mediator	Pressure from interdependent relationship
4. Evaluation of the mediator's contribution	Aid on substantive issues	Aid on process so that parties can resolve substance
Observed role behaviors		
1. Formal role presentations to the parties	To make a deal	To develop a dialogue
2. How mediators channel interparty communications	Indirectly	Directly
a. How proposals are conveyed	Via the mediator	Joint meetings preferred
b. Contents of message conveyed	Embellished	Pared down
c. Preferred communication role	Advocate	Conduit
3. Changes in role over the case	Logical persuader → headbanger	Dumb questioner → gatekeeper

Contrast these comments with federal mediator Allen's on the Alfred Corporation case: "I'm a gatekeeper here. I'm trying to get them to buckle down, get them to meet. I'm just letting things sit, trying to let the pressures they exert on each other build." And on another case reported to me by Allen: "I was a conduit there. I try to represent their positions as best I can."

Observation of mediators Allen and Richards on their other cases further supports the lexical consistency of their respective role descriptions. Each acted on these other cases in ways that were remarkably close to his behavior in the Reed School Committee or Albion Broadcasting case. Richards, in the Regis School Committee case, tried to make a deal by pressuring the committee to drop the work-rule changes it proposed. In the Rutgers School Committee case he worked through the spokesmen to make a deal and visited the full committees only occasionally. Yet the Regis and Rutgers cases differed in important respects from the Reed case. In both the Regis and Rutgers School Committee cases, the teachers were judged to have considerable bargaining leverage. Further, the union and management committees in both cases were represented by chief spokesmen who had extensive negotiating experience and had worked with mediator Richards before. Richards seems to behave the same in a variety of situations.

For mediator Allen, too, there is some consistency across varied cases. In the Alfred Corporation case, only the union representative had collective-bargaining experience, and neither party had ever worked with Allen before. The circumstances of the Alfred case were also quite different from those in the Albion Broadcasting case. In the former, a tentative agreement reached in negotiations had been rejected by the union membership, and the parties sought mediation on only one issue—the procedure for determining the cost-of-living adjustments. Mediator Allen's orchestration of the case was directed toward keeping the union at the bargaining table; they kept threatening to strike. In contrast to his behavior in the Albion case, he did make some of his own proposals for resolving the single issue, none of which were accepted. Despite these variations, the play of mediator Allen's case resembled the Albion Broadcasting case far more than it did those cases conducted by mediator Richards. In sum, then, the roles mediators Allen and Richards played in these other cases were adjusted to mesh with the features of these cases, but more as variations on the themes of orchestrating and dealmaking than as de novo constructions tailored to the situations.

Given that a particular mediator's role seems to be enacted and described consistently across his caseload, the next question is whether these are merely differences in personal style. Recall that each mediator is alleged to develop his own unique philosophy and approach to mediation. Does this explain the differences in roles favored by Allen and Richards? If we look at what some of the other mediators in the two agencies say about their roles, we can determine whether observed role differences are individual or seem to reflect a group perspective rooted in the social practices of the agencies and the characteristics of the bargaining environments served. In essence, that task is what the succeeding chapters set out to accomplish. In the present chapter the discussion of shared perspectives focuses only on the verbal descriptions the other mediators gave of their roles.

Dealmaking

Each of the state mediators described to me his version of the mediator's role in terms that were similar, often identical, to those used by Richards. Mediator Shaw described his activity in the context of the Sheridan Firefighters case: "The role of the mediator is to make a deal." He then elaborated on his role in that case, which he described as "a great one": "This is real mediation. I played an active role on the union side. I was a definite input into their thinking. I actively manipulated them." In the context of the Ulster School Committee case, mediator Unger commented, "Mediation is where the parties tell the mediator to make this deal or that deal." Mediator Thomas, on the Taft Teachers case, described "real mediation" in a similar vein, an elaboration of what dealmaking means in practice: "This is real mediation. You fashion a package acceptable to both sides based on what you know about other contracts." Thomas lends credence to the notion that mediators develop particular approaches, in this instance dealmaking, that are enacted in similar ways over a range of cases: "After ten–fifteen years, you find yourself developing a pattern of mediation. My style is to try to get the bottom line from both sides. You may have to sweat it out of them. Then you get compromises, from each side and from yourself. . . . I play an active role. The passive stance means that you transmit messages as they are given to you. They give me the parameters, but I don't necessarily adhere." Mediator Vance, in the context of the Vanderbilt School Committee case, described his activities in terms that mirror Richards's actions in the Reed case: "My role is to explore and look for flexibility on both sides. I try to get them to move on issues which are clearly unreasonable and on those where comparisons can be made with other units."

To summarize, three of the five state mediators described the mediator as one who makes a deal. Further, each of the five, in the context of the full ten cases, acted and described the process of mediation as the active search for priority issues and the use of direct persuasion on these substantive issues, resulting in a deal that bears the imprint of the mediator as much as it does the parties. These are all behaviors associated with a dealmaking role. Although these mediators have their unique styles—some were casual, others formal; some were coarse, others refined; some were humorous and others grave—their perspectives on the process resembled each other more than they differed. I never observed a state case conducted according to the orchestrating mode.

Orchestrating

The federal mediators eschewed a dealmaking role as incongruent with mediation. Mediator Baker made this quite clear: "The parties aren't here for you to make a deal. If you think that, you are all wrong." The other three federal mediators described the role of mediator in terms quite similar to what mediator Allen discussed in Albion Broadcasting. Mediators Carr and Dixon, in the contexts of Carroll University and Duke Hospital, respectively, commented as follows:

Mediator Carr: The service I provided was to keep the ball rolling. I provided a forum for the parties to meet. They wouldn't have been able to resolve it, if they didn't meet across the table to talk about it.

Mediator Dixon: I'm a gatekeeper here. That's typical. Often you're a gatekeeper, providing a forum for the parties to meet.

Mediator Baker elaborated on the activities associated with the orchestrator role in Bard Manufacturing: "I assist the union and management to work out their agreements. We get a dialogue across the table, and then I may give them my input, but only after they have narrowed it down themselves." On the desirability of such a role in Bates, Inc., Baker said, "I ask you. Is it better for me to go over it point by point and pressure them to change their position or should I tell them to do it themselves? I tell them that they have to do it. That way, I haven't tried to convince them to change their positions on issues that may be unimportant."

One mediator summed up the essence of how he views mediation with a story he told the parties after they had reached a settlement and extended congratulations to him on his work: "You know, there's a story people tell in mediation. Nobody can find the mediator. Both sides think that he's been with the opposite side. Meanwhile, he's been at the bar, having a drink. But in the meantime, both sides have been working, and when he comes back, they have reached a settlement."

These differing descriptions of the roles they play—dealmaker or orchestrator—reflect the perspective each group of mediators holds about how disputes between the parties will be resolved. State mediators typically attempt to make a deal, believing that a successful outcome in the case, that is, an acceptable deal, is a direct result of their efforts to forge the elements of that deal. Working primarily in the public sector, state mediators tend to credit their knowledge of other settlements in the geographical area, their understanding of the proper language in common contractual clauses, their ability to gauge the components of a "reasonable" package (a skill the parties are not seen to possess), and their talents for explaining and persuading the parties to agree to the package as explanations for why a dispute is settled. For the federal mediators, settlement is achieved by providing a forum for the parties to come together to "explore their differences," with only intermittent, well-timed "injections of reality" or "input" from the mediator.

Orchestrators and Dealmakers: Some Indirect Validation

When state and federal mediators describe their preferences for cases and distinguish between those they experience as easy or difficult, the differences in perspective are supported. For the state mediators, easy cases are those where the parties are "reasonable," that is, are open to arguments presented by the mediator. Two state mediators described the epitome of an enjoyable case where they function like factfinders—they formally present to the parties their version of a package, which the parties agree to accept. A hard case, for example, Reed School Committee, is the opposite; that is, the committee "would not listen to reason."

In contrast, the federal mediators described easy cases as ones where the key actors are in basic agreement or have saved "something for mediation," so that the assistance they require from the mediator is to help sell the package to the full committee. As one mediator said, "We want them to settle it themselves." A difficult mediation is one where the hostility between the parties precludes their meeting directly across the table. "Joe and I had a case where we spent the whole day shuttling back and forth. Now that was a touchy one." Obviously, intransigence and unwillingness to make concessions make a case difficult, but the federal mediators seem to believe that if the parties can meet directly, with time they can negotiate their differences.

Also of interest is the fact that when these state and federal mediators speak of one another, they are clearly aware of the differences in approach and perspective that distinguish them. They view the approach of the other with disdain. Federal mediators describe the state mediators as so active in their "pursuit of a deal" that they ignore the preferences of the parties and continually demonstrate their naiveté about how the process works. "The state mediators don't listen. It's always what should be done by their standards, not the parties'."

State mediators often claim that the federal mediators are "passive," that all they do is let the parties meet. One state mediator commented about his working relationship with the federal mediators. "They don't like to work with me because they think I take over, and I do." Indeed, the state mediators allege that the federal mediators are almost superfluous to the settlement process because their private-sector caseload makes less demands on them. "The private sector is easier. You know that one side will eventually cave—it's inevitable. The parties do not really need the mediator, but they are required to use him by law. So all the mediator does is let the parties negotiate. But in the public sector, we do not let the parties off the hook; we hammer away. We are a part of the settlement process."

These lines of evidence—the preferences and perceptions of the mediators—though they support the verbal accounts the sample of mediators presented of their roles, are in themselves verbal accounts. To test the generalizability of the perspectives and role behaviors of Allen and Richards on their cases, material from other cases needs to be investigated.[3] Further, the meanings of such cognitive differences need to be sought in the social practices of mediators mediating.

3

Arranging the Mediation Forum: Intervention and Negotiating Patterns

Mediators spend most of their case time in meetings. Across the table, separately with the parties, and off the record with chief negotiators, the substantive issues in dispute are introduced, discussed, and, perhaps, resolved. The purposeful arrangement of these meetings serves to structure the settings within which these substantive issues are addressed. In the management of these meeting forums, the mediator influences the parties' participation, regulates the flow of information, and therefore projects his own preferred view of the proceedings. Indeed, mediators view this control over the meeting forum as a strategic resource just as integral to their efforts as substantive tactics more commonly associated with the process.

Meeting arrangements as a strategic element have been all but ignored in the empirical work on mediation. Knowledge of the rules governing meeting use comes, therefore, from the writings of practitioners. Guidebooks by mediators (Maggiolo, 1971; Simkin, 1971; Robins and Denenberg, 1976) make it quite clear that no fixed rules exist on meeting arrangements, but they do suggest that certain forums are more appropriate at certain stages in the process and in the face of particular circumstances. For example, joint meetings are to be preferred at the commencement of a mediation. At these opening meetings, mediators are urged to introduce themselves, to learn the issues that separate the parties, and to set ground rules to cover subsequent meetings. Joint meetings are also recommended to conclude the mediation, in order to give the parties time to review the agreed-upon provisions, prior to the final ratification.

During the middle phases of mediation, separate meetings with the parties presumably enable the mediator to learn more truthfully the parties' priorities and to permit him to "try on," without commitment, alternative solutions to the dispute (Simkin, 1971).

Situational considerations also apparently guide the choice of forum. For small negotiating committees, joint meetings are preferred. But when face-to-face discussions become heated and/or direct negotiations become stymied, the mediator is advised to separate the parties (Maggiolo, 1971). The choice of forum may be based on other strategic purposes. Stevens (1963) suggests that when a "contract settlement zone" is obscured by too many possible solutions, separate meetings allow the parties to engage in tacit bargaining, which may highlight certain prominent solutions over others.

In summary, these guidebooks describe certain conventions about meeting arrangements in terms of time and purpose, but they do not consider the ways in which meeting patterns may be used as a strategic resource by mediators to structure their own, and control others', participation in the proceedings. Since the mediators in this study seem to articulate different roles for themselves and consider meeting arrangements a part of their strategic repertoires, even these minimal conventions are unlikely to be slavishly followed in like form by all mediators. Patterns of meeting use will reflect the mediator's perspective on what forums work best for what purposes, taking into account the exigencies of the particular dispute. Orchestrators and dealmakers, as expected, arrange their meetings differently.

Variations in Meeting Arrangements

Mediators work on cases that are defined within the context of the face-to-face sessions and meetings they hold with the parties.[1] Prior to the first session the mediator has with the bargaining committees or spokesmen, the case has existed in docket form only, an assignment from a thirty-day notice or petition of impasse. If the mediator works for the state agency, that assignment typically leads directly, once matters of time and location are settled, to the first session of the case. A federal mediator may keep the case assignment in his files, monitoring negotiations over the telephone until a contract-expiration deadline is imminent and no agreement has yet been reached. Once the mediator convenes the first session with the parties, the case becomes a sequence of meetings where the work of mediation is done. The case exists until a tentative agreement is reached or until the mediator removes himself, by choice or suggestion, from the proceedings.

A case may span several sessions (discrete occasions that are separated in time), during which the mediator meets with the full bargaining committees or subgroups of them. Within each session, a variety of meeting formats is available to the mediator—the joint or separate meeting, the caucus held without the mediator present, and the off-the-record encounter with chief spokesmen. In joint meetings the parties meet, if space permits, "across the table" with the mediator at the "neutral head."[2] The mediator may separate the parties into different rooms and work with the union or management committee out of hearing of the other. Or the parties may caucus separately without the mediator present, either at his or their request. There are also off-the-record meetings held in a hallway or office, where the mediator meets separately or jointly with the chief negotiators, encounters that may be initiated by the spokesmen or the mediator. These meeting formats are the raw materials from which the mediator, by himself or in concert with the negotiators, can arrange the case proceedings. Recurrent meeting patterns are observable elements of a case that can be tabulated and analyzed to illustrate the different perspectives on practice introduced by the mediators in their verbal accounts of their roles. Consider the meeting arrangements in the following cases.

Sheridan Firefighters: An Intervention Arrangement in a State Case

Mediator Shaw convened only one session in connection with the Sheridan Firefighters dispute. Agreement was reached by the end of the session, though the full union membership failed to ratify it. Ultimately, the case was decided in final-offer arbitration, where, according to Shaw, the union realized fewer of its demands than it had in mediation.

The Sheridan town bargaining committee of two selectmen, the fire chief, and a labor-relations attorney crowded into the mediator's office. The union committee—the president of the local, two members of the unit, and their spokesman, a general-practice attorney—met in the hearing room, down the hall from the mediator's office. The mediator met first with the town committee, where the spokesman, well known to the mediator, presented both the town's and the union's most recent proposals, as well as some background information on other settlements in the town. The union's proposals included an increase in wages of 6 percent for the first year of the contract and 7 percent for the second, increases in the clothing allowance, education incentive payments, and the stipend for Emergency Medical Treatment. In addition, it asked for two shifts as personal leave and release time for the union president. Management offered a 1 percent increase in the first year and 2 percent in the second and proposed to delete the minimum manning provision in the contract.

The mediator started the separate meeting with the union committee by reviewing with it the proposal he had received from the town's spokesmen. On each of the demands, Shaw questioned the committee about its rationale—why it wanted it, how much it had had before, and what the police received. After reviewing the proposals and their "merits," Shaw described his version of mediation: "I will conduct mediation in the usual way, keeping you both separated unless it is necessary to bring you together. My philosophy is that mediation is a fluid process—whatever works, do it. If that means pulling your attorney out, I hope you will have enough faith to trust him and me."

Continuing with the union, he attempted to gauge its priorities: "What are you looking for on duration, wages, and the safety issue?" As they reviewed the proposal to identify other priority items, the mediator suggested, for their consideration, some possible trade-offs. After this discussion, he concluded the meeting: "I'm not going to ask you to alter your present proposals; I'll see if they are generous enough to do it. But you should be thinking along the lines I've suggested so we can get something going. We can drag this out over the summer, meeting every week, but I'd rather just go at it."

After a brief phone call concerning another case, the mediator came upon the two spokesmen, who had, they claimed, been looking for him. They were in the hall discussing two of the outstanding issues—minimum manning and wages. The mediator participated in their off-the-record meeting. He asked them both directly about their off-the-record positions on wages. After some evasive responses, in which the spokesmen reiterated their table positions, the mediator announced his intention to concentrate his efforts on the union committee. The town spokesman requested that the mediator meet first with his committee to reiterate his own position that more money would need to be forthcoming in the second year of the contract. The mediator did so: "Unless you are prepared to offer more money in the second year of the contract, I think I had better certify you to factfinding."

While the town committee polled absent members, the two spokesmen, myself, and the mediator adjourned for lunch. Lunch became an off-the-record meeting where the spokesmen reached an informal accord on some of the issues, which the mediator would try to get the union to accept. After lunch the mediator checked briefly with the town committee to learn the result of the poll, and armed with its revised wage proposal, went to "work" on the union committee. He presented the management offer as somewhat less than it, in fact, was. The union was far from pleased with the offer and suggested other areas of the contract that were important to it but had not been addressed by the town. During the discussion the union attorney called the mediator into the hall to give his "reading" on the committee and to suggest a proposal on another issue that had not been discussed at lunch.

The mediator met with the town committee and presented the union's proposal as given by the attorney and got, in return, a concession on other issues. Shaw then called the town attorney into the hall to ask what other concessions the town was willing to make and was told, "None." Before the mediator could report the counterproposal from management to the union, the union attorney requested a private meeting with the mediator to inform him that management's lunchtime proposal was considerably less than acceptable to the union. Shaw then "pulled" the town attorney from his committee for a joint off-the-record meeting. During the meeting, the management attorney agreed to some of the union positions but claimed that they would require considerable selling on his part. The mediator, in concert with the spokesmen, worked out a strategy to "ease the union into a settlement": "Why not this. I'll come back with 4 percent/3 percent, clothing, and the rewrite on manning. Then we let them counterpropose as close as possible. They'll want more than this, and then I'll come back with less. Then they may hit it the next time. I'll tell them the other issues are silly, and if this isn't settled in mediation, they'll lose the manning. Then you [union attorney] send me out and lay it on them and call me back when the package is ready."

This "script" as described was then acted out. The mediator met with the union, presented the first proposal, and left the union with its attorney to caucus. The attorney, in an off-the-record meeting, gave the mediator a counterproposal, which the mediator took to a "mock" meeting with the town. After a believable interval elapsed, he returned to the union with the next installment of the proposal, got one in return from the union, which he took to the town committee. A further concession from the town was added at this stage. The mediator returned to the union meeting with a package that had 1 percent less in wages in the second year than was actually there. The union counterproposed the additional 1 percent, which the mediator took to the town committee.

The management attorney was already typing the memo of agreement that included a wage increase of 4 percent in both years, a compromise on the manning provision that compelled the fire chief to keep the force at a certain level but reserved the right to deploy them, and an increase in both the clothing allowance and the educational incentive.

For the purpose of comparative analysis, we can summarize the meeting format used by the mediator and the spokesmen in Sheridan. Six separate meetings with the union and seven with the town committee, two caucuses—one by the union as it pondered management's proposal and one by management as it polled the entire board of selectmen during lunch—were officially held.[3] There were a total of seven off-the-record meetings; three of these, with the union spokesman, were held at his request, and one, with the management attorney, was convened at the mediator's request. Three joint off-the-record meetings occurred—the one the mediator came upon early in the case and the two he arranged later.

Bates, Inc.: A Negotiating Arrangement in a Federal Case

Bates, Inc., was settled in the early morning hours at the conclusion of the fourth session, four hours after the contract expired. Bates, a division of a larger corporation, had on its management committee a representative from the corporate office and four members from the local Bates plant: the plant manager and three support members from the financial and industrial-relations departments. The union committee was led by the regional representative of the union and five employees, all of whom were officials in the local. The first meeting lasted two hours. In monitoring the case, the mediator learned that the union had a proposal of some fifty to sixty items. He met separately with the union for the first session in order for it to present this voluminous proposal, which included wage increases of 7 percent for each of three years, increases in the cost-of-living formula, pension contribution, and insurance. In addition, the union wanted an extra holiday, increased vacation, provision for sick days, funeral leave, a different system for job bidding and training, as well as an overtime allocation system based on seniority. The mediator instructed it at the conclusion of this session to prepare a counterproposal for the next session that was more manageable.

The mediator convened the second session in a joint meeting where both sides presented their most recent proposals, the union's being substantially the same as the one presented to the mediator during the first session. Due to the bulk, the meeting was quite lengthy. The mediator confined the meeting to a mere presentation of issues.

To get the union to start "lowering its sights," the mediator met briefly with the committee and instructed it to caucus and "come up with a counterproposal that brings this thing into focus." The caucus, which took the better part of a day, resulted in a proposal that reduced the number of demands by half. The union proposal was presented to management in a joint session, and the second session ended.

Management started the third session of the case in a caucus where it continued, according to the mediator, to consider the union's proposal.

Prior to the upcoming joint meeting, the management spokesman came into mediator Baker's office to announce his plan for that meeting: "The game plan has changed. I'm going to read them a speech on our economic position. We'll let them meet and then together we'll go through the language items one at a time to give them an indication about where we'll move."

Baker convened the joint meeting and turned it over to the management rep, who read the prepared statement and presented the company's current proposal. Discussion, sometimes heated, between the union and management reps ensued about the veracity of the statement and some of the work practices management had proposed. The mediator instructed the union to caucus and to consider management's statement and proposal. Leaving the union to caucus, he met with management to discuss the implications of some of the work practices discussed in the joint meeting.

Following the meeting with management, the mediator met with the union to reiterate management's statement on its financial position. He instructed it to reconsider its proposal and to develop one that reflected their priorities, taking management's statement into account.

Based on the suggestion from the management spokesman, the mediator convened a joint meeting for the discussion of noneconomic issues. During the meeting, the mediator tried to move the discussion along, suggesting that they consider the next issue when discussions on one appeared at a stalemate. Often these suggestions were linked to possible trade-offs they might consider: "On either one, the cost on the Richter scale is nothing. Why don't you drop jury duty, and they'll give bereavement, and we can move on."

During the lunch recess, the union rep told the mediator in the privacy of his office that he was under instructions from the membership that no ratification meeting could be held until the typed agreement was in the hands of the members. This was a departure from previous practice.

Just as the joint meeting was to reconvene after lunch, the mediator was called to the telephone on another case. The parties ran the joint meeting without him, continuing their discussion of the noneconomic issues. After he returned he let the discussion continue as it had without him. When the talk ceased, he instructed the union to caucus to consider possible changes in the noneconomic package: "What you need to do, Joe, is bat this around and come back with a counterproposal on the economic and noneconomic issues. You need to bring this thing into focus. They [management] don't know what you want." He suggested further that to facilitate management's response, they might want to propose a duration of thirty-six months, so that the parties would have a common framework for negotiations. While the union caucused, the mediator met with the management committee and made some strategic suggestions. On the issues where it had no substantive objections, it would be "strategically wise" to concede. And that when it received the union's refined proposal, it should caucus for only a few minutes and request time to review it. In that way, it would not waste a move. The session ended in just the way the mediator described, a joint meeting and then a short caucus.

The fourth session commenced in a joint meeting. Management presented its position, and both sides, in the joint meeting, discussed the changed proposals on the noneconomic items. The mediator then met with the union and calculated for it how much the combination of the cost-of-living adjustment (COLA) and wage increases would net it, a figure he deemed unattainable. He instructed it to prepare a proposal that would be more "realistic."

Such a counterproposal was presented to management in a joint meeting. The mediator instructed management, as he had the union, to "review the proposal and work on a response." The representative from the plant came to the mediator's office during the caucus to give his reading on the areas of movement. Baker listened but later commented, "That's his bottom line. His committee may not agree. That's why I don't want to know it."

Management presented its proposal to the union in joint session. The mediator remained with the union and again instructed it to refine its proposal in caucus. This proposal was presented in joint meeting, and the mediator then met with management to instruct it to consider the union's refined proposal carefully. Management caucused, presented its proposal in joint session, and the mediator met with the union to reiterate the unrealizable dollar value of its wage demand and COLA. He left it to caucus, and its proposal was again presented in joint session. After that the mediator met with management, where agreement was reached to split the wage increase demanded by the union. This proposal was presented in joint session. In this last round the mediator spent a long time with the union and worked in concert with the union spokesman to develop a final proposal that would be acceptable to management. Management accepted after a brief caucus. Both sides came together in a final joint meeting, where management announced its acceptance. The union attained a 5 percent wage increase in each of the three years, modest increases in cost of living, pension contribution and insurance, an additional half-holiday, funeral leave, and overtime based partially on seniority. The mediator later claimed that the economic package resembled the contract they had negotiated three years previously, and a settlement at the wire was also replayed. The contract was ratified by the membership.

There were fifteen joint meetings convened in the Bates case. On twelve occasions, the mediator met separately with the committees—seven times with the union and five with management. Thirteen caucuses were held without the mediator, all at his instruction. Four meetings were held off the record,[4] all initiated by the spokesmen—three with the management negotiator and one with his opposite number from the union.

Analysis of Meeting Arrangements

Inspection of the meeting configurations and sequences in the Sheridan and Bates cases suggests some interesting contrasts in format. Mediator Shaw initiated the mediation session in separate meetings, first with the town and then with the union. Not once during the case did he bring them together in a joint meeting. The separate meeting forum, however, was in reality a screen for the off-the-record meetings where the mediator and the spokesmen discussed and cemented the elements of the agreement. To compare these observations with those in Bates, frequency distributions can be constructed that capture some of these facets of meeting arrangements. Twenty-two discrete meetings were held in the Sheridan case. Of these more than half (59 percent, $N=13$) were separate meetings Shaw had with the parties. Nine percent ($N=2$) of the total were caucuses held without the mediator present, and 32 percent ($N=7$) were meetings held off the record. Over half of the time, then, Shaw was meeting separately with the parties.

Mediator Shaw's description of his role in Sheridan Firefighters puts this format into context: "This is real mediation. I played an active role on the union side. I was a definite input into their thinking. I actively manipulated them." The role he described and the meeting pattern that emerged complemented and reinforced each other. Off-the-record meetings provided the forum for the creation of the deal, and separate meetings, particularly with the union, enabled him to "sell the deal" to the committee.

Baker started the mediation in a separate session with the union. At the request of the union negotiator, only the union was present at this initial session. This enabled the mediator and the committee to review their fifty-item proposal, a review that would have taken considerably longer if it had been conducted across the table. From there, the Bates case followed a different pattern in its subsequent sessions. Proposals were presented during joint meetings, and at the conclusions of these meetings, Baker instructed one side or the other to caucus for the purpose of presenting a counterproposal.

Joint meetings were also the forum for direct negotiations on non-economic issues. Baker also met separately with the parties in order to instruct them to clarify issues, to answer questions, and to make suggestions and in order to exert pressure on them to move. But the actual development of the proposals was accomplished in caucus without the mediator present. Though the meetings were not timed, it was clear that the time spent in separate meetings, particularly with the union, increased as the case neared resolution. The final separate meeting with the union lasted two hours; the "instruction" meetings held earlier in the case each lasted five minutes.

Over the four sessions of Bates, Inc., some forty-four different meetings were held. Thirty-four percent ($N=15$) of these were held across the table using the joint meeting format. Separate meetings with the parties occurred 25 percent ($N=12$) of the time, and 30 percent ($N=13$) were caucuses without the mediator present. Off-the-record meetings, primarily for procedural purposes—to discuss management's plan and the delay in ratification—comprised 9 percent ($N=4$) of the total. In contrast to mediator Shaw's emphasis on separate meetings in Sheridan Firefighters, Baker in the Bates case used caucuses and joint and separate meetings about equally. This format is given meaning in the context of Baker's articulated role in the case:

I brought them together. The process is to bring into focus which issues are the priority ones, but with the sheer volume, you can't tell. I don't work with them separately unless they are at each other's throats or unless they're on strike. I make them tell it to management across the table. I won't take it for them. It would take me forty-five minutes to write everything down and then forty-five minutes to report it. The process is to let them caucus and cut it down themselves. I ask you, is it better for me to go over it point by point and pressure them or tell them to do it themselves? It's the latter.

Like mediator Allen in the Albion Broadcasting case, Baker suggested that relying on joint meetings for the presentation of proposals and caucuses for their preparation, with input from the mediator in separate meetings, encourages the parties to continue their negotiations in a new forum. Mediator Baker felt this was particularly important in the Bates case, precisely because premediation negotiations had been ineffective, a conclusion that he drew from the size of the union proposal.

The comparative analysis of meeting patterns in Sheridan Fire-fighters and Bates, Inc., suggests differences in the frequencies of particular forums and the intentions for their use and has implications for how the mediator enacts his role. These observations can be translated into a set of inferences about meeting arrangements and the role of the mediator that can be tested for their general applicability across mediators, cases, and agencies. Abstracted from the analysis of Sheridan and Bates, the elements of meeting arrangement would include the following dimensions.

1. The frequency distribution of meeting types that involve the full committees—joint and separate meetings and caucuses—provides an overview of the arrangement and indicates, on balance, the forums in which discussions and decisionmaking are likely to occur.

2. The use of different meeting forums at various phases in the case and for particular purposes—learning the issues, exchanging proposals, and consummating the final agreement—has implications for understanding the mediator's position in the flow of communications. Based on data from Sheridan and Bates, it seems clear that separate meetings position the mediator as the major communication link between the parties, whereas the joint meeting, particularly for the exchange of proposals, has the parties communicating directly with each other.

3. The frequency of caucuses held without the mediator is an observable indicator of the opportunity the mediator has to be a significant contributor to the parties' deliberations. If the parties are left to caucus by themselves, by implication the mediator has less opportunity to become involved in the actual formulation of proposals. When the mediator is present at all deliberations, he has a forum continually to present his own views on the content of a particular proposal, and as the expert he will experience pressure to do so. The decision to adjourn to this forum may be made by the mediator or the negotiators. The balance between these two options serves to indicate the mediator's preference on this issue—whether, like Shaw, he wants to help shape the content or, like Baker, thinks it is better to have the parties do it themselves.

4. The frequency of off-the-record meetings and the source of their initiation are indicators of how the mediator views participation of bargaining-committee members and chief negotiators. In Sheridan Firefighters, off-the-record meetings provided the occasions for constructing a deal between the chief negotiators, a package that was scripted and sold to the union committee. Off-the-record meetings were a less significant component in the Bates case, in part because Baker believed that involvement of the bargaining committees was necessary to the creation of an acceptable package.

Table 3.1
Meeting patterns in Sheridan Firefighters and Bates, Inc.

Dimensions of meeting arrangements	Bates, Inc.	Sheridan Firefighters
1. Predominate meeting forum	Approximately equal	Separate
2. Frequencies (%)	$N = 40$	$N = 15$
Joint	38	0
Separate	30	87
Caucus	32	13
3. Use of meetings for various purposes		
To start mediation	Separate	Separate
To convey proposals	Joint	Separate, off the record
To agree on final package	Joint	Separate
4. Who initiates caucuses	Mediator	Mediator[a]
5. Frequency of off-the-record meetings (compared to total meetings)	Low (9%)[b]	High (32%)[b]
6. Initiators of off-the-record meetings	Parties	Parties and mediator

a. As part of his strategy, Shaw initiated the union caucuses. This approach was not observed in other cases, nor were the state mediators prone to initiate caucuses. See table 6.4.
b. Total meetings ($N=44$ for Bates, $N=22$ for Sheridan) is the sum of joint and separate meetings, caucuses, and off-the-record meetings.

Analysis of these four facets of meeting arrangement suggests two rather distinct patterns. In the Bates case, Baker used a *negotiating arrangement*, one that gave the parties maximal exposure to each other in joint meetings and ample opportunity, in caucuses, to construct their own proposals with assistance from the mediator proferred in separate meetings (see table 3.1). The label "negotiating arrangement" seems appropriate because it suggests that in orchestrating the case, the mediator is encouraging the parties to continue their negotiations in a new forum. In the *intervention arrangement*, observed in the Sheridan Firefighters case, the mediator is more of an active participant in the construction of proposals and their transmittal. In this arrangement, the committees have less opportunity to interact with each other and spend less time on their own without the mediator present. The negotiating and intervention arrangements were observed in other cases as well and serve to distinguish further the differences between orchestrating and dealmaking.

Across cases, federal mediators tended to exhibit the negotiating form of meeting arrangement with the distribution among forums approximately equal (see table 3.2). The intervention pattern is more in evidence in the state cases; on average, 75 percent of the meetings that occurred in the state cases were conducted separately. Federal mediators used separate meetings, too, an average of 44 percent of the time, but with considerably less frequency than was the case with the state mediators. The federal mediators balanced their use of separate meetings with approximately equal numbers of joint meetings and caucuses. Like mediator Baker, the federal mediators seem to favor joint meetings and caucuses as the preferred settings in which to conduct major parts of mediation. There were four other state cases that were like Sheridan Firefighters, in that no joint meetings were held, and two state cases where no caucuses were convened.

Evidence of the negotiating and intervention meeting patterns may also be observed in the intentional use of the forums to accomplish particular purposes. All but two of the state mediators convened the initial session in separate meetings, and used this forum to learn the issues in dispute (see table 3.3). The reverse was true for the federal mediators, of whom all but two learned the issues in dispute from the parties sitting across the table from each other, and all favored that forum for the exchange and discussion of proposals throughout the case. Like Shaw, the state mediators tended to shuttle proposals back and forth to separate meetings or to hand them to spokesmen in the hall. The patterns on concluding the case, where the parties signal their assent to the tentative agreement, are not as clearly divergent. The federal mediators tended to end their cases in joint forum, consistent with the view that consummation of the final agreement is simply the transmission of another proposal, the final one. Some of the state mediators also used the joint forum to review the elements of the tentative agreement, while others preferred to report it to the separate meetings.

Caucuses were a more consistent feature of the federal mediators' negotiating arrangement (see table 3.4). More often than not, these caucuses were held at the insistence of the mediator. The state mediators allowed the parties to caucus without them, but rarely initiated these forums themselves. Indeed, in the Rutgers School

Table 3.2
Frequency distributions of meeting types by case and agency

Case	(a) Joint meetings (%)	(b) Separate meetings (%)	(c) Caucuses (%)	Total meetings (T) in case (T=a+b+c)
State agency				
Reed School Committee	0	90	10	N=10
Regis School Committee	0	100	0	N=6[a]
Rutgers School Committee	0	42	58	N=7[a]
Scripps School Committee	27	62	11	N=26
Sheridan Firefighters	0	87	13	N=15
Taft School Committee	9	82	9	N=11
Tulane Firefighters	12	76	12	N=25
Ulster School Committee	9	64	27	N=22
Urbana Housing Authority	0	100	0	N=7
Vanderbilt School Committee	43	43	14	N=7[a]
Average	10.0	74.6	15.4	13.6
FMCS office				
Albion Broadcasting	14	53	33	N=51
Alfred Corporation	23	69	8	N=13
Bard Manufacturing	32	36	32	N=22
Bates, Inc.	38	30	32	N=40
Carroll University	40	30	30	N=27
Duke Hospital	29	43	29	N=7[a]
Average	29.3	43.5	25.3	26.7

a. These cases were not observed in their entirety:

	Number of sessions in case	Number of sessions observed
Duke Hospital	4	1
Regis School Committee	5	3
Rutgers School Committee	3	1
Vanderbilt School Committee	3	1

Table 3.3
The use of joint meetings to learn issues, to exchange proposals, and to conclude by case and agency

Case	Learn issues	Exchange proposals	End of case
State agency			
Reed School Committee	No	No	No
Regis School Committee	No	No	NA[a]
Rutgers School Committee	NA	No	No
Scripps School Committee	Yes	No	Yes
Sheridan Firefighters	No	No	No
Taft School Committee	No	No	Yes
Tulane Firefighters	No	No	Yes
Ulster School Committee	No	No	No
Urbana Housing Authority	No	No	No[b]
Vanderbilt School Committee	Yes	No	NA
FMCS office			
Albion Broadcasting	Yes	Mixed	Yes
Alfred Corporation	Yes	Mixed	Yes
Bard Manufacturing	Yes	Yes	Yes
Bates, Inc.	No	Yes	Yes
Carroll University	Yes	Yes	Yes
Duke Hospital	No[c]	Yes	NA

a. NA indicates that the case was not observed at the stage in question.
b. These cases were not resolved in mediation and went to factfinding. By definition, the finale was not observed.
c. Although the initial meeting was not observed, discussion with the mediator served as the source for this item.

Table 3.4
Distribution and use of caucuses by case and agency

Case	Caucuses (% of meetings)	Caucuses (#)	Party-initiated caucuses (%)	Mediator-initiated caucuses (%)
State agency				
Reed School Committee	10	N=1	100	0
Regis School Committee	0	—	—	—
Rutgers School Committee	58	N=4	100	0
Scripps School Committee	11	N=3	100	0
Sheridan Firefighters	13	N=2	0	100
Taft School Committee	9	N=3	100	0
Tulane Firefighters	12	N=3	67	33
Ulster School Committee	27	N=6	100	0
Urbana Housing Authority	0	—	—	—
Vanderbilt School Committee	27	N=1	100	0
Average	15.4	2.3	83.3	16.6
FMCS office				
Albion Broadcasting	27	N=16	25	75
Alfred Corporation	8	N=1	0	100
Bard Manufacturing	32	N=6	17	83
Bates, Inc.	32	N=13	20	80
Carroll University	29	N=7	14	86
Duke Hospital	29	N=3	50	50
Average	25.3	7.5	21	79

Committee case, where caucuses were a prominent feature, the mediator was barred by the parties from meeting separately or jointly with them.

Differences in off-the-record meeting practice were quite striking in the Sheridan and Bates cases. For the entire sample of cases, the pattern of divergence is not as distinct (see table 3.5). In their deal-making efforts, the state mediators made use of off-the-record meetings and tended to suggest that they be held. Although the federal mediators may also be observed meeting off the record, it is more often because the spokesmen have requested such an encounter. These patterns in off-the-record discussions can be understood in the context of the relationship the mediators have with these chief negotiators (see chapter 5).

In summary, then, the distinctions between the negotiating and intervention meeting arrangements observed in the Sheridan and Bates cases seem to be in evidence in other cases as well. The federal mediators orchestrate a case by arranging meetings in such a way that the parties are able to confront each other on their issues directly. In joint meetings, issues are learned, agreements are consummated, and proposals are discussed and exchanged. Although separate meetings with the parties are extensively used, so are caucuses where the parties are expected to meet without the mediator. Off-the-record meetings occur, but typically because the spokesman wants to meet with the mediator away from his committee.

In state cases, an intervention meeting arrangement is the pattern most in evidence. The state mediators appear to spend most of their time meeting separately with the parties, holding discussions with them, and transmitting proposals prepared in their presence back and forth between the separate meetings. There are occasions when the parties caucus without the mediator, but these tend to be at the parties' request, whereas the off-the-record meetings tend to occur more often than not at the mediator's initiative.[5] These observed patterns can be understood in the context of the mediators' accounts for why they arrange forums the way they do.

To Prove the Rule: Accounts and Variations

Neither the negotiating nor the intervention pattern of meeting arrangement appears in precisely the same form in every case. Personal preferences of individual mediators and the special circum-

Table 3.5
Initiation and use of off-the-record meetings by case and agency

Case	Off-the-record meetings (%)	Off-the-record meetings (#)	Spokesman-initiated meetings (%)	Mediator-initiated meetings (%)
State agency				
Reed School Committee	23	$N=3$	100	0
Regis School Committee	40	$N=4$	50	50
Rutgers School Committee	59	$N=10$	60	40
Scripps School Committee	7	$N=2$	0	100
Sheridan Firefighters	32	$N=7$	58	42
Taft School Committee	0	—	—	—
Tulane Firefighters	8	$N=2$	50	50
Ulster School Committee	39	$N=14$	36	64
Urbana Housing Authority	22	$N=2$	0	100
Vanderbilt School Committee	0	—	—	—
Average	23.0	4.4	44.2	55.8
FMCS office				
Albion Broadcasting	16	$N=9$	100	0
Alfred Corporation	7	$N=1$	100	0
Bard Manufacturing	18	$N=5$	80	20
Bates, Inc.	9	$N=6$	100	0
Carroll University	21	$N=7$	86	14
Duke Hospital	22	$N=2$	50	50
Average	15.5	5.0	86.0	14.0

stances of cases give rise to variations in pattern. But in the accounts they give for preferring one arrangement over another, and in the exceptions to practice they identify, it seems apparent that the observed patterns are not random, but an integral part of the way orchestrators and dealmakers mediate.

State Mediators

The state mediators allege that joint meetings are, for the most part, unworkable, unproductive, and likely to exacerbate hostilities. Their preference is for separate meetings supplemented with off-the-record meetings with chief negotiators, where, they claim, they can more objectively and efficiently learn the parties' true positions. This approach enables them to create a deal that is acceptable to both sides. These are their reasons:

Mediator Shaw: Most of the work is done in separate meetings; otherwise the parties fight with each other across the table. You rarely get any place with it.

Mediator Richards: Remember these people are at impasse. A joint meeting is a confrontation, and an ill-spoken word can blow it apart. Separating them cools them down.

Mediator Thomas: Separate meetings reduce the personality clashes and arrests the former bargaining style which was ineffective; that's why they are at impasse.

Mediator Unger: It's [separate meetings] the most efficient way to learn the facts.

In part, these perceptions are based on characteristics of the sector in which they practice—especially the possibility that the parties in the public sector will go to the prescribed next step, factfinding or arbitration, if mediation fails to yield a settlement. If this should occur, mediator Richards suggests that separate meetings protect the parties' bargaining leverage: "If I can't settle this case, they go to factfinding. If they make a proposal across the table, they may be bound to it in the next stage. If they give it to me and I take it and then I can't settle it, they are free to return to their premediation positions."

The minimal use of caucuses by the state mediators is related to their justification for separate meetings and is based, in the view of the mediators, on another characteristic of their sector, the parties' lack of bargaining expertise. As one mediator claimed, "The parties can't do it themselves. If they could, they wouldn't be at impasse."

This perception of the parties' inexperience surely has some of its roots in the mediator's case experience, but tends to be reinforced by the statutory procedures for mediator notification. One or both parties, in filing their petition for mediation, formally certify that they are at a bargaining impasse. The state mediators' tendency to assume, therefore, that the negotiations are at a stalemate and that the parties have been ineffective at resolving their dispute is based in part on the parties' certification that this is so.[6]

The state mediators' use of off-the-record meetings is further related to their perceptions of the parties and their negotiations. Whereas bargaining committees are seen to lack experience and expertise, certain of their chief negotiators are judged to be quite competent at bargaining. These spokesmen are known as professionals, and when they represent the parties, the mediator is likely to work with them off the record to formulate the elements of a deal and to plan strategy to sell the package to the bargaining committees. This is what occurred in Sheridan Firefighters, an approach that was not unique to that case. Mediator Thomas decribed this type of relationship: "When you work with professionals, you hardly have to talk to the total committee because the professional tells you where they are all the way through. They tell you what you have to do; it's a real team effort."

The intervention arrangement, then, is seen by the state mediators as the appropriate meeting pattern, given the character of the parties they tend to work with in the public sector. It provides the ideal setting in which a deal may be struck.

But not every case is run according to the intervention arrangement. Personal preferences of particular mediators as well as the special circumstances in the case frequently result in variations on the meeting pattern.

1. *Mediator preferences* Two of the state mediators had their own preferences for the use of joint meetings. Mediator Thomas, for example, claims that he always uses (and indeed was observed using) a joint meeting at the end of the case to review the agreement and to make sure that both parties understand and accept it: "I use the joint meetings to verify the package. That way there are no misunderstandings about what was agreed to." On the other hand, mediator Vance uses a joint meeting to start the case: "I like to bring them together to learn the issues." Vance also used a joint meeting on procedural matters to work out the scheduling details for the next case sessions. But for the purpose of proposal exchange,

these two mediators, like their colleagues, relied on separate sessions with each party, where the mediators acted as go-betweens.

2. *Nature of the issues* When the issues themselves are complex or quite technical, state mediators report that they will often encourage the parties to work jointly to straighten out the technicalities. Mediator Shaw, for example, remarks, "Last week in Yorktown there was an issue of health insurance. It was an issue that everybody knew better than I did. So I brought them in to talk about it. Otherwise you find yourself in a situation where the groups are saying, 'What if we did that?' I wouldn't know what they meant." Three of the state mediators explicitly linked their use of joint meetings to issues they thought were "ridiculous, irrational, or naive," positions that they would not convey. Mediator Unger states, "If I don't think the issue has merit, I won't take it in to the other side. I let them do that themselves."

3. *Apparent preferences of the parties* Bargaining committees may directly or indirectly express a desire for a particular meeting format. State mediators, for the most part, willingly permitted such deviations from practice. For example, in the Scripps School Committee case, the mediator found the parties together when he arrived at the town hall. Since they were together, he started the session in a joint meeting: "What I want to do initially is get the positions of the parties and since you're together, we can get them together. I usually separate the parties and work with you individually."

Similarly, at the start of the second session he found the parties in the same room. The purpose of this session was a review of the negotiating status of the contract. He kept them together as he found them and commented after the session, "The usual procedure is to separate the parties, but they didn't give me any reason to separate them, since they seemed to be able to talk to each other and were making moves." A request by the union to make a presentation directly to the school committee in the third session and an agenda for further negotiations to take place without the mediator in the fourth session were other "atypical" examples of joint meetings in this case. A request from the management spokesman to rectify a misunderstanding between the parties provided the occasion for the joint meetings in the Tulane Firefighters case.

In other situations, the parties requested joint meetings in order to communicate with each other directly about their positions. The full school committee in Ulster secured the cooperation of the mediator to convene a joint session for it to present its proposal. The union then caucused and presented its proposal directly to the attorney for the school committee. This return to direct negotiations, without the mediator, continued for the duration of the case, and indeed, the parties returned to bilateral negotiations without the mediator after two sessions with him. The situation in the Rutgers

School Committee case was somewhat different. Observations on meeting use were drawn from only the last session of a three-session case, and therefore the fraction of caucuses may be over-stated. This contention is supported in the account mediator Richards gave to explain why the parties were caucusing while he was standing in the hall: "I came on very strong the last meeting and may have outstayed my welcome. I can't do any more. I'll have to leave it to the attorney to bring it home." For these two state mediators, the extensive incidence of caucuses was seen as an indication that they were no longer playing an active dealmaking role. Excluded from the caucuses, they had to content themselves with off-the-record meetings as a way to keep apprised of case progress.

From the justifications the state mediators provide and the occasions that give rise to variations, it seems apparent that the intervention arrangement, with its extensive use of separate meetings and minimal use of caucuses, is not random. Rather, the arrangement stems directly from the perceptions these mediators have of the public-sector parties they work with and their own perspective on the mediator's role. Mediators deviate from the pattern in practice, but prefer the intervention arrangement. This is not the case for the federal mediators.

Federal Mediators

The state mediators allege that they prefer separate meetings because they believe the parties are more truthful and objective in that forum. The federal mediators claim just the opposite. They argue that in joint meetings the parties are more objective and truthful because they stare at their opposing numbers across the table. Mediator Baker argues that "you have to bring them together at the beginning to get the facts. Both parties need to agree where to disagree." Mediator Allen reasons that "they are more truthful in joint meetings because they have to look each other in the eye." Further, say the federal mediators, the joint meeting is a better reflection of the enduring relationship between the parties. Comments mediator Dixon, "The joint conference is best. I hate it when I'm forced to split it up. It's better to keep together, even if they are somewhat antagonistic. They have to live together when the mediator is gone." Joint meetings also place less of a burden on the mediator and diminish the chances for errors. In the Albion Broadcasting case, mediator Allen favored joint meetings because he was less likely to make a mistake in transmitting proposals. Mediator

Baker in the Bates case alluded to the unnecessary work involved in transcribing positions for 45 minutes and then reporting them to the other side for 45 minutes. Further, the federal mediators claim that using joint meetings for the exchange of proposals aids the chief spokesman in the work he has to do with his committee:

Mediator Baker: It helps the union rep, when his committee hears no across the table from management.

Mediator Carr: When they heard that response from management, they knew they could believe what their rep had been saying.

Mediator Dixon: When Jim [management spokesman] took the offensive, he was telling the union to take a hard look. That gives Joe [union spokesman] a way to get his committee moving.

Federal mediators' extensive use of caucuses complements their use of joint meetings and is related to their perception of the parties. Although bargaining committees may or may not be expert in the intricacies of collective bargaining, the chief negotiators who represent them more often than not do have such expertise. These professionals, who have often worked for years in the private sector, and frequently know the mediator professionally and personally, are seen by the federal mediators as pivotal actors in the process. In the work with their committees, these negotiators, according to mediator Allen, are the ones who move the parties toward settlement: "Pros know as much as I do about where these contracts should settle. But they have to bring their committees along. You know that they'll move them when they think the time is right." The federal mediators instruct the parties to caucus, for it is in this forum that the chief negotiators can work with their committees. This perception also partially explains why the federal mediators are reluctant to initiate off-the-record meetings, except for procedural matters. In order for the negotiator to maintain his credibility with his committee, the federal mediators believe that he must remain with it. Otherwise the impression may be created that he is making a deal behind its back. Federal mediators, then, use a negotiating arrangement in order to orchestrate the concession process. Such an arrangement, the mediators allege, encourages the parties to continue, in essence, their bilateral negotiations, with the mediator there as a resource to help the spokesmen when needed.

Federal mediators, like their state counterparts, also vary the arrangement of meetings. Federal mediators seemed to display less individual diversity than their state counterparts in their beliefs about what forums work best for particular ends. But they do alter their approach when they judge that circumstances warrant a change or the parties request it.

1. *Apparent preferences of the parties* Federal mediators claim that if the hostility between the parties becomes blatant, they will abandon joint meetings in favor of separate ones. But at what point does such a separation occur? If the observations in the sample are indicative, joint meetings will be abandoned only when the parties request the change themselves. For example, in the Albion Broadcasting case, the management committee felt that it took undue abuse in the joint meeting and requested that the mediator adjourn the parties to separate forums. Mediator Allen acceded to this request, but continued to encourage them to return to joint meetings. Whereas the state mediators seem to base their use of separate meetings on the assumption that antagonistic feelings between the parties preclude across-the-table discussion, the federal mediators seem to wait until such behavior occurs, and even then will not abandon the forum unless the parties insist.

Extensive off-the-record meetings observed in the Albion and Bard cases likewise reflect the preferences of the parties. In the Albion case, the final agreement was worked out in a five-person off-the-record meeting that was suggested by the chief spokesmen, but implemented by the mediator. So, too, in Bard Manufacturing, the final agreement was developed in the mediator's office at the instigation of the chief negotiators. Mediator Baker commented on the unusual arrangement in that case: "I wish they were all this way, but it is not the typical way to go. Usually you go the whole committee route. You can only do this if you have 'pros' who are trusted by their committees." Federal mediators, it seems, will use off-the-record meetings only when the spokesmen signal that they feel free to meet away from their committees. Sometimes this signaling occurs in the state practice, but at other times it does not.

2. *Issues* The issues in the case provide the other impetus for the federal mediators to abandon the use of joint meetings and caucuses. It was not the nature of the issues that resulted in the exception, but rather the number. In the Alfred case, there were too few issues, and in Bates and Duke Hospital, there were too many. The Alfred case came to mediation after a contract rejection. The parties requested mediation for the sole purpose of resolving one issue. In this situation the parties were not working from full proposals, but rather from suggestions by the mediator and the parties themselves on the single issue. Mediator Allen carried these suggestions back and forth to separate meetings: "With a one issue case like this, you are working from suggestions, not proposals, and neither side

wants to get committed. So you carry them back and forth and present them as your own."

The minimal use of caucuses in the Alfred case reflects the mediator's strategy for offering the parties' suggestions and some of his own in separate meetings. In Bates, Inc., and Duke Hospital, mediators Baker and Dixon, at the request of the spokesmen, used other forums besides the joint meeting to learn the issues in dispute. Baker met separately with the union committee because he and its spokesman felt that the fifty-item proposal would take too long to cover thoroughly in joint meeting. Dixon used an off-the-record joint meeting to view the voluminous proposal brought by the union. The spokesmen, who had never met before, asked for this meeting as a way to get acquainted with each other and the issues: "This is quite atypical at this stage of the game. But they wanted to do it, so I went along." And further, "The union rep [new to mediation] requested that we continue this way, but I said no. This was just a review, because there were so many issues and it would save time."

Like their state counterparts, the federal mediators seem to have distinct preferences for a particular meeting format. These preferences are based on what they believe works most effectively for their cases. When conditions appear different or change during the case, so will their arrangements, but with the demurral that these new arrangements are a departure from the usual and preferred.

Meeting Arrangements and the Enactment of Role

The state and federal mediators describe their roles as, respectively, dealmakers and orchestrators. They arrange their case sessions differently. Orchestrators favor a negotiating arrangement and dealmakers an intervention format. These patterns are not chance occurrences. The rationales the mediators provide, as well as their descriptions of exceptions, suggest that preferences for one pattern over another are based on deeply held convictions about the parties, their needs and expertise, and what works most effectively given the circumstances. These convictions are integral to the perspectives these mediators have developed about the process and their role in it.

State dealmakers attempt to arrange a mediation so that their access to information and their ability to influence the development of the package and to push the settlement in a particular direction are facilitated. They make these arrangements because they believe that the parties, frequently new to collective bargaining, have been ineffective in their premediation negotiation efforts and need, therefore, the mediator's sustained presence and continued substantive advice in order to reach an agreement. There is scant evidence to suggest that the parties see the situation any differently. With few exceptions (noted in the tables and text), spokesmen and committees willingly collaborated and worked within the meeting arrangements the state mediators imposed.

In contrast, the federal orchestrators use a negotiation arrangement that minimizes the mediator's sustained presence and maximizes the opportunities for spokesmen to work with their committees and for the parties to communicate directly with each other. The federal mediators seem to use this format as a way to further, in a new forum, the negotiations that preceded mediation. They argue that the interdependent relationship that binds the parties to each other and the potential threat of a strike create pressure for settlement. These pressures are best harnessed, the mediators claim, in direct, face-to-face encounters. Although sometimes the parties may balk, as some of the exceptions to the pattern indicate, most appear willing to accept the federal mediator's arrangements.

It is clear that the state and federal mediators play different roles and, in their enactments, create different meeting arrangements. But this is only a partial depiction of how the orchestrating and dealmaking roles differ in enactment. We have yet to consider what occurs in the context of these meetings. It is in the strategies and tactics, their form, content, and the circumstances of their use, that the differing roles can be fully appreciated.

4

Mediator Strategies: Building and Narrowing

To observe a mediator at work is to watch him talk. What, where, to whom, and when he says something are the basic tactical elements from which strategies are fashioned.[1] A strategy refers to the generalized plan or approach the mediator has for bringing the parties to settlement and allows him to impose a modicum of order on the process. It suggests to him the critical features of a case, highlights the problems he can anticipate, and allows him to exercise control over the process in order to maximize the chances that his objective of settlement can be achieved.

Mediators enter a case with a strategy in mind, one that is tied to their definition of role. The state mediators, intent on making a deal, seek to accomplish this by using a building strategy. Using the intervention meeting arrangement, they attempt to identify priority issues around which an acceptable package or deal can be formed. Dealmakers then use their powers of persuasion and pressure to convince the committees to make concessions on these priority issues. Federal mediators seem to favor a narrowing strategy.[2] They seek to orchestrate the continual exchange of proposals in such a way that the parties successively reduce the differences that exist between them. Powers of persuasion and pressure are reserved until the parties are unable to make further moves themselves.

What a mediator is observed doing in the pursuit of an articulated strategy can be called his tactics.[3] Whereas overall strategies derive from the role perspective the mediator brings to a case, his tactics are more situational in character.[4] That is, what a mediator says

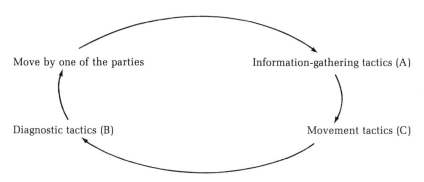

Move by one of the parties   Information-gathering tactics (A)

Diagnostic tactics (B)   Movement tactics (C)

Figure 4.1
Cyclical scheme of mediator's strategic activity.

and when he says it will be based on his immediate diagnosis of
the situation. As a result, it is difficult to extrapolate from the
isolated use of a tactic how it meshes with overall strategy. However,
in the frequency with which particular tactics are used, the purposes
for which they are intended, and the timing of these actions, certain
patterns of tactical behavior may be observed. Indeed, by considering
these patterns, one can infer the underlying strategies of which
they are a part.

Two Examples

Tactics and the strategies of which they are a part cover the full
spectrum of activities mediators undertake to settle disputes. Existing strategic models of mediation make sense of this complexity
by bracketing tactics into mediatory stages (Stevens, 1963; Kressel,
1972; Kochan and Jick, 1978).[5] In this view, a mediator seeks to
establish credibility and to learn priorities early in the case, to use
tactics to foster discussion during the middle stages, and to press
for concessions near the conclusion. Observation of mediators at
work suggest that this conception of chronological action is not
scrupulously followed. The mediator seeks information about
priorities throughout a case and employs tactical maneuvers to press
for movement right from the start. For mediators, the game of strategy is one of securing information, interpreting it, and making tactical moves on the basis of these diagnoses (Gulliver, 1979). It is in
this context of iterative diagnostic and movement cycles that tactical
patterns may be observed (see figure 4.1).

During the case, the mediator is continually engaged in diagnosing the potential for settlement and the probable elements of the agreement. These diagnoses take the following form. Information is both sought and given about priorities (A). These data are evaluated according to certain diagnostic categories that allow the mediator to make predictions about the case and suggest to him the kinds of tactics he will use to press the parties for concessions (B). Movement tactics are the observable actions the mediator takes to encourage such movement (C). The conclusion of a cycle will typically be a move by one of the parties that yields new information that the mediator uses to refine his diagnosis. With each move, the cycle starts anew and the process of information gathering, diagnosis, and tactical moves continues until at best a settlement is reached, or at worst, an impasse thwarts further movement.

These basic elements of the strategic cycles—gathering information, diagnosis, and encouraging movement—were observed in every case. Given contrasting strategies, however, the tactical patterns associated with each phase of the cycle differed between the state and federal mediators. During the early iterations of the cycle, the state mediators, as part of their building strategy, actively sought information about priorities and diagnosed these issues according to their conformity with certain patterns of practice. These mediators freely gave their opinions, advice, and suggestions about moves the parties should make on these issues. The federal mediators had less interest in identifying the priority issues during the early iterations of the strategic cycle and used movement tactics that encouraged the parties to narrow the differences between them on whatever issues they chose. Although they continually diagnosed the potential for settlement, the federal mediators rarely made direct use of this insight in their movement tactics until requested to do so. The following examples illustrate these differences.

Tulane Firefighters: A Building Strategy in a State Case

The first session of the Tulane Firefighters case convened in two separate rooms in the Tulane town library late in the afternoon. Though it was the first case mediator Thomas had with the unit, he had mediated other cases in Tulane and surrounding towns and was acquainted, therefore, with the counsel for the town, whom he regarded as "sophisticated in the workings and practice of labor negotiations." He had not met directly with the attorney representing the union, but knew from conversations with the town attorney that labor negotiations was a new field for him. Thomas indicated that he planned to consider the first session preliminary, his intent being to learn the facts of the case.

The formal session began in a separate meeting with the union. On the bargaining committee sat the president of the local, three members of the unit, and, in absentia, its attorney, who was ill. Though the union president was concerned at the attorney's absence and suggested a postponement until he could attend, the mediator assured the entire committee that the meeting was only preliminary and the attorney's presence would not, therefore, be missed. Because the members present had never been in mediation, Thomas described his style: "I do everything informally and I will explain what I am doing as we go along. Mediation is a confidential process; I will be telling you things in confidence and you will tell me things in confidence. You will, if you want a settlement. If we just go by the formalized procedures, there won't be any settlement, and that will hurt you. I think I know my job. I have been doing it for 30 years. I think I can get you a contract in the least damaging way possible."

Thomas then attempted to ascertain the facts. His first questions concerned the composition and relative power of the town bargaining committee: who was on it; who was the personnel assistant; did he speak for the mayor; how long had the fire chief been chief; who called the shots, the attorney or the personnel assistant? The next topic was the history of this negotiating round, where Thomas learned that a tentative agreement between the union and town attorneys was rejected by the mayor. Thomas requested and obtained the provisions of that agreement and the union's analysis of the mayor's rejection rationale. The mayor himself was also of interest to the mediator—his tenure, campaign platform, and previous job history. For intercommunity comparison, Thomas requested information about the tax rate, property valuation, and the budget-making process. Thomas declined the union president's offer to give him a refined proposal based on the rejection: "I am not interested in that now. I will be later. You can't just think of what you want. You have to think of your proposal's comparability to firefighters in other towns."

With instructions to the union to phone its attorney and to identify some future meeting dates, Thomas left it to meet with the town. After a warm exchange of greetings, Thomas described to the town committee his meeting with the union: "I went into a long dissertation with them about what is happening here because they are totally unschooled in collective bargaining and their attorney is sick. I indicated to them that this is an introductory session so that we can start to bring it to a head."

Thomas presented the union's position that a tentative agreement was vetoed by the mayor and gave his "reading" that such an agreement represented the union's settlement point. The town attorney denied that such an agreement ever existed and agreed to state this position directly to the union. The mediator then returned to the union to prepare for this confrontation: "I will tell you that there is a problem and we have to get to the bottom of it. You made reference to a tentative agreement. Management denies it. I've got to get to the bottom of this, so I am going to bring them in. On this occasion I have to."

At the joint meeting, the town attorney stated his position. After some heated discussion on both sides, the mediator adjourned the joint meeting because the absence of the union's counsel precluded "getting to the bottom of the misunderstanding." Thomas remained with the union to reiterate the need to schedule another session with its attorney present.

In the ensuing separate meeting with management, the mediator and management discussed the "root of the problem" and agreed that the inexperienced union attorney and the "green" committee were the cause. The mediator started to discuss the "supposed" tentative agreement: "I understand the monetary pattern, but I am a little amazed at the Emergency Medical Treatment (EMT) situation. I know and you know the way we keep EMT available is to pay a stipend, and $400 is on the low end of the stipends being paid. I get another negative from you that surprises me, the sick leave pool."

The sick leave pool was the first item of discussion. The mediator suggested ways that the town could control its use, but the attorney, basing his argument on the atypical duty tours, remained negative. EMT was the next provision discussed, and the enumeration of its assets by the mediator and liabilities by the attorney occupied the remainder of the session. Against a series of nays from the town attorney, the mediator made the case for an EMT stipend from a number of different perspectives: "It is common practice in other cities and towns. Its legitimacy is evident from its wide usage. EMT is dirty work and needs a sugar coating. EMT is a burden to the firefighters so they need to be paid for it. Firefighters will intentionally fail the qualifying exam unless paid. It is an important issue to the union and they won't concede it."

The town attorney ended the session with a compliment to the mediator: "What you have to find, as a talented and exemplary mediator, is some little area to settle this thing. There is no way we can give more than the wage pattern in the town."

Thomas checked in with the union and requested that its attorney phone him before the next session. The session adjourned and Thomas discussed with me his rendition of the first cycle:

This deal can be put together. If I read the town attorney right, the sick pool is off. I agreed with him. Given the structure of their duty tours [two twenty-four-hour-duty tours per week], it is not viable. You see I was testing the viability of that issue by asking for the reasons he disapproved.

On EMT I think the town is starting to veer toward my conception. Other towns do it. I think there is room there. I understand the town on money; you can't depart from the pattern. Later I'll tell the union, based on my experience, what a good settlement the wages are, relative to other towns. Of course, that depends on the comparability of the bases. That's why I wasn't interested in the union's proposal. It makes no sense unless it's compared with firefighters in other cities and towns. That's why I think the town attorney will go along with EMT—it makes sense comparability-wise. What I was trying to do was get the parameters. They gave me some, but like with EMT, I don't necessarily adhere. My goal always up front is to make a contract, and I think EMT will do it here.

Between the first and second sessions, the mediator learned the "root of the misunderstanding." Apparently the union attorney interpreted the town attorney's statement that the union's last proposal was "fair" to mean that he accepted it. Clarification of the misunderstanding was essential, said Thomas, to reassure the town attorney that the union attorney could be trusted in future dealings. Thomas described his suggestion: "I came up with the idea of a joint meeting where the attorney can clarify the situation with his own people, cool them down, and, in a half-hearted way, apologize to the management attorney. Then we will split up and go into bargaining. I told the union attorney that if the union takes the wage pattern and the town does something fair on EMT, we'll have a contract. By meeting with the attorney, it gives the impression that I am helping the union more, and that always helps."

The mediator began the second session with the union, announced his intention to convene a joint meeting to clarify the misunderstanding, and suggested that EMT was the most likely issue for discussion. The union presented its refined proposal on EMT and the mediator reported management's rejection and rationale on the sick-leave pool.

Thomas met with management, made his suggestion for a joint clarification meeting, and summed up his "reading" of the situation, based on the union's move: "I think if we can do something fair on EMT, we can make a contract." The management attorney responded, "We can't. Think in another direction." Thomas argued that the union's EMT proposal was fair and comparable to practices in other communities. When the personnel manager, using published data, challenged the universality of the EMT stipend, the mediator responded: "That's not the right measure. No factfinder would agree to that. You look only at your geographic area. You can't go outside your economic universe. I think if we don't do something fair on EMT, we won't be able to settle."

The joint-apology meeting was held, and at its conclusion the mediator remained with the town committee. He reported the entire union proposal, which included longevity payments, sick-leave accumulation, and a clothing allowance. He learned that apparently the longevity and sick-leave-accumulation provisions given to other units in the town had been accepted by the union. Thomas reiterated his "reading" of the settlement possibility: "Something small on the clothing allowance, EMT, and the money. I have a strong feeling that if we get a fair EMT proposal, we can get the salary down to the other unit's settlement. So the key rests entirely on EMT."

The town attorney said he would not consider EMT. After a brief discussion of the clothing allowance, the mediator returned to the topic of EMT. He claimed that since it was a nearly universal practice in other communities, refusal to consider it was sufficient reason to certify the dispute to factfinding. When the attorney suggested that the unique duty tours in Tulane made comparisons with other towns irrelevant, the mediator asked whether he could use the duty tours as a "quid pro quo" to pressure the union to concede EMT. The attorney vetoed such a tactic and presented a proposal on the clothing allowance.

Thomas: I've read them long and clear; EMT will be a stumbling block. Let's see if I read them wrong.

Attorney: You don't have to read them. Just convince them like you tried to do us on EMT.

Thomas: I'm not convinced. If you want to put out the quid pro quo on duty tours in exchange for EMT, that's something else.

The mediator met with the union and reported that longevity and sick-leave accumulation would follow the town pattern.

I haven't gotten too deeply into salary with them. My feeling is that they will give what the police got. The biggest surprise to me is that there is nothing on EMT. It appears they are totally unconcerned that most other towns do it, and though not a threat, they do throw out to you that you do have a good deal on the duty tours. The attorney indicated that he supports EMT, but the mayor is opposed. All I can say to you is that you would have to take a calculated risk in going further with this. You know the situation on EMT and the detriments of losing the duty tours. You know the bargaining climate and the procedures. I can't in conscience go further than that. You have to make up your own minds.

The union requested a caucus and at the conclusion presented a new proposal that verified agreement on longevity and sick-leave accumulation, reduced the wage offer, dropped the clothing allowance, and kept the EMT proposal the same. After some discouraging words on EMT, the mediator carried the proposal to management: "I know I will get a no from you. But I'd like to see your rebuttal."

Management requested a caucus, and at its conclusion the attorney gave the mediator a proposal for clothing allowance in the first year. En route to the union, the mediator discussed his strategy: "I am going to try to get the clothing allowance for both years. It's a little sweetener. The attorney knows he needs some sweetener." Thomas presented the proposal for clothing allowance in the first year and the union accepted it and altered its EMT proposal to defer its enactment to the second year of the contract.

Thomas reported to management, "I don't have a table position, but I have an indication that we can work around the problem to agree on the clothing allowance as you outlined it and probably agree on wages. Concerning EMT, they would consider postponing it a year because they feel it's a deserved stipend." The management attorney said that EMT was out of the question, that the city council and the mayor were opposed. The mediator stayed with EMT, arguing again for its merit and initiating discussions of its cost to the town and finally suggesting a reopener on it. The attorney ended the discussion: "There is no way to build anything in."

Thomas reported to the union his further efforts to get something for them on EMT: "I have given them all the warnings, but they want to tough it out." When the union asked his advice on what it should do, he suggested it take time to think it over and try to exert pressure on the mayor. In response to questions about taking the dispute to the next steps, Thomas painted a gloomy picture about the time it would take to get a settlement either in factfinding or arbitration. The session ended in a short meeting with management at which Thomas reported that the union wanted another session and suggested that it, the town committee, exploit its contacts in the interim.

Thomas was disappointed in the performance of the management attorney: "These people on both sides are inexperienced. What I'm trying to do is educate them, to show them that comparisons are the only objective means to decide what is fair. I've worked in 100 towns and to use comparisons is to introduce justice into the situation. The town attorney reneged. He should have pressured the mayor to do the fair thing on EMT."

Based on a phone call with the union attorney between the second and third sessions, the mediator learned that the union planned to accept the town's offer. At the start of the third session, the mediator met with the union and formally obtained the tentative proposal, which had been presented to the union membership as a mediator's proposal and agreed to. The union's proposal called for retroactivity on the clothing allowance. At the mediator's suggestion, this was vetoed by management, and management's proposal from the second session was agreed to in its entirety. Thomas concluded the session with a joint meeting to review the contents of the agreement.

Thomas used a building strategy in this case. Based on his diagnosis of the priority issues, he determined, during the first iteration of the cycle, that the final package should contain the town pattern on wages and longevity and include an EMT stipend, a practice he claimed was widespread. In order to press the town to concede on this issue, he used a wide range of movement tactics. When he was thwarted in this movement effort, he was forced by the management attorney to redirect his tactics and to persuade the union committee to drop EMT and accept the clothing allowance. In summing up the case, Thomas credited the settlement to two major factors: his introduction of the possibility that the union might lose its attractive work schedule if it continued to press for EMT, and his discouraging portrayal of its options if it failed to make the concession.

Bard Manufacturing: A Narrowing Strategy in a Federal Case

The union committee, five members of the unit and a representative from the International arrived first at the FMCS office. The mediator assigned them a front room and, at the request of the representative, allowed them time to caucus. When the management committee arrived, Bard's director of industrial relations, four technical support staff and their attorney, the mediator informed them that the union was in caucus. In the mediator's office, the management attorney told Baker, the mediator, that the case looked as if it would settle, the central issue being health insurance. The union rep announced that the union was ready.

A joint meeting was convened. The mediator asked the union to present first: "Okay, Charlie [union rep], why don't you give me a summary of where you are. Then Bill [management attorney] can tell me. We need to agree on where to disagree. The number one item as I understand it is the health and welfare."

The union presented its proposal on health and welfare (H&W). The discuussion that ensued on this issue was cut short by the mediator: "Obviously, we have to talk more about H&W. Next item, COLA (cost-of-living adjustment)." On each of the issues, the mediator had the union present its position and followed with some clarifying questions: "Your proposal on COLA, is it to continue as now constituted? You're both talking a two-year contract? How is the pension formula figured? Any sick leave now? How many holidays do you have now? What kind of bonus was it? A Christmas deal?" After the union finished its presentation, the mediator turned to the management attorney: "Bill, I'd like the benefit of your comments." Management presented its proposal along with its justification for certain of its positions. The mediator checked to see whether there were other issues and announced his intention to meet with the union first.

Baker began his meeting with the union by describing the posture of FMCS vis-à-vis the voluntary wage/price guidelines that had just been issued: "We are not enforcers. We are neutral. All we do is provide you with the necessary information. Because Bard has government contracts, I have to warn you that you run a risk with wages that exceed it. But remember the fringes are folded into the base. So it isn't just 7 percent of the standard average hourly rate. My function is to assist you to reach agreement."

After some calculations and discussion on the precise dollar-amount increase that would fall within the wage/price guidelines, Baker instructed the union to caucus: "You need to run down all the issues. You need a caucus, with or without the guidelines. No way you'll get the 10 percent and with 1 percent (from COLA), that's 11 percent. No way. That can't be firm. Charlie, what you have to do is go over each item individually and frame up a counter. Include your proposal on H&W, include just what you want. You want to keep COLA, put it in. You have to give them [management] a complete proposal so they can respond."

While the union caucused, the mediator gave me his diagnoses of the case:

The union needs to get its act together, shape up their position on H&W and cut the wages down. Then this thing can come into focus. If they're asking 10 percent and COLA, that's 11 percent. They have as much chance of getting that as flying. Other things will have to come off—sick leave—there's no chance. They don't have it in manufacturing, it's covered in the weekly Sickness and Accident (S&A). There are a few more items they can cut. But the next move is for the union to cut down their proposal. At a point, we'll recess to give the union time to get its act together.

A joint meeting was held. There the union presented its proposal, noteworthy for a complete H&W plan and a 1 percent reduction in the wage demand. The session adjourned because the mediator had another case in progress.

At the start of the second session, the management attorney drifted back into the mediator's office for some informal talk. The mediator suggested that management respond to the union's proposal, particularly the H&W plan, so that the union could caucus again. The attorney left and Baker commented on the union's H&W plan that called for full company participation: "Charlie knows the company won't buy it, but he had to pursue it. He took this case over from another rep so he couldn't just come in and pull the whole proposal down in one session. He had to show his committee he tried. That's why nothing happened in the first session, he needed time. Today, we'll get Bill's answer that full participation is out. That will show the committee Charlie tried, but management said no. Then I'll spend some time with the union committee to get them to make a counterproposal."

The joint meeting was convened. Baker asked the management attorney for the response to the union's proposal. After it was given, the mediator remained with the union: "At this juncture you see that bringing in all employees is out. You showed the cost savings and they still say no. Now in light of that you should look at your proposal and prepare a response."

The union rep requested that the mediator obtain the cost of the company's fringe benefits in order to prepare a response within the guidelines. The mediator agreed and further instructed the union committee: "Charlie, your job is to work to bring this into focus."

En route to management's room, Baker commented that it helped the union rep to have no said directly across the table on the H&W participation.

Baker met with management and requested the cost figures. It gave him total cost, but he pressed for itemized costs, which it needed time to get.

The mediator returned to his office and was joined by the union rep, who did want the itemized costs. However, his purpose in meeting with the mediator was to request that the next mediation session be deferred until after the upcoming holiday because ratification meetings were hard to schedule at that time. The rep went on to report that his relationship with his committee was much improved, that they were listening to him. The mediator asked the management attorney to join them in his office to discuss deferring the next session. The attorney agreed to this and after some reluctance also agreed to provide the itemized fringe costs. They planned that the mediator would meet with the union and give it the total cost, the rep would ask for cost breakdowns, and they would arrange for the union to meet in the interim to prepare a proposal based on these costs. While the attorney checked dates with his committee, the mediator suggested that the union rep return to his also: "Incidentally, does your committee know you're in here? Maybe you should go back and tell them I called you in."

After the rep left, the mediator discussed the meeting between the spokesmen:

This is unusual. You can't do it with everybody. I know these guys. People think this kind of thing happens in the majority of cases. It doesn't, but it would be nice if it did. But here the principals are both "pros." They've been in the business a long time. There are no emotions. But you have to remember that they are negotiating with each other and with me too. They represent their constituencies very well. If you think they're here for you to make a deal, your're wrong. Charlie gets what is best for his committee.

After the management attorney set a date for the transmittal of the cost data, the mediator met with the union to report: "We're finished with the logistics part. I pointed out to Bill that it was essential to get the breakdowns. Charlie, the plant manager will give them to you and then you can get in touch with your guys to work out a counterproposal. During that time, you can meet at our offices if you want."

Baker adjourned the session and explained his final meeting with the union committee:

When you do a lot of one on one, you have to update the committee and let them know what you are doing. The bottom line in this thing is rati-

fication of the contract. And you can't get to that unless you have a recommendation from the full committee. If you don't keep them up to date,
they will balk. So when you short-circuit, you have to inform the committee.
You never short-circuit their participation in the process because they have
to recommend it. In the ideal situation, you try to get the last move from
the union with their recommendation. Then you are asking people to ratify
their position, not the company's.

The third session started with a union caucus. Although it had met in
the interim, the union rep said he needed more time. Shortly after the
start of the session, the rep asked the mediator to meet with his committee
to talk about its proposal, which was written on the blackboard.

Mediator: You haven't changed anything since last time. You're still at 9
percent and you've gone backward on the pensions.

Union Rep: We're prepared to do more.

Mediator: When? Do you want to be here all night? In terms of bringing
this into focus, this is nothing. The people in the other room may look at
this and say, that's it—take it or leave it. Now you guys know me. It would
be easy for me to sit here silent. But I have to give you my reaction. My
reaction is that you are going backwards. Now I don't have to tell you,
Charlie. You know the game better than I do. We're looking at the same
stuff as two weeks ago. They'll think, what encouragement do they have
to change their position? You are doing yourself an injustice with this kind
of proposal. Now before you caucus, let me say that this is your version.
It's your proposal, but you asked for my opinion. It's easy for me to sit
silent. So take a few minutes to kick this thing around.

Baker left the union to caucus, and back in his office discussed what
had transpired in the union meeting: "Charlie was having trouble with his
committee, so I helped. Yes, I used a bullet in there. You see you let them
go to the extent that they can drop things by themselves. You have to
massage, but you don't use your ammunition too soon."

Later the union rep came into Baker's office and complimented him.
"You really do fine work. We changed the figures. I was playing straight
for them, giving you the numbers. Then you came in and said it was crazy.
I love FMCS."

The mediator met with the union, reviewed its proposal, and called a
joint meeting for its presentation. Management stated that it had already
done the best it could, but agreed to take another look. The rep indicated
the union's willingness to modify further, but it too was not far from where
it hoped to settle.

The mediator met briefly with management to clarify some questions it
seemed to have on the new proposal: "Just to keep the dialogue going, look
at what your premiums are now and what they are proposing. I'm just
trying to clarify this."

While management caucused, the union rep drifted into the mediator's
office to chat about old friends, but at the mediator's suggestion returned

to his committee. "Procedurally, I think it's a good idea to stay with your troops because I may be calling you out later."

The management attorney told Baker that his committee had made some improvements on their proposals, but that little was left after that. Baker suggested that it present its proposal in joint session and then get the union rep out to decide what to do next. The joint meeting was held, and the mediator instructed the union to caucus and call him when it was ready.

At this juncture, the mediator considered a strike unlikely because most of the major issues had been addressed by management. When the union rep came into Baker's office to use the phone, he and Baker discussed the procedure. Said Baker, "I think it might be helpful for you and me and Bill to sit down. Unless Bill is playing poker with me, I don't think there's much more. What are you going to do in your counter? It looks to me like you'll get the bonus and something on the pension, and that's the ball game, but it's a good ball game."

After some discussion the mediator suggested that the rep return to his committee. The rep replied, "I'll go back and tell them I have been on the phone."

A joint meeting was held, and the union presented its proposal. Again the rep needed to use the phone to ask some questions about benefits, and this provided the occasion for a three way off-the-record meeting. Baker began it with the comment that "the time has come to talk. Put yourself on dial-a-prayer, Charlie."

The spokesmen discussed certain aspects of the H&W plan, employee contributions, and the changing costs. Baker participated only to ask questions about things he did not understand. The union rep introduced the remaining issues that had yet to be resolved:

Attorney: You want me to tell you. I will if you make a commitment. I'll tell you the most we'll give if you promise you won't chisel for any more. Earlier, you said that when I give you my bottom line, you can always come up with more. That hurt. I won't tell you if you are still talking about some of these other issues. If that's the case, there's no point.

Union Rep: I know I can't bleed a stone.

Mediator: What's the best way to get this on the table?

Union Rep: Didn't you get the last proposal?

Mediator: This either has to be the final-final, or Charlie, maybe you can get your troops to do it.

Attorney: [To Baker] You can give it without commitment.

Mediator: I have no compunction about telling them that this is it, that you don't have it yet but are willing to do the work for it.

Attorney: That's what I like about mediator recommendations. It's not a new plateau.

The mediator wrote down his understanding of management's proposal and checked it with both spokesmen. He rechecked the proposal and reviewed how he would present it. The union rep claimed it was going to be difficult to sell it to his committee. Both spokesmen left, and the mediator explained why he thought his actions were likely to succeed: "This is why the process of narrowing down is so important. The wage offer is the union's. The complete H&W is theirs. They got the bonus and COLA they asked for. When you get them to narrow down a lot, the issues are theirs."

Before going into the union meeting, the mediator checked the proposal again with the management attorney. He then met with the union:

To get to the bottom of this, while Charlie was on the phone I called Bill into my office. He was firm about the last proposal. I told him there were still some areas he should address—the pension and the bonus. He justified his position. To make a long story short, I told him to keep talking. The way he tells it, he'll give the pension and bonus, your proposal on H&W and S&A. I called Charlie in and he made an impassioned plea for the vacation and personal leave. No way. Bill doesn't even have this, but he said he'll work for it. I don't have it either. He told me with Charlie there that if this represents an agreement, he would try to get it. But only up to this point. His people said no more.

The mediator reiterated the monetary benefits the union would receive, how hard Charlie had tried for the other issues, and that these concessions were based on the union's proposals: "In my humble opinion, this is the best chance to get the three big things. But if that doesn't do it, I'll tell him not to waste our time. As I told you, Charlie, I can't guarantee it. He has it sell it."

The mediator left the union to caucus. Some time later the union spokesman came out to call the mediator in. Vacations were still a sticking point. The mediator argued that it couldn't get them. If it did, the demand would represent 1 percent of the total package, which would affect only fifteen members of the unit. Further, if it struck over it, the last formal position, without the bonus and pension, would hold, and it was not assured of recouping them after a strike. With further discussion along these lines, the union agreed to recommend the package unanimously. The proposal was presented at a joint meeting. Management caucused and accepted.

Two weeks later the union membership ratified the contract.

Baker used a narrowing strategy in this case. Each cycle was concluded with a formal, across-the-table exchange of proposals. Baker's knowledge about priorities came primarily from these exchanges. During the early iterations of the cycle, Baker emphasized tactics that encouraged the parties to refine their proposals without discussing extensively with them the form such refinements should take. Later in the case, after an agreement had been reached off the record, he then used tactics to persuade the union to make the

Table 4.1
Information sought at first meeting

	Tulane Firefighters	Bard Manufacturing
Purpose of first meeting	Learn the facts	Learn the issues
Forum for starting the case	Separate meetings	Joint meeting
Topics addressed at initial meeting	(1) Basics of proposal; (2) mechanics of some provisions; (3) negotiating history; (4) political climate of town; (5) tax status; (6) budgetary process; (7) composition, personality, and authority of bargaining committees	(1) Last proposal from each side; (2) mechanics of some provisions; (3) status of provisions under existing contract

final concession. Baker believed that his narrowing strategy was effective because the two chief negotiators were able to oversee it. They knew what the important issues were, stuck to them, and encouraged their committees to drop the others.

Analysis of Strategies and Tactical Patterns in Tulane Firefighters and Bard Manufacturing

By the mediators' standards, the Tulane and Bard cases were successful. At their conclusions, the parties had acceptable packages that were subsequently ratified and approved. The strategies and the tactical patterns associated with the development of these packages differed, however, at each phase of the cycles and over their iterations. These differences are noted first in the initial meetings the mediators held with the parties for the purpose of learning the issues in dispute.

In these initial meetings, the mediators sought to gather the kind of data necessary to implement their strategies. To build a package, Thomas claimed that he needed to understand the political and economic constraints that existed in the town. To that end he asked a series of direct questions about these facts (see table 4.1). Baker's agenda for his initial meeting with the parties was somewhat different. He simply wanted to be sure that the range of issues on which the parties disagreed was introduced at the outset. For he claimed that his narrowing strategy could be upset if extraneous issues surfaced later in the case.

At the conclusion of these initial meetings, both mediators had a sense, and could discuss, what they thought the relevant issues were and what form the final settlements might take. The remainder of the cases may be understood in a similar manner. Information about priorities was sought by the mediator and given by the parties. These data were interpreted by the mediator and used to diagnose the potential for settlement and the probable content of the agreement. Tactical moves were made by the mediators based on these diagnoses, and then the actual moves became a new source of data by which settlement potential could be judged. These reflective and reiterative patterns are the tactical elements of strategy.

Gathering Information from the Parties about Priorities (A)

Baker and Thomas were interested in the parties' priorities. Priorities mean several things in this context. In terms of the demands that comprise a proposal, priorities mean those issues that are crucial or "musts," as opposed to issues that may be "nice, but are not necessary." Wages are usually considered priority issues. Work rules, such as shift preference and manning levels, and fringe benifits, such as medical plans, vacations, and maternity leaves, may or may not be priority issues, depending upon the particular situation. But priorities do not refer solely to the issues themselves; they also include the level of benefit sought—that is, how many vacation days, what wage increase. What interests the mediator, then, are those issues the parties consider top priority and the level at which they are to be compensated. It is obvious that if the mediator were privy to all this information, he would know the parties' "bottom lines." Baker and Thomas had differing opinions about how much information they needed and when this information had to be forthcoming.

In order to build a package, Thomas claimed that learning priorities early in the case was crucial. Just prior to the case, he articulated this view: "You try to get the bottom line, realizing that it changes. You may have to sweat it out of them. You keep asking directly and keep hammering it down. You keep asking what the priorities are." And after the first session he reaffirmed this view: "You need to get the core of the matter, and often the parties don't know what it is. So priority issues are not what they say they are, but your experience about what's important and your determination of what is obtainable." In the Tulane case, EMT was deemed the priority issue.

Baker also claimed that he needed to know priorities, but believed they were not knowable until later in the case. This was true, Baker said, because the union was unsure about what it wanted and management, though probably clear about its goals, was unlikely to reveal them until the union position was clarified. As Baker said, "I know from experience what the key issues are, but it's their priorities that are important. They have to get a fix on what they want and they can't do it until they bring their proposal into focus." On the need to know the bottom line, Baker commented several times: "I don't want to know it. It may not do it. Besides, they don't know yet what they really want. As for management, they'll tell me when the time is right."

Starting from rather different postures on the "need-to-know" priorities, Thomas and Baker seemed to emphasize different tactics in order to learn what they needed to know. Thomas sought information on priorities by discussing each issue separately, a tactic he called "testing the viability" of an issue. This tactic was used in several ways. He would *ask* directly. For example, on the tours of duty, he asked the town whether they intended to put that informal work practice into the contract. He felt that this should be a union priority (it did not appear to be); therefore he wanted to determine what the town's position was on it. If a committee voiced an objection to a demand, he made a *suggestion* as to how to solve the problem it identified. If it still was unconvinced, he judged that it was not viable. For example, when the management attorney claimed that the cost of a sick leave bank would be excessive, Thomas offered some examples of how the clause could be written to prevent its abuse. When the response was still no, he judged the issue "dead": "You see, I showed him [management attorney] how we could 'condition' it to take care of his problems. When he still said no, I knew it was off the table."

Thomas's major attempt at viability testing concerned the issue of EMT. Convinced that it should be a priority, he tried to offer suggestions and to argue for its inclusion in order to determine how strong management's objections were. What characterized these efforts is the emphasis he placed on these active information-seeking tactics during the early iteration of the cycle.

Later on in the case, information about priorities tended to come more from *moves* the parties made and from *confidences* given him by the management attorney. From formal proposals prepared by the union, he learned that EMT had indeed become a priority issue. During the second iteration of the cycle, the union dropped its demand for the clothing allowance in order to strengthen the case for EMT and, in the next cycle, proposed to defer the stipend until the second year of the contract. In off-the-record encounters, Thomas was informed by the negotiators of changes in their positions. He learned from the union attorney that if management would concede EMT, the union would drop its other outstanding demands and agree to follow the town pattern on wages and longevity. And from the management attorney he learned, off the record, that EMT was definitely not a consideration, but that compromise was possible on the clothing allowance.

Baker's posture with regard to priorities was somewhat different. For most of the Bard case, his information about priorities came not as a result of direct tactics to secure it, but rather from formal *moves* and spokesman *confidences*. Before the first joint meeting, the management attorney indicated, off the record, what management's priorities were—employee contribution to the health insurance plan and wages within the limits of the federal guidelines. During subsequent cycles, priorities were revealed primarily as the parties presented their refined proposals to each other. The highlights of these proposals were frequently reported off the record to the mediator just before they were formally presented.

Baker learned the bottom line in an off-the-record meeting, held near the end of the case, wherein the elements of the final agreement were discussed by the chief negotiators in his presence. The timing of this meeting is important to note. In a similar one held during an earlier cycle, both the parties and the mediator were reluctant to discuss the bottom line:

Attorney: You and I should settle it.

Rep: You haven't told me your bottom line. You're waltzing with me.

Attorney: I told you—no vacations, no bonus.

Rep: No vacations? Your bottom line always changes.

The mediator commented on this interchange: "What Charlie [union representative] was saying was, I don't want your bottom line. It's too soon. He doesn't know what his troops will take."

Even in this forum, presumably conducive to honest talking, the emergent quality of priorities and positions can be observed. From Baker's perspective, ultimate positions or settlement points were less important than the parties' willingness to keep meeting, talking, and negotiating. After the union failed to make a substantive move, Baker gave voice to this concern: "As long as they keep talking to each other, that's what I monitor. You worry that a move like that, management will say, that's it."

In summary, Thomas, the state mediator, felt he needed to know the parties' priorities. On balance, therefore, he was more likely to seek this information directly, early in the case, than to wait for such data to be divulged. In contrast, Baker seemed more concerned that the parties demonstrate that they were narrowing their differences than that he ascertain the precise nature of their substantive priorities, particularly early in the case.

Diagnosis of Potential and Priorities (B)

As mediators learn of the parties' intentions and develop a sense of the priorities each side has for settlement, they begin to make predictions about whether the parties are likely to settle, and if so, what form the agreements will take. To make such predictions, mediators rely on interpretive categories that enable them to make sense of what they hear.[6] Three categories seem to be of general concern in the Tulane and Bard cases and appear to underlie the mediators' tactical moves.

First, the relative *bargaining power* of the parties was assessed. Relative bargaining power refers to the mediator's assessment of which side is more likely to realize its demands, and complementarily, which party will have to "move the furthest" for a settlement to be reached. The mediators' estimation of bargaining power seems to be based on two intertwined criteria: (1) how critical the employees are to the functioning of the organization and, relatedly, (2) how capable the union is of striking and management of withstanding this action.

Second, the relationship between the demands and "*patterns and standards of practice*" was considered. Whereas estimations of bargaining power help the mediator predict the shape of the final agreement, mediators tend to assume that the form of the agreement, that is, the contract provisions, will conform to certain patterns and standards of practice. When mediators use the term patterns, they refer to historical settlement ranges, wage scales, and practices with regard to fringe benefits and work rules in comparable industries and/or contiguous communities. Thus as demands are introduced and modified, they are diagnosed by the mediator according to their conformity to or deviation from what are thought to be patterns.

Third, mediators develop an assessment of the *chief negotiators*, based on firsthand knowledge and reputation. Statements from chief negotiators, particularly those who are seen as competent professionals, have the power to modify the mediator's diagnosis about settlement and contract provisions that were based on relative bargaining power and patterns.

Relative Bargaining Power

Tulane Firefighters was a public-sector case, as indeed are most of the cases Thomas mediates. As a result, Thomas entered the case with certain assumptions about bargaining power and its relationship to the final package. These assumptions influenced his tactical behavior. Because public-sector unions are denied the right to strike, Thomas claimed that the balance in negotiations is always tipped in favor of management. He believed, therefore, that much effort would be devoted to moving the union committee, because it would have more concessions to make. In addition, he expected to aid the union by pressing its positions with management, for he felt that without such efforts the union would be unlikely to realize its demands. Indeed, Thomas's efforts early in the case to press for EMT must be understood against this background.

For Baker, diagnoses of bargaining power depended on the specific circumstances of the Bard case. The union had the right to strike and had exercised this right during the previous negotiations. Prior to the start of the case, therefore, Baker was unclear about the power relationships. Early in the case, he learned that the company had decentralized its operations, leaving only one of its three plants unionized. In the event of a strike, the company would be able to shift its operations to the nonunion plants. Therefore the company was in a stronger bargaining position than it had been in the past, and as a result, Baker expected that the final agreement would reflect this power. Given this changed power configuration, Baker predicted that the union would not strike, a position that was affirmed by the union negotiator. Baker's evaluation of management's bargaining power vis-à-vis the union led him to expect that later in the case, he would have to become directly involved in the efforts to exert pressure on the union committee to make the final concessions.

Patterns

Whereas assessments of bargaining power helped the mediators to predict whose positions the final agreement would reflect, evaluation of patterns suggests the range of settlement on particular issues. Patterns have a particular meaning in this context. In major sectors of the U.S. economy, particular patterns on wages and other economic benefits seem to exist. Among and within certain industries, notably trucking, autos, rubber, and steel, the parties to negotiations appear to follow patterns set by others (Ross, 1948; Dunlop, 1957; Bourdon, 1979). The patterns invoked by mediators are not so stringent or systematically apparent, but seem to be looser and more intuitively divined. But as loosely constructed as they are, patterns seem to have an existence in the mind of the mediator apart from the particular context and appear to him as an "objective" standard to apply to any dispute. Patterns and standard practice represent the "fair," "rational," and "logical" position for the parties to consider and adopt. Indeed, both Baker and Thomas made continual reference to patterns and practice and tended to evaluate many of the issues according to their conformity with or deviation from such standards.

For Thomas, patterns were of overriding importance in his assessment of the issues. From the start of the case, Thomas based his evaluation of the issues on their conformity with patterns set by other units in the town and practices in contiguous communities, and he sought to build a package based primarily on these assessments. Because the firefighters were the last unit in the town to settle, he assumed throughout the case that wages, longevity payments, and sick-leave accumulation would follow the town patterns. This meant that Thomas never discussed these issues with the union, even though for most of the negotiations, their demands were higher than the pattern. His identification of EMT as the issue that would settle the contract was likewise based on his perception that the payment of a stipend for EMT was a pattern observed in other communities. Management's challenge to the universality of this practice, and Thomas's rebuttal—"You are looking at the wrong communities"—only serves to demonstrate how loose is the construction of patterns.

For a mediator like Thomas, who works extensively in the public sector and whose caseload exposes him continually to similar occupational groups in contiguous communities, it seemed quite natural to make comparisons between demands in this case and similar settlements in other towns. Thomas gave voice to this tendency when the union wanted to present its initial proposal at the start of the first session. He told it he did not want to consider the proposal until it had supporting documentation from other communities: "In the public sector, we are very primitive, but we do have a first measure—to compare your proposals with agreements in other towns."

Baker also assessed the issues with reference to patterns and standard practices. In terms of wages, the government's wage/price guidelines was one pattern of note. Baker learned early in the case that the company had a number of government contracts, information that led him to predict correctly that the wages would fall within the guidelines. The other economic provisions, particularly the bonus and COLA, were assessed by Baker in terms of precedent established in previous contracts. He predicted throughout that at some point management would offer the same terms on these issues as it had in the past. For fringe benefits, such as vacations and holidays, Baker compared the union's demands with industry averages and judged their likely inclusion in the final agreement accordingly. Finally, the union's demands for sick days and personal leave were judged by Baker as unattainable because they were not common practice in the industrial sector.

Baker's references to patterns as a way to put demands into a manageable and predictive context were, like Thomas's, casual and vague. Some were based on his recent experience on other cases, while the rest came from his perusal of standard reports furnished by FMCS. Although he undoubtedly read these sources, his recollection was selective and less than complete. In contrast to Thomas, however, Baker's allusions to these patterns were not made to the parties directly until late in the case. Although they were clearly a category of diagnosis, references to patterns were not translated directly into tactical moves.

People

If the only thing the mediator had to concern himself with was the issues, a package based on patterns could be easily fashioned. But the issues belong to the parties, and how the parties act with regard to them further influences the mediator's diagnosis of potential and priorities. Thomas made certain assumptions about the parties, a few of which had to be revised later in the case. He viewed the union committee and its negotiator as inexperienced, which meant, he claimed, that it would be anxious for his guidance about the "right" kind of settlement. He seemed correct in this assumption, for the union was guided throughout by his advice—it embraced his EMT suggestions and settled for the clothing allowance when he assured it that EMT could not be attained.

His perception of management changed during the case. Having worked with the management attorney previously, he viewed him as competent, and as someone who would recognize the merits of his pattern-based arguments. Because of this initial perception, Thomas accepted without question the attorney's rejection of certain issues—in particular, the sick-leave bank—and believed his version of the illusory tentative agreement, that the union attorney had misunderstood him. Based on these perceptions, Thomas predicted, until he was proved wrong, that the final package would include an EMT stipend. When, despite Thomas's best efforts, the attorney continued to reject EMT, the mediator's assessment of him changed. He began to doubt the attorney's expertise and referred to him as a "reneger" and was forced to revise his diagnosis of the package that could be built.[7]

From Baker's perspective, the presence of two able chief negotiators was a distinguishing characteristic of the Bard case. Off-the-record indications from them that the case looked settlable (based on a comment from the management attorney and the union negotiator's affirmation that he did not expect a strike) led the mediator to expect that an agreement would be reached in mediation. Further, because the spokesmen knew each other well and had worked together in the past, Baker expected that they would eventually consummate an agreement off the record. His sense of the process, therefore, was based on the presence of these professionals. So too was his diagnosis of the issues.

Baker could never be sure exactly how "straight" the negotiators were with him, but comments they made to him tended to influence his assessment of the issues. For example, the management attorney claimed that the company, as a matter of philosophy, would insist to the end that the employees make a contribution to their health plans. Baker was convinced that this provision would be part of the final contract, a prediction that proved only partially correct. So, too, the mediator expected that the employer's contribution formula would have to be changed because he knew from the union negotiator that certain fixed amounts were needed to cover the costs of the plan.

In addition to the indications that the spokesmen gave regarding specific issues, Baker also predicted that certain moves would be made because these men were well versed in the game of negotiations. For example, the mediator throughout predicted that the bonus and COLA provisions present in the existing contract would eventually be conceded by management: "Bill's [management spokesman] smart. He knows he has to put them in because they were there last time. But he's saving them until the union makes substantial moves." Similarly, he expected that minor issues, or those that affected only a few union members—for example, vacations and personal leave—would be dropped because the union representative would convince his committee accordingly. These predictions about the ways the spokesmen would behave were similar to those made by Thomas concerning the management attorney. Yet, for whatever the reason, Baker's predictions proved more reliable.

These categories of relevance—power, patterns, and people—constituted the major criteria by which Baker and Thomas diagnosed process and issues and predicted the form of the package. As the examples make clear, these categories are not mutually exclusive; indeed, they overlap to a considerable degree. In the Tulane case, the union's lack of bargaining power meant that Thomas felt he had to convince management on EMT, the one issue he felt they should concede because of its presumed widespread existence in other communities. Baker's prediction that the COLA and bonus would be in the final package, based on the precedent of the past agreement, was reinforced by his perception of the management attorney, who was sophisticated enough to concede it, but astute enough to save it until the end.

Diagnostic categories are not used with equal frequency during a case. Asssessment of the issues according to pattern seems to predominate early in the case. The mediators appear to use this "objective" criterion as a way to orient themselves to the issues in dispute. As a case unfolds, the diagnosis seems to shift from how the demands deviate from pattern to a consideration of how the parties will behave with regard to these issues. Mediators continually test and revise the assumptions they bring to a case about people and bargaining power.[8] As the parties argue for and justify their positions, this type of contextual data tends to supplement and often supplant the diagnoses that were initially based solely on patterns.

The changing character of these diagnoses has implications for understanding the strategies and tactics of Thomas and Baker. Thomas, intent on building a package, started to shape one early in the case and in these efforts relied on arguments based primarily on patterns. He actively encouraged both the union and management committees to make moves on EMT and this issue alone. Baker spent the early part of the Bard case monitoring the narrowing process. Although he made assessments about pattern conformity, he made no direct use of these diagnoses until later in the case, at which point more information about relative bargaining power and the intentions of the parties had been revealed. For example, he never discussed the fact that he considered the union's vacation demand to be above average until the end of the case. By that time he knew from the union negotiator that three of the five members of the bargaining committee were personally affected and from the management attorney that the company president refused to grant additional vacation time. When the union's demand for additional vacation was the only outstanding issue separating the parties, he could marshal all these arguments to convince the union committee to concede this final issue.

Movement Tactics (C)

The third element in the cycle of strategic activity is movement tactics: those actions the mediator takes to encourage the parties to make concessions. The particular tactic a mediator uses emerges from the diagnosis he has made of the power relationships, the people, and the issues. How and when the mediator uses these tactics are influenced, however, by the strategy he chooses to pursue. Ten basic movement tactics were observed in these two cases, and these seem to cluster into three basic categories: communication tactics, substantive tactics, and procedural tactics (Simkin, 1971).

Communication tactics refer to the actions taken by the mediator that allow the parties to communicate more effectively with each other, even when they are not in the same room. This is accomplished chiefly through the mediator's position as an intermediary and his efforts to secure information for the parties or to clarify their misunderstandings. Communication tactics are of several sorts. The mediator can use a *conduit tactic* (1) and merely report the positions exactly as prepared by one bargaining committee to the other. He can use a *surrogate tactic* (2) and present, in addition to the position, the proposing committee's justification for the proposal. Through the use of this tactic, the mediator tries to get each side to appreciate the other's constraints and limitations. *Reshaping tactics* (3) are more extreme. When a mediator uses such a tactic, he knowingly alters or embellishes the positions he carries as a way to inject his own ideas. In this way, he uses the basic proposal mechanism as an occasion to "try on" his own formulation of how the issue(s) might be resolved. The parties may be aware of this tactic or not. The mediator may use a *clarification tactic* (4) when the parties have questions to which they seek a response. The mediator may secure the answer from the other party or directly respond himself. The tactic may also be observed when the mediator seeks to reiterate or highlight something that has already been stated.

Substantive tactics refer to specific, usually mediator-initiated, commentary about some facet of the issues in dispute. The mediator may *assess the costs of demands* (5). By translating what appear to be noncomparable issues into unidimensional terms, he assists the parties to assess the relative trade-offs among issues. Highlighting how demands *deviate from patterns* (6) is a tactic that can be a compelling inducement for the parties to bring their proposals into conformity without significant loss of face. When the mediator gives his *opinion* (7) about an issue or position, he tries to use his position to shape the committee's thinking about its issues. Finally, the mediator can be even more forceful in offering his point of view by making *suggestions* or *recommendations* (8) for how the parties should reformulate their issues.

Procedural tactics refer to the actions the mediator takes to facilitate the process, as distinct from the substance. Arranging the meeting forum is a tactic of this sort. In addition, the mediator can offer *strategic suggestions* (9) or advice on concession strategy, timing of responses, or extra-mediation activities, such as outside meetings

Table 4.2
Movement tactics in Bard Manufacturing and Tulane Firefighters: incidence, purpose, timing

	Bard Manufacturing			Tulane Firefighters		
	Observed	Purpose	Timing	Observed	Purpose	Timing
Communication tactics						
1. Conduit	+	Pressure for concession	Session 3	0	—	—
2. Surrogate	+	Pressure for concession	Session 3	+	Pressure for concession	Throughout
3. Reshaping	0	—	—	+	Pressure for concession	Throughout
4. Clarification	+	Explain confusing issues	Throughout	+	Start negotiation	Session 1
Substantive tactics						
5. Calculate costs	+	(a) Facilitate proposal preparation (b) Pressure for concession	Sessions 1, 2 Session 3	+	Pressure for concessions	Session 2
6. Identify pattern deviations	+	Facilitate proposal preparation	Throughout	+	Pressure for concession	Sessions 1, 2
7. Give opinions	+	Keep process moving Pressure for concession	Session 3	+	Pressure for concession	Throughout
8. Substantive suggestion	0	—	Session 3	+	Pressure for concession	Throughout

Procedural tactics

9. Strategic suggestion	+	Keep process moving	Throughout	+	Bring pressure on management	Sessions 1, 2
10. Threats	0	—	—	+	Pressure for concession	Session 2

or lobbying activities. A mediator may also use *threats* (10) to withdraw his service, to convene excessive meetings, or to certify the dispute to factfinding. These threats are intended to create pressure on the parties.

These ten tactics constituted the major ways Thomas and Baker sought to encourage the parties to make moves and concessions. Although the two mediators drew from the same tactical pool, there were significant contrasts between them in the frequency with which they used certain tactics, the purposes for which these tactics were intended, and the chronological points in the case when these tactics were employed. These differences reflect the underlying divergent strategies the mediators had for resolving the dispute.

Baker organized his movement tactics around the preparation of proposals and emphasized those tactics that would facilitate their preparation. Primarily, he clarified what had been said in joint meetings, helped the parties ascertain the costs of certain demands, identified pattern deviations when relevant, and gave strategic suggestions. For example, after management rejected the union's proposal to bring all the employees into the union's health plan, Baker started the separate meeting with a clarification: "At this juncture, you see that bringing in all the others is out. You showed them the cost savings and they still say no. Now in light of this, you should look at your proposal and make a response." When management had to respond to the union's proposal, Baker helped put it in context by calculating certain costs that allowed him to highlight a pattern: "Let me think for a minute. You say that the standard average hourly rate is $5.40. What's the total fringe cost? $1.20? That's about 22–23 percent of wages. That's about right. The standard is usually 25 percent of wages. I thought $1.20 was low, but that's about right."

This type of tactical input into the preparation of proposals was prominent throughout the case (see table 4.2). There were two occasions, however, when Baker made more direct use of substantive tactics. At the request of the union negotiator, he spoke to the union committee and gave it his opinion that its proposal might jeopardize the negotiations. It is interesting to note that Baker apologized several times to the committee for being so direct with it. The other occasion in which a substantive tactic was prominent occurred when Baker calculated the costs of vacations and gave his own opinion to pressure the union to accept the final package agreed to by the chief negotiators.

Thomas made extensive use of all the tactics, primarily to pressure the parties to make concessions on particular issues. To persuade the union to lower its wage and longevity demands, he referred it to patterns set by other units in the town. With management, on EMT, he emphasized patterns, offered opinions, and made substantive as well as strategic suggestions. For example, he calculated the cost of EMT to persuade management that it was not expensive: "In a single 24-hour period, you have two men. Work it from two men who work seven days. At 365 days, you get 712 tours, times $5. So you have $3,560 as a cost factor." When management still refused to move on EMT, Thomas tried to offer suggestions that might make it more palatable: starting in the second year of the agreement and including a provision to reopen the contract on just this issue. Finally, he made a threat: "I think failure to move on this issue is sufficient to warrant sending this to factfinding."

There is considerable overlap in the tactics used by these two mediators. Yet the incidence of similar actions belies the differences in purpose and strategy (see table 4.2). For example, Baker used strategic suggestions as a way to keep the negotiating process moving, whereas Thomas's strategic suggestion to the union about lobbying the mayor was intended to create pressure on management to concede EMT. Thomas highlighted patterns as a tactic to pressure the parties to make concessions on specific issues. Baker used the tactic primarily to help the parties to identify the parameters of the settlement. Thomas calculated the costs of EMT to bolster his own arguments, whereas Baker used the same tactic to clarify the monetary relationships, among the issues. Only in the last cycle did he use it to press for a particular concession, vacations.

The timing of tactical choices differed in these two cases as well. Thomas relied on communication and substantive tactics during the formative stages of the case—session one and part of session two. After EMT was off the table, Thomas seemed to back away from the substantive tactics and confined his efforts primarily to communication tactics, transmitting offers on the clothing allowance from one side to the other. Baker emphasized communication tactics and also procedural and certain substantive tactics to keep the narrowing process moving and to facilitate proposal preparation for most of the first, second, and indeed, the third sessions of the case. Only near the conclusion did he explicitly use substantive tactics as a way to pressure for specific concessions.

The building and narrowing strategies and their tactical correlates observed in these cases seem to be rooted in the differing perspectives these two mediators have about how they help parties reach a settlement. Thomas's strategy—to build a package through the use of directive and aggressive tactics early in the case—seems to be based on the view that the parties, because of their inexperience and the union's lack of bargaining power, needed his active assistance to structure an agreement. Further, he claimed that the strategic position of the mediator means that he is uniquely placed to achieve this end. Thomas made the following comment on this position: "Parties camouflage their positions with each other, but with the mediator they are more open to discussing things directly. You cut right to the heart of the matter and are in a unique position to guide the direction a package takes." In contrast, Baker looked more to the parties themselves, particularly the chief negotiators, to structure a package that was agreeable to them: "These guys know as much as I do about where this thing should settle. I don't have to draw pictures for them. They'll move their committees when the time is right." In this way, Baker claimed, the parties could create a package largely of their own design, a process that would facilitate its ratification. The strategies of building a package, or narrowing proposals until a package is left, are seen, therefore, by these two mediators as appropriate strategic responses to the contingencies they faced in Tulane and Bard.

Building and Narrowing in Other Cases

The specific tactics used by Baker and Thomas are in a real sense unique to these mediators and these cases. The precise words they uttered and the actions they took will probably never be replicated in another case. This is not to suggest, however, that strategies and tactics are based solely on the unique circumstances of a case. There are major elements of strategic activity that probably will be the same in other cases conducted by these two mediators, for they are rooted in these mediators' perspectives on the process. This fact is illustrated in the way the major elements of strategy are made manifest in two other cases conducted by Baker and Thomas.

In the Taft School Committee case, Thomas had mediated with both parties before and resolved the Taft case in just one session. During the first meeting with the union, Thomas questioned the committee about its demands, the membership's feelings about them, the union committee's assessment of the management team, and management's response to previous proposals—in particular, the union's intention to use the budgeted funds available for wage increases in order to equalize the salary schedule. Based on the committee's responses to these questions, the order in which the demands were presented, and his own knowledge of the settlements in Taft and its neighboring communities, Thomas made a preliminary diagnosis of the package. In his first meeting with management, he gave it his assessment and suggested specific responses on each of the issues. Management's response to the union's proposal was based almost entirely on these suggestions, which Thomas then conveyed to the union.

He remained with the union to answer some of its questions, and then, at its request, left it to caucus. The revised proposal it gave him reflected priorities that were somewhat different from Thomas's initial assessment. He tried to dissuade the union from pursuing these "minor issues," arguing that the wage package would be lower if it continued to insist on them. The union held firm, and the mediator shared this information with the school committee to develop a counterproposal. In formulating this proposal, Thomas recommended that management lower its wage offer because "I'm working from the assumption that they [the union members] don't know what they are doing. I want to move things around on the salary schedule a bit." Thomas reported this proposal to the union members and left them to discuss it. The union committee accepted the proposal and achieved, therefore, less in wages than management had been prepared to give.

The outlines of Thomas's tactical moves in the Taft School Committee case largely paralleled the building strategy in Tulane Firefighters, with certain notable exceptions. Thomas eagerly sought to learn priorities in this case because they were the building blocks he used to construct the two management proposals. His interpretation of the priority issues were based on wage patterns for teachers and the policies on sick leave and maternity leave in neighboring communities. His tactical efforts to move the parties were also similar to the other case, although the Taft management seemed more cooperative than the committee in Tulane. Thomas made specific suggestions on each issue, suggestions that management adopted. In his meetings with the union, he freely gave it his opinions, made extensive reference to patterns, and threatened it with a lower wage if it did not drop its "minor" issues. Finally, as in Tulane, Thomas started his building of the package as soon as he had made his initial assessment of the union's priorities, during his first meeting with it.

In Bates, Inc., the other case mediated by Baker, the narrowing strategy is even more apparent than in Bard. Because the union's proposal was so lengthy, considerable narrowing was required. Further, the chief negotiators in Bates were strangers to each other, which meant that most of the proceedings were confined to formal channels. Finally, the traditional practice of these parties to settle close to the contract expiration deadline meant that the narrowing process in this case moved even slower than in the Bard case. Although a few proposals were exchanged during the first two sessions, the union spent considerable time in caucuses with its representative, narrowing its own demands. During this time, the mediator knew from spokesman confidences that one issue was a priority—funding of the pension—but learned the rest of the priorities as they emerged from the proposals. These proposals were assessed in light of the past contract, industry patterns, actions of the spokesmen, and the power relationship between the union and the company. He held negotiations across the table on the non-economic issues, another difference between Bates, Inc., and Bard. In part, these meetings were a tactic that postponed discussions of wages until the point at which final moves could be made. Movement was achieved primarily by giving the spokesmen time to work with their committees on proposals, and the joint exchange of offers was a tactic used to create mutual pressure on the parties. Tactically, Baker offered strategic suggestions, ascertained the cost of certain elements of the package, introduced relevant patterns, and made some substantive suggestions, primarily on the noneconomic issues and work practices.

The specific tactics used in Taft School Committee and Bates, Inc., were clearly not exact replicas of those observed in Tulane Firefighters and Bard Manufacturing. But certain aspects of strategy were. Thomas built a package for management relying on what the union had told him and on his own diagnosis of the issues that the final package should contain. Baker used a narrowing strategy that encouraged the parties to develop and to refine the proposals themselves, offering his tactical aid as needed. Although describing four

Table 4.3
Information sought at first meeting: observations by case[a]

	Number of state cases in which tactic was observed $(N=9)$[b]	Number of federal cases in which tactic was observed $(N=5)$[b]
Forum for learning the facts or issues		
Joint meeting	2	4
Separate meeting	7	1
Information sought		
Last proposal from each side	2	5
Mechanics of provisions	3	4
Negotiating history	9	1
Personalities on the other side	8	—
Financial status of company or town	6	—
Status of provisions in current contract	8	3

a. In each case, multiple types of information may be sought in the first meeting. Thus the types of information sought do not constitute mutually exclusive categories.
b. I was not present at the first sessions of one state and one federal case.

cases does not constitute proof, it does appear that these two mediators rather consistently employ different strategies. Whether these differences are unique to Baker and Thomas or are rooted in the social practices and dispute environment of these two agencies is an issue that can be addressed by considering the strategic activities of the other mediators in the study.

Given the verbal character of mediation, it is difficult to make direct tactical comparisons across cases.[9] However, using commentary from the mediators and crude tabulations of observations, it is possible to compare certain features of strategy and tactical patterns. In the initial meetings the federal and state mediators held with the parties, either jointly or separately, differences in information sought and tactics used may be observed (see table 4.3).

Like Thomas, the other state mediators tended to cover a wide range of topics as they sought to learn the basic facts of the cases. In the building strategy, learning the issues, gauging priorities, and even tentative movement tactics are often tightly coupled because they occur in the same forum. In contrast, the federal mediators seemed to confine their introductory sessions to learning the issues and getting the parties to agree on the issues in dispute. If narrowing is to occur, the parties and the mediator must be sure that they are working from the same baseline. These joint meetings are typically followed by separate meetings where priorities, history, and constraints are discussed. Finding a consensus on the issues is uncoupled, therefore, from attempts to gather information on priorities or to encourage movement. This nicety means, in practice, that the parties continually work from the same agreed-upon areas of disagreement. In the building strategy, the parties will often be involved in making moves before they have agreed upon the issues in dispute.

Like Thomas, the other state mediators appear to be eager to know about the parties' priorities and to ask for information directly. The following attempts were culled from interactions with state mediators and the parties.

Mediator Richards (Regis School Committee): What will it take to get a settlement?

Mediator Shaw (Scripps School Committee): I can't do anything until you tell me what you are willing to take.

Mediator Unger (Ulster School Committee): Here's my roadmap of the issues. You have to tell me if I am in the ball park.

Mediator Vance (Vanderbilt School Committee): How far can you go on the wages?

In contrast, the federal mediators, like Baker, seemed more likely to gather information about priorities from formal moves and confidences given by parties (see table 4.4). As mediator Carr said in the Carroll University case, "I learn where they are going based on what they tell me."

The state mediators, intent on building a package, tended to dissect the parties' proposals into their component issues and relied on patterns as the most prominent criteria in diagnosing the potential of a package. In six of the state cases, this discrete issue-by-issue analysis was observed. The state mediators tended to use more movement tactics and a greater variety of them as they attempted to move the parties issue by issue (see table 4.5). Since they prefer to keep the bargaining committees separate from each other, the state mediators usually carry positions and proposals themselves. As a result, they typically use surrogate tactics, at a minimum, and more often reshaping ones as well. Substantively, the state mediators

Table 4.4
Tactics to learn priorities: observations by case[a]

Tactic	Number of state cases in which tactic was observed (N=10)	Number of federal cases in which tactic was observed (N=6)
Learn priorities from formal proposals	4	5
Spokesmen's confidences	4	5
Ask for priorities	7	1
Ask procedural questions	1	3
Make suggestion and see response	8	2
Make an argument and see response	3	—

a. The tactics used to learn priorities and the categories of interpretation are not mutually exclusive. A mediator may use any or all of the listed tactics and interpret the information according to multiple categories.

made extensive reference to geographical patterns and quite liberally offered their own opinions and suggestions for compromise. When they made strategic suggestions, this advice often related to lobbying activities the party might undertake. For example, mediator Shaw gave the following strategic advice to a union committee in the Scripps case: "You said you have some friends in the town. Now is the time to contact them and publicize your position. They won't move on the salary schedule without some pressure. Maybe you need to light some fires."

The federal mediators, in contrast, most frequently work with full proposals and judge priorities according to their assessments of the negotiators and their relative bargaining powers, as well as patterns. Tactically, the federal mediators seek to help the parties to clarify areas of misunderstanding or confusion and to get them to appreciate the rationale and reasoning that underlie an offer. The substantive tactics they use seem to be tailored primarily to proposal preparation, for example, making cost calculations and identifying pattern deviations.[10] Similarly, their strategic suggestions relate to the exchange process as well. For example, "It's getting late today. When they come back with their counter, why don't you caucus for a few minutes and tell them that you want more time to consider it. If you rush through and present a counter, you'll waste a move."

The strategic implications of trying to move parties one issue at a time can be better appreciated by considering a case that seemed

Table 4.5
Tactics used to encourage movement: observations by case, average use, and range across cases

	Federal cases (N=6)			State cases (N=10)		
	Number of federal cases[a] in which tactic was observed (N=6)	Average use of tactic across all federal cases[b]	Range of use across all federal cases[c]	Number of state cases[a] in which tactic was observed (N=10)	Average use of tactic across all state cases[b]	Range of use across all state cases[c]
Communication tactics						
1. Present proposal as given (conduit)	6	4.0	(1–9)	5	1.3	(0–3)
2. Provide rationale behind position (surrogate)	6	7.8	(4–12)	10	8.2	(2–13)
3. Reshape position	1	0.2	(0–1)	10	7.0	(3–13)
4. Obtain clarifications and responses to questions	6	9.0	(3–16)	10	1.4	(1–8)
Substantive tactics						
5. Calculate costs	6	5.8	(1–12)	10	5.9	(1–14)
6. Identify pattern deviations	5	3.8	(0–5)	10	8.9	(2–15)
7. Give opinions	6	4.8	(1–8)	10	12.9	(4–18)
8. Make substantive suggestions or recommendations	6	2.6	(1–7)	10	9.7	(5–17)

Procedural tactics

9. Strategic suggestions	6	12.6	(9–17)	10	3.9	(1–9)
10. Threats	0	0	(0)	6	2.2	(0–7)

a. Multiple tactics were observed in the case.
b. The sum across the cases of the total number of times the tactic was observed in each case divided by the number of cases.
c. The range in the number of times the tactic was observed in each case across the caseload.

to depart from the federal narrowing pattern. In the Alfred Corporation case, the parties were in mediation after the union had rejected an earlier agreement. The union members rejected the contract because they were dissatisfied with the cost-of-living formula. Mediation was requested for the purpose of resolving this one issue. In this one-session, single-issue case, mediator Allen was observed using and timing his movement tactics in ways that were more characteristic of the state mediators. Early in the session he sought to learn the basis for the rejection, asked each party directly for its bottom line on the issue, and used this information to offer, right from the start of the case, suggestions and alternative formulations that might resolve this one issue. He commented afterward, "With a one-issue case like this, you are working from suggestions, not proposals, and neither side wants to get committed. So you carry the suggestions back and forth and present them as your own. They also looked to me to come up with some ideas, and I did."

If mediator Allen's behavior in the Alfred case is indicative of what occurs when a mediator confronts a single issue, it suggests that a single issue leads the mediator rather directly to use more substantive and persuasive tactics. The parties seem to expect it, and the mediator has few other options available. The strategic approach of the state mediators of dissecting proposals into component issues and applying tactics to these discrete issues creates a series of single-issue situations. In this context, the parties' expectations and mediator's strategy push him to use his opinions, suggestions, and recommendations as the primary means of moving the parties. When proposals are considered in their entirety, the expectations of the parties are less, and the pressure for resolution rests more with them than with the mediator.[11]

The timing in the use of these movement tactics also seems to show a rather consistent pattern between the state and federal mediators. Early in a case, the state mediators consider the proposals on an issue-by-issue basis and use substantive tactics to encourage the parties to make particular moves on the priority issues. Later in the case, these priority issues may be incorporated into a package that the mediator conveys from one committee to the other. In a few cases, during this phase the parties reverted to bilateral negotiations without the mediator present. The process seems to be reversed for the federal mediators. During the early stages of a case, they work from full proposals, emphasizing communication and selected substantive tactics as they encourage the parties to narrow their differences. Later in their cases, when certain issues remained, the mediators' tactical efforts tended to be devoted to convincing the parties to make concessions on those outstanding issues.

These contrasts in timing reflect differing perspectives on how the mediator facilitates the concession process. The state mediators try to build momentum. They believe that the parties, who have typically made only minimal progress in their negotiations prior to mediation, need to see results quickly. Therefore the state mediators start to build a package early in the case by pressuring the parties to make substantive moves on the major issues. Analysis of the proposals on an issue-by-issue basis serves to identify those areas in which movement is most likely and allows the mediator to play a formative role in shaping the elements of the agreement. The intervention meeting arrangement further facilitates these activities.

The federal mediators believe that settlements result from incremental moves that continually narrow the differences between the parties. To that end, the union in particular, whose livelihood is the subject of negotiations, needs time to lower its aspirations. The engineer of this movement is the chief negotiator, and the federal mediator seems to look to him for guidance in the planning and timing of his own tactical moves. In sum, the mediator's strategy and tactics seem to be inseparable from the perceptions he has of his own role and that of the other players. By the meeting arrangement that he adopts and the tactics that he uses, the different roles are enacted and made real in the case context. To make a deal is to build a package, whereas to orchestrate is to oversee the narrowing of proposals until an agreement is achieved.

The particular role a mediator adopts and the strategies he uses have consequences for how the other actors play their parts and for how credibly the mediator can perform his own. Orchestrating the development of an agreement through narrowing has the effects of aiding chief negotiators with their committees and protecting the federal mediators from mistakes they might make through over-zealousness. This presumes, of course, that the negotiators are able to move their committees and that substantive assistance from the mediator is not directly required until late in the case. Dealmaking by building a package requires access to accurate information about priorities and is aided by spokesmen who are willing and able to collaborate in the construction of the agreement. When this is not the situation, the spokesman's relationship with his committee may be harmed, and the mediator's credibility challenged as well. These are the consequences of different mediation strategies.

5

Mediators and Spokesmen: Complementary Strategic Roles

As mediators tell it, it is the people in the case that make the difference. Disputes may be marked by disagreements about the issues, but the actual demands, claim the mediators, tend to fall into fairly standard and predictable patterns. The union wants higher wages and increased benefits; management wants productivity increases and changes in problematic work practices. The numbers change and the work practices may differ, but in only two instances were truly unique issues the reasons the parties in this study sought mediation assistance. It is not, therefore, the issues that give a case its unique character, but rather the people involved in it and how they act with regard to the issues, the process, and the mediator.[1]

The people in the case figure prominently in the mediator's strategic thinking and tactical activity. Roles are justified on the basis of the parties' needs. Meetings are arranged with relationships between the parties and within the bargaining committees in mind. The tactical elements of strategy derive from assessments of which of the people involved bear primary responsibility for shaping and developing an acceptable package. Differences in how the mediators evaluate the people in mediation and interact with them serve to distinguish further the strategic approaches of the state and federal mediators.

Of all the people potentially concerned with the outcomes of mediation, only a small fraction are physically present at the proceedings. The rank-and-file union membership and the company management or elected town officials, who hold ultimate power either to ratify or to reject an agreement, do not directly participate in mediation.[2] Except in unusual circumstances, these constituencies seem to play only a minimal role in the mediator's strategic thinking and behavior.[3]

The union and management bargaining committees are composed of individuals who represent different departments or coalitions of the constituent organizations. It is these people who are charged with responsibility for formulating, with the mediator's assistance, the tentative agreement. Despite the near-universal gesture of having committee members indicate their names and titles on a sign-in sheet, the mediators typically know very little about the composition of these committees.[4] Rather, the mediators tend to refer to the bargaining committees by rather stereotypical and sweeping generalizations. For example, union committees are usually described as inexperienced and undisciplined, noted for their lengthy initial proposals and reluctance to make moves or to delegate bargaining authority to their representatives. Private-sector management is frequently depicted as hierarchical and controlled, whereas the state mediators describe the public-sector management committees as political and fragmented.[5] Although the mediators make extensive reference to these committee attributes when they justify their roles, the particular characteristics of a bargaining committee seem to be less important to their strategic decisionmaking. The chief negotiators who represent these committees, however, are critical.

Chief Negotiators: Background and Strategic Roles

The union and management committees in both sectors are usually led by spokesmen or chief negotiators who, as their titles indicate, speak for their committees in mediation.[6] During meetings, most of the formal communications about positions and much of the informal discussion about the issues take place between the mediator and these chief negotiators. Indeed, mediators define a well-disciplined committee as one whose only spokesman when outsiders are present is its chief negotiator. These chief negotiators play complementary strategic roles in mediation.[7] The state mediators view chief negotiators as potential resources who facilitate their efforts to build a package. In contrast, the federal mediators see themselves more as resources to the negotiators, who bear primary responsibility for moving their committees toward settlement.

In most of the cases I observed, the union and management committees were led by spokesmen who had backgrounds related to labor law or industrial relations (see table 5.1). Typically, management committees in both caseloads were represented by attorneys employed by law firms that specialize in labor/management relations (eleven out of sixteen cases). On the union side, some of the negotiators were attorneys, but a substantial number were representatives (reps) of national unions (N=11). These reps are employed, not by the local bargaining unit, but by its parent union and are assigned to the local union to aid them in negotiations and mediation. Despite differences in background and organizational allegiance, these spokesmen share a common fate—they are outsiders. They are hired or assigned, often on a regular basis, for the purpose of leading the negotiating committees.

Some of these spokesmen were labeled pros by the mediators (indicated in table 5.1 by capital letters). The pro has certain attributes that make him a valued asset on a case. By virtue of his work, he is experienced in the ways of negotiations. Pros work for either a law firm, union, or corporation in positions that give them primary responsibility for conducting contract negotiations in concert with the local client or unit. Because his job is negotiations, the pro knows mediation; he has been in it often and frequently knows the mediator personally.

The mediator meets the pro regularly in his round of cases. A case with a particular company, local, or town may come to mediation only once every two or three years, but the pro may have a case with the mediator monthly or even weekly. The term pro, however, describes more than the experience of the negotiator or his familiarity with mediation. Pro is a value-laden label that carries with it a wealth of meaning about the relationship the mediator has with the spokesman. To be called a pro by the mediator, a spokesman has necessarily to be experienced; but he must also be able to work with the mediator in such a way that each complements the other in the strategic task of developing an acceptable package.

A majority of the union and management negotiators in both the federal and state cases has the requisite job experience to be considered pros. Yet not all of these negotiators were labeled pros by the mediators. Some were relatively new to their jobs and were, therefore, still learning their role. But others, although they had worked with the mediators many times before, did not, during the

Table 5.1
Chief negotiators: occupational backgrounds and designations of pros[a]

Case	Management	Union
State cases		
Reed School Committee	LR attorney[b]	Union rep
Regis School Committee	LR ATTORNEY	UNION REP
Rutgers School Committee	LR ATTORNEY	UNION REP
Scripps School Committee	LR attorney	Union rep[b]
Sheridan Firefighters	LR ATTORNEY	LR attorney
Taft School Committee	School superintendent	Union rep
Tulane Firefighters	GP attorney	LR attorney[c]
Ulster School Committee	LR ATTORNEY	LR ATTORNEY
Urbana Housing Authority	Housing Authority director	LR ATTORNEY
Vanderbilt School Committee	LR attorney	LR attorney[c]
Federal cases		
Albion Broadcasting	LR ATTORNEY	UNION REP
Alfred Corporation	GP attorney	UNION REP
Bard Manufacturing	LR ATTORNEY	UNION REP
Bates, Inc.	VP, INDUSTRIAL RELATIONS	UNION REP
Carroll University	LR ATTORNEY	UNION REP
Duke Hospital	LR ATTORNEY	Union rep[c]

a. LR attorney: lawyer employed full time by a law firm that specializes in labor/management relations. Union rep: outside bargaining representative assigned by the national union to aid the local unit in negotiations. GP attorney: general-practice lawyer who may or may not have experience with labor negotiations. Chief negotiators who were labeled pros by the mediators are indicated by capital letters.
b. These chief negotiators were not present for the entire case.
c. These chief negotiators were in mediation for the first time.

cases, play the kind of strategic role the mediators had come to expect of a pro. This was particularly evident in the state cases.

Pros in the State Cases

Pros can help a state mediator build a package. They do this by providing information to the mediator about priorities, sharing a common definition of what makes for a "fair and reasonable" settlement, and then working with the mediator to "sell" such a deal to their committees. These expectations, although they were frequently articulated, were not as often realized in practice. This lack of collaboration did not appear to present major impediments to the mediator's building strategy, however, which appeared to work independently of the negotiator's assistance. Pros make the task easier, but did not seem to be essential to its implementation.

The state mediators seem to expect that if the parties are represented by pros, then their efforts to learn priorities will be facilitated. In off-the-record meetings, the mediators anticipate that the pro will distinguish between the committee's priority and minor issues and reveal its bottom line on wages. From these data, the mediator can then determine how proximate the true positions are and plan his tactical moves accordingly. For example, in Sheridan Firefighters, mediator Shaw asked the management pro "how far are you willing to go on wages?" The pro told him, and his reply became the basis for setting the goal toward which the mediator worked in his meetings with the union.

During the early part of the first session in the Ulster School Committee case, mediator Unger separately engaged both pros in off-the-record meetings and asked them several times how firm their wage positions were and whether they would consider alternative formulations for splitting the difference between them. He commented afterwards, "With the attorneys, when we are alone, I usually ask them how far they can go." Mediator Richards, in the Rutgers School Committee case, used separate off-the-record meetings with both pros to learn their bottom-line positions: "You have to tell me what you will take. I can't do anything until you give me the percentage. How about 16 percent for the two years? Will that do it?" Information about issues other than wages is sought in similar fashion. Again, in the Ulster case, Unger questioned the management attorney in the hall: "Listen, I've been talking with them [the union]. What are some of the areas you can move on?

How about Greek Orthodox Good Friday? The release time for the union president? The extracurricular stipend?"

Off-the-record meetings also give the pros opportunities to initiate their own confidences. In these meetings, pros would often tell the mediator about priorities, report on progress they were making, and identify those areas where they might need the mediator's persuasive assistance. Indeed, in those cases where both committees were represented by pros (Regis, Rutgers, and Ulster School Committees) the average off-the-record meeting frequency was 46 percent, as compared with 23 percent for the entire sample of state cases (see table 5.2). The average off-the-record frequency for cases where at least one committee was served by a pro is 38 percent. It appears, therefore, that when pros are present on a case, there is considerably more off-the-record activity, that is, discussions initiated both by the mediators and the spokesmen.

But the mediator's efforts to engage the pro in a discussion of priorities is not confined solely to these off-the-record forums. In separate meetings with the parties, the state mediators often involved the pro in discussion of priorities. In the Regis case, mediator Richards sat next to the union pro and asked him to review the proposal and indicate which issues were most important: "Joe, you know the way I work. I know all twenty-six of these are important, but which are more important than the others? Which ones would really make a difference? Why don't I go through these and you whisper in my ear what can go." So, too, mediator Unger sat next to the union pro in a separate meeting and asked him to review the union's proposal: "I want to verify my road map. Why don't you check the ones that are most important."

These overtures to the chief negotiators for information about priorities were a common feature of the state mediators' tactical activities. Sometimes this information was forthcoming, and at other times it was not. Indeed, part of the state mediator's definition of a pro is based on whether he willingly provides such data. The other attribute of a pro is that he helps the mediator construct and sell a package.

The state mediators are greatly influenced, in their conception of a package, by its conformity to patterns and standards of practice. Accordingly, they expect pros, who are likewise knowledgeable about these criteria, to share a similar definition about the components of a "fair and reasonable" settlement and to support the

Table 5.2
Off-the-record meeting frequency in cases with and without pros by case and agency

Case	Off-the-record meetings as percentage of meeting types	Number of off-the-record meetings	As percentage of meeting types in cases with pros
State cases			
Reed School Committee	23	3	—
Regis School Committee	40	10	40
Rutgers School Committee	59	4	59
Scripps School Committee	7	2	—
Sheridan Firefighters	32	7	32
Taft School Committee	0	0	—
Tulane Firefighters	8	2	—
Ulster School Committee	39	14	39
Urbana Housing Authority	22	2	22
Vanderbilt School Committee	0	0	—
Average off-the-record frequency	23	4.4	38
Federal cases			
Albion Broadcasting	16	9	16
Alfred Corporation	7	1	7
Bard Manufacturing	18	5	18
Bates, Inc.	9	6	9
Carroll University	21	7	21
Duke Hospital	22	2	22
Average off-the-record frequency	15.5	5.0	15.5

mediator's efforts to convince their committees of its merit. In the context of the Rutgers case, for example, mediator Richards reviewed his "selling" collaboration with the management pro: "He knows a fair settlement and tries to bring it in. He supports me. He realizes he's giving me insight as to where his committee is going, but he needs me to talk about other settlements, to tell them the wages they are offering aren't that good. He gives me latitude to do it. He lets me work on his committee and seldom stops me. Whatever I want to present, he won't fight me. Then he uses it to sell them on what he and I have already agreed to." Mediator Shaw in the context of Sheridan Firefighters, where an off-the-record deal was made and sold, described how pros work:

He's a real pro. He isn't wishy-washy. If the three people, the spokesmen and the mediator, are a team, the issue is the strategy to get what we want, since we already know what we want. With pros, they're willing to work for what they don't have. They go further than what the committee gives them. Then they use me to help sell it. When I tell Dave [management pro] that we need more money, he tries to get it. Or he'll say to me in private that I'll have to work on his people. He'll refer back to what I've said. We use each other for support.

Mediator Thomas contrasted the management attorney in Tulane Firefighters with the kind of behavior he would expect from a pro: "The mark of a true pro is that he doesn't confine himself to the parameters he is given but is willing to go further. He's willing to take a gambit on a reasonable package and then sell it."

Sheridan Firefighters and Rutgers School Committee were two cases in which the pros behaved in line with the mediators' expectations. Off-the-record deals were constructed over the course of several cycles based on confidential information given the mediator by the pros. These pros demonstrated their willingness to collaborate openly with the mediator and then work with him to sell the deal to their committees. But there were also occasions when known pros failed to behave according to the mediator's expectation.

Sometimes a pro was unwilling to meet off the record. In the Regis case, the pro decided to remain with his committee. Richards commented on this behavior: "The problem with Jack is he's too honest. He puts everything out in front of his people. He doesn't give me any room to move in and make a deal." In the Urbana

Housing Authority case, special circumstances precluded further off-the-record participation. The union pro explained his reasons to the mediator: "I can't leave any more. The committee doesn't trust me. It was on my advice that they accepted the last offer and then the members rejected it. I thought it was their best shot, but they still blame me." The union attorney in the Ulster case wanted the mediator to convince the entire school committee (not just the negotiating subcommittee) to attend the sessions. Until that occurred, he was unwilling to meet off the record or discuss priorities with the mediator. When the mediator sat next to him and urged him to place priorities on the issues, the pro refused: "Our proposal states our position."

Sometimes a pro collaborated on an off-the-record deal, but then failed to convince his committee to go along. This is what occurred in the Regis School Committee case. Mediator Richards reviewed what happened: "I put the whole thing together—maternity, jury duty, the grievances, and 7 percent. Then Dave [management pro] goes to his committee and he can't get them to buy it. I tell the teachers that I don't have it yet, but if I could get it, would they take it? The union president says what makes you think we'll settle for 7 percent. I guess Bill [union pro] misread them. So it's off. But I have another plan."

From the mediators' perspective, there are reasons why pros do not or cannot always act in ways that suit the mediator's strategic plans. When pros disappointed them, therefore, the mediators could well understand and justify the circumstances that precluded their collaboration in dealmaking. Other (nonpro) negotiators, however, were rather severely criticized by the mediators for their disappointing behavior.[8] In the Scripps School Committee case, mediator Shaw described the management attorney's unprofessional behavior: "I've worked with him before. He doesn't confide in the mediator. He never has any authority. On the last case I had with him, nothing happened until the full school committee was there. He just can't deliver." Mediator Thomas described a similar problem in Tulane Firefighters: "If the management attorney had been a pro, he would have gone along with EMT. See, it's not just the experience that makes a pro, but does he have the authority to bargain? And for the true pro, if he doesn't have that authority, he'll grab it. He'll demand it as a condition of his employment."

If the cases in this study are indicative, state mediators are more likely to work with spokesmen they consider to be less than effective. Such spokesmen tend to play "close to the vest," are bound by their committees, and are afraid to push for what they know is reasonable and justified. Combined with the state mediator's sense that committees are inexperienced, are vague about their priorities, and are reluctant to delegate full negotiating authority to their spokesmen, the mediator is fully able to justify his own role and strategic approach. He must build a package using whatever assistance he can get. He "educates" the parties about the realities of mediation by demonstrating how a "reasonable" package is built. In this way, the state mediators suggest, the committees will become more adept at doing it themselves in future negotiations. In his interactions with chief negotiators whom he expects to encounter more often, the state mediator likewise tries to teach them about how a pro should behave.[9]

Pros in the Federal Cases

Pros were a more consistent feature in the federal cases. Not only did these negotiators have the requisite occupational position to be so labeled, but like the pros in the state cases, they acted in ways that complemented the mediator's strategy. The nature of this complementary role was somewhat different, however. Whereas the state mediators define pro-like behavior largely in terms of pro/mediator collaboration on the construction and sale of a deal, the federal mediators seem to see pros as the crucial actors in the narrowing process. It is the pro who bears primary responsibility for moving his committee toward settlement.

To the federal mediator, the pro is an experienced, knowledgeable, effective negotiator who is well acquainted with the elements of a reasonable package and often better informed than the mediator about the local character of the issues in dispute. Since all pros are outsiders to the particular local or company they represent, federal mediators believe that they require time, space, and assistance from the mediator to establish themselves with their committees. This perception of the pro/committee relationship colors the mediator's expectations about how much information the pro is privy to and how much he might be willing to transmit to the mediator.

Consistent with his view that management acts in a businesslike way, knows its priorities, plans for timely concessions, and has a centralized decisionmaking structure, the federal mediator expects that a pro representing management is privy to this information—in fact, has aided in the planning of positions and concession strategy. But the mediator does not necessarily expect that this information will be shared with him, particularly early in the case. Rather, the federal mediator tends to assume that the management pro is in control and that all actions he takes are deliberate. Mediator Dixon described the management pro in the Duke Hospital case: "I'm a little surprised that he put so much out at this stage. But he knows what he's doing. He took the offensive and threw the gauntlet down with the real stuff. Nothing was held back. He was forcing the issue, telling the union that they really needed to take another look and start making moves." Mediator Baker, in the Bates case, also tended to attribute strategic motives to the management pro: "I'm surprised he spelled out the company's financial position in such detail. It was too soon. It's not time for the financial position. But it told the union that management is serious and that they better buckle down. He handled it well and it worked." The federal mediator expects that the management pro is in control of his committee, has planned his strategy well, and will, if problems arise, ask for help: "You have to remember, he's representing his clients. He's good at it. I don't expect him to confide in me. He's negotiating with Joe [union pro] and he's negotiating with me."

Management pros do keep the mediators informed, however. Prior to the presentation of a proposal, managment pros frequently stopped by the mediator's office to tell him what they intended to do in the upcoming joint meeting: "The game plan has changed. I'm going to read them a speech on our position, our economic position. Then we'll let them meet and after that we'll go through the language items, item by item and we'll give them indications of where we'll move. They are very naive about industrial relations, so we have to get them ready to settle."

The federal mediator's perception of the union pro's relationship with his committee is somewhat different. The union committee, with its often diffuse, democratic composition, combined with a lack of sophistication and vagueness of priorities, indicates to the mediator that the union pro may be unclear himself about the direction his committee will take. According to the federal mediators, the priorities emerge from the process itself: "I don't know what they want. Joe [union pro] doesn't know what they want.

Their proposal hasn't been refined enough yet." Further, even if the pro knows what his committee might settle for, his presence as an outsider may portend problems of trust. Mediator Carr described this situation in the Carroll University case: "Jack told me he didn't want to leave his committee. This is a touchy issue. He's running that committee, but they don't trust him. They think a deal is being made." Mediator Baker spoke of the trust problem as well: "You don't usually pull people out. He's an outsider. He needs time to establish himself with his committee. You have to be careful to keep the committee involved, to convince them that their spokesman isn't working on a deal behind their back."

The contrast between off-the-record meeting frequency on cases with and without pros is impossible to make on federal cases because each case had at least one, and many had two, pros. But compared to the state mediator's use of off-the-record meetings with pros present, the federal mediators used such meetings considerably less frequently (see table 5.2). This divergence is consistent with the federal mediator's view that negotiators, particularly union pros, have minimal information to share about priorities and that remaining with their committees, particularly during the early phases of the case, is critical to their efforts to establish a trusting relationship with the members.

Union pros did confide in the mediators about intended alterations in their proposals just prior to presentation; they reported on their relationships with their committees and indicated which areas were of paramount concern. For example, the union pro told the mediator in the Bates case that an increase in the pension contribution was necessary to bring the union's pension plan into conformity with federal law, and in the Albion case, the management pro told Allen that the work schedule was the "crunch" issue.

Finally, the federal mediators seem to expect that pros will meet with each other outside of mediation and discuss strategy among themselves. Indeed, the federal mediators often encourage this. For example, mediator Dixon discussed his use of an initial joint off-the-record meeting between the management attorney and the union negotiator as a way to foster this behavior: "This kind of meeting is unusual. There are so many issues that I wanted them to mutually identify the crunch ones for dialogue. It's desirable to get the two spokesmen talking among themselves, so I provided the initial forum to do it." At the end of the second session, Dixon suggested that the union negotiator meet with the management attorney to work out a settlement.[10] Reference was continually made to such extra-mediation dialogues and the existence of scripts and scenarios being played out to which the mediator was not privy.

Mediator Carr: There's a scenario being played out here. I'm sure he's [union rep] been in communication with management all along. These scenarios are acted out all the time, and I'm not privy to the information.

Mediator Allen: Pros may have a script worked out. They may have all the moves mapped out—what they are going to do and how. But they don't tell you about them. So I wait. They'll ask for help when they need it.

In summary, the federal mediators look to the pros, not to provide specific information about the direction of settlement, but rather to manage proposal presentation so that priorities can emerge. Movement is but an extension of the same process.

The federal mediators expect the pros to move their committees. Since they have extensive exposure to labor negotiations, pros are assumed by the federal mediators to know as much as the mediator about settlement patterns and to be capable of identifying the level of wages and benefits that would comprise a "good" settlement. Therefore, the pros and the mediator could coolly and rationally develop the substance of a reasonable package, but the de facto existence of such a package, as equitable and reasonable as it might be, in no way ensures that it will become an acceptable settlement. Acceptance of the package rests first with the committees, who must be so invested, committed, and "sold" on the package, so that they can enthusiastically and actively endorse its ratification to their constituencies. Only then is there a settlement. Narrowing is the process by which the priority issues are defined and commitment built. The chief engineer of this process is the pro working with his committee. Commented mediator Allen, "I like working with pros. They are realistic. They know the settlements and bring reason to the case. They act as a steadying force and move their committees when the time is right." Although they move their committees, they are limited in terms of how quickly they can do so: "He's a pro. He is moving that committee, but you have to remember that he has to live with them. He knows the settlements, but he's got a five-man committee, and there is a limit as to how much they can drop at any point."

As well informed as the mediator, the pro can make the same arguments, suggestions, and recommendations that the mediator can. To the degree that the pros do move their committees unaided, the mediator is able to husband his "bullets" until they are really needed and protect himself, thereby, from egregious errors of timing or judgment.

Mediator Allen: Pros protect you. See, he could have asked me, dragged me in on the settlement size. One of my jobs is to explain all that, but he did it for me. That way if they need me later on, I can come in fresh.

Mediator Baker: He's doing most of the work. With a guy like that, he's saying the same things I am. He's elected and they get tired of listening to him. So I come in and say the same things. But it's a new voice and I'm neutral. They believe me when I say it's idiotic.

In addition to fostering movement on the committees, the mark of the true pro is that he acts like a "closer," one who uses his expertise in negotiating, knowledge of settlements, and familiarity with local circumstances to suggest options when negotiations reach a stalemate. Mediator Carr described closing: "Both sides need pros who are closers. Closers are people who are capable or have the ability to close the agreement. You get pros who can negotiate, but does he know how to close. Jim was a closer here. He came up with the alternatives. He was strong; he pushed them to close it." Pros also know how and when to ask for assistance from the mediator. "Pros aren't afraid to ask for help. But they use us in the right way and don't involve us too soon." Requests for help do not always come directly, but are frequently signaled to the mediator. For example, in Bard Manufacturing the union asked the mediator to talk to his committee about their "backward movement." The mediator read the signal as a request for help. The union pro later reaffirmed this: "They were giving me trouble. But we changed the figures. I was playing straight for them, giving you the numbers. Then you came in and said it was crazy. I love FMCS."

Of course, pros do not always act in such exemplary fashion. There were occasions in the observed cases where the pro was not a stabilizing force, but acted to incite his committee: "He's not acting like a pro. I'm really concerned when a guy pushes his people to strike because he's upset at the company. He's not doing his job. He's not being a leader, and he's making matters worse with that rhetoric." Or a management pro, who did not encourage his one-member committee to move was commented on in these terms: "He's not acting like a pro. He's letting the manager call the shots, which is inciting the union. He doesn't have much clout." Some pros are not closers: "He's not a closer, a fast resolver. A closer would move it. If he couldn't, he'd take another tack. Two years won't do it, so in what other areas can we move?" One union pro confided his strategy to the mediator, which later compromised the mediator when the information proved erroneous: "He curve balled me. He told me what he wanted and then wouldn't take it when I brought it in. It was a charade and I'm the shill."

The interesting feature about each of these examples was that like the state mediators, federal mediators were able to construct plausible reasons for why three of the four pros acted as they did. Concerning the pro who incited his committee, mediator Allen commented, "He must not have a lot of strength and has to prove it. It was just rhetoric and it was a way to give his people the choice to fish or cut bait." Of the management pro without clout mediator Allen said, "The problem is the manager. He's playing close to the vest and not telling his attorney what's on his mind. He wants to keep control. There's nothing an attorney can do in that situation." The noncloser was absolved by the kinds of cases he gets, where there is minimal room for maneuvering: "I've worked with him before. He gets some dud cases where there's nothing to negotiate, like here. The last time it was a textile company that was going bankrupt." Only the pro who manipulated the mediator was criticized to the end: "This was a charade. He sold his committee out. Then he wanted me to tell them that they got a good deal, but they didn't. That's why I was so noncommittal." Apparently, to fail to act consistently like a pro is understandable in light of specific circumstances, provided such activities do not have the effect of compromising the mediator.[11] When they do, a response in kind may be forthcoming.

Both the state and federal mediators hold their roles and strategies to be responsive to the needs of the parties with whom they work. Because public-sector bargaining committees are seen as inexperienced and not consistently represented by pros, responsibility falls to the state mediator to build a package that meets the mutual needs of the parties and concurrently prepares them for the future. When pros represent the parties, the building strategy becomes more of a collaborative effort conducted extensively off the record.

As one mediator put it, "When pros are on a case, you hardly have to talk to the total group because the pro tells you where they are all the way through." But the basic tactical elements of the building strategy seemed to take a similar form whether pros were present or not. All that differed was the mediator's sense that he had more accurate information about priorities and was on "surer footing" in making and selling a deal. This contributed to the mediators' perception that the presence of pros makes for a more efficient and satisfactory process.

This was not the situation with the federal mediators. Pros are essential to the narrowing strategy, for it is the pro who moves his committee to alter its positions and it is the pro who closes the deal.[12] If a pro is not present, then the mediator will have to push and prod himself, tactics the federal mediators do not appear to relish. For, they argue, if they are forced to push actively for concessions early in the case, whatever persuasive ammunition they have can be used up prematurely.

Helping the Pro

The orchestrating role the federal mediators play and the strategic activities associated with it are planned and executed with the pro in mind. Federal mediators allege that one of their major functions is to lend credibility and assistance to the pros of both sides as they work with their committees trying to "close" a deal. Each situation presents its unique demands and challenges to the pro. The mediators claim that the businesslike character and hierarchical authority structure of the management committees mean that such a committee is most likely to heed the advice of its pro. The management pro is, therefore, less likely to require much direct assistance from the mediator. Union committees, however, with their diverse composition and their long proposals, frequently pose long and hard work for the pro, work that requires the help of the mediator.

The nature of the assistance the federal mediator provides the pro is a set of tactics that support the pro's efforts to move his committee toward settlement. These helping tactics are considered by federal mediators an integral part of their narrowing strategy. Indeed, to isolate these helping tactics from other components of this strategy would be to misinterpret the federal mediator's efforts.

Many of the tactical elements of narrowing are used precisely because they have the added advantage of helping the pro.

Calling sessions According to the federal mediators, the very act of convening mediation sessions at the FMCS offices signals the severity of the situation to the committees and gives them the chance to meet, an opportunity they otherwise will not have. Mediator Carr commented on this: "The company wanted a forum for meeting. Without the mediator, they might not have had as many meetings. The union rep has a touchy situation. He needs time to meet. That's what I gave him—a forum to meet." The assignment of rooms within the field office is also made with an eye to helping the pro: "I put Joe [union pro] in the front room. He may need to use my telephone or talk to me and I want to be sure his committee can't hear." The federal mediators keep short notes on what transpires during a case, and even this practice is often justified by its assistance to the pro: "I don't keep detailed notes, so they can't be used as evidence to hurt somebody. We usually deal with people we know. I don't want to have notes. That way I won't be able to say anything that might hurt Dick. We have to work together."

Joint meetings for proposal exchange The federal mediators prefer the joint meeting for the exchange of proposals, in part because a direct response from management has more impact on a committee than one delivered by an intermediary or speculated upon by the pro or the mediator: "You see, it helps Joe [union pro] with his committee to have Sam [management pro] present it across the table. The committee can see that Joe tried. He gave it his best effort and management said no way. Joe knew it all along, but he had to satisfy his committee that he tried." By using formal proposals as the vehicle for movement, the pro need only move his committee incrementally. This presumably makes the pro's task easier and minimizes the chances that the committee members will decide to strike against the advice of the pro: "When you shape a package, you want to be sure not to take bites that are too big at one time. As you narrow it down more and more, it becomes less likely for either side to take a walk. Nobody wants a strike here." Further, the incremental moves the parties make in their proposals mean that the final package will reflect many positions that the union has proposed. This serves to build their commitment and makes ratification, a process that the pro oversees, more likely.

For such gradual movement to occur, the pro needs time to work with his committee. The federal mediator gives him time for additional sessions and for lengthy caucuses, sometimes over the impatient objections of the other committee. For example, in Bard Manufacturing, the mediator viewed the purpose of the first session as providing the time for both pros to establish themselves with their committees: "I knew nothing was going to happen the first day. He's [union rep] new on the case. Somebody had it before. It's hard for him to come in and pull down the whole proposal in one session." In another case, when a management spokesman complained at the amount of time the union was taking with its response, the mediator reported, "He's having some trouble with his committee. He doesn't usually, but he is today. You know you can pick your members, but he has no control. He's just got to live with them. They'll move, but it's going to take some time." Though not as common, there were occasions when a union committee complained of management's pace and the mediator made a similar gesture: "It's going to take some time for them to pull those figures together. They're on the phone with the plant now." The federal mediators also employed specific tactics whose sole purpose was to support and help the pro.

Calling attention to the pro's expertise The federal mediators publicly defer to and honor the pro as an experienced negotiator in front of his committee. They refer to the pro as an expert, on familiar terms with important people in the local industrial-relations community, schooled in the mechanics of collective bargaining, and knowledgeable in current typical settlements. For example, as the mediator explained to a union committee that their proposal was still up on "cloud nine," he turned to the pro and said, "Joe, you know the settlements as well as I do."

Calling attention to the pro's position as committee leader The federal mediators reinforce the pro's position as leader of the bargaining committee, the person to take charge of the process. Instructions to the committee to meet, to gather information, or to develop a counterproposal are frequently addressed to the pro directly, in the presence of his committee: "Dick [union rep], what your team has to do is take their [management] input and develop a proposal in a framework the other side can respond to." This practice, claim the mediators, helps the pro keep the meetings on track.

Enhancing the trust between pro and committee The federal mediators continually help the pro gain and maintain the trust of his committee. It is essential, according to the federal mediators, to convey to the committees the impression that they are integrally involved in making the decisions at each stage of the process so that a feeling does not develop among them that a deal is being made behind their backs. The federal mediators, therefore, explicitly use tactics that foster the committees' involvement. Names of the committee members are learned and used. Off-the-record meetings are rarely instigated by the mediator, except on procedural matters. Such meetings are held, of course (frequently at the behest of the pro), and the mediator offers plausible reasons to the committees to justify them. When "trust" is deemed a problem, a pretended phone call or other artifice may be used as subterfuge to camouflage off-the-record meetings. During these meetings, whether in problem situations or not, the mediator monitors the pro's time away from his committee (intermittently, but carefully), and after "reasonable" lapses he will often suggest that the pro return to his committee. Some unions eschew off-the-record meetings entirely, so that pros from these unions are never pulled out, even if management deems it essential.

Responding to signals for assistance The federal mediators are alert to the direct as well as the indirect signals from the pro for assistance. The pro and the mediator review the pro's relationship with his committee, in the words of the mediator, to see whether they are yet "waltzing together." If the pro requires assistance to move his committee, to explain something to them, or to argue a point, the federal mediator, in most situations, does so. Often this assistance is merely a restatement of the argument already articulated by the pro. For example, in Bard Manufacturing, the pro signaled the mediator; he asked him to join the union caucus and to comment on the proposal written on the blackboard. The mediator interpreted this cue as a request for help from the pro, who was "having trouble with his committee." The mediator did meet with the committee and gave his opinion on its position. He was certain, he commented afterward, that he had only repeated what the pro had already told it. On another case, a management pro reported that he was having trouble with his committee. At the nearest opportunity, in a separate meeting, the mediator argued a specific point with the "trouble-maker" on the committee: "Jack [management pro] said he was having trouble convincing his committee, so I helped. Besides, what they are doing on the job bidding is clearly an unfair labor practice."

In sum, the federal mediator's narrowing strategy is predicated on the participation and collaboration of pros. To separate these expressive tactics, which help the pro, from the more substantive ones, which address the issues in dispute, would be to make a distinction the federal mediators do not themselves recognize. For them, helping the pro is a major way they facilitate the concessionary process.

Since the state mediators do not work with as many spokesmen they consider pros, and since they see them as helpful but not essential in building a package, helping a spokesman, whether a pro or not, was not a central feature of the state mediator's strategic activities. There were isolated examples of a mediator providing assistance when asked. In Sheridan Firefighters, when an initial wage deal was made, the management pro told the mediator he would have to work on the management committee, and the mediator did. In a few instances, when a pro was criticized by the opposing committee, the mediator would defend the pro's action. For example, in the Ulster School Committee case, the union pro blamed the management pro for the "insulting" wage offer. The mediator responded, "No, it came off the computer that way. Allan [management pro] tried to tell them that you would take it this way, but the school committee wouldn't listen."

But these were isolated examples. For the most part, a state mediator tended to criticize, to insult, and openly to embarrass spokesmen in front of their committees for their failure, in the mediator's eyes, to collaborate with his building efforts. One mediator described this tactic: "He won't do anything without the consent of his committee. The only way I can get him to cooperate is to shoot him down." Another mediator described a similar practice: "What I tried to do was embarrass him. Now he has to weigh whether he should put up with my embarrassing him or try to get the school committee to move off dead center." In the Vanderbilt School Committee case, the management spokesman was criticized by the mediator for his lack of preparation: "You should have met with them before you came to mediation. This is not the time for a caucus." Spokesmen were "pulled" from their committees with apparent disregard for its effect. On a few occasions, the mediator asked the spokesman whether his committee trusted him, but these instances were rare.

State mediators, however, do believe that they help chief negotiators in two ways. They provide them with arguments that they can use to convince their committees: "He needs me to talk about other settlements to say the wages aren't good. Then he can take over and refer back to what I've said. He'll say, what the mediator said is true." Also, and probably more useful to the spokesmen, according to the state mediators, is the settlement the mediator brings in, one that is "responsive and fair," which proves to the committees that in hiring or using their spokesmen, they have been well served. This view that the elements of the settlement are the yardstick by which a spokesman is judged is lent support by a union pro in one of the cases: "The administrative ratio is the reason I'm here. Last time they gave it away late one night, and they want it this time. If we don't get it, I may be out."

There is an interesting paradox implied in the different ways state and federal mediators interact with chief negotiators. Although the federal mediators claim that they are not interested in making an off-the-record deal, their narrowing strategy, which has the effect of helping the pro's relationship with his committee, sometimes creates a situation where a deal can be made and then sold to the bargaining committees. In Bard Manufacturing, for example, after the parties narrowed some of the differences, the final package was cemented off the record and then "sold" by the mediator, working with the pro, to the union committee. A similar process was observed in Albion Broadcasting.

The state mediators, in their efforts to construct a deal, may inadvertently jeopardize the pro's relationship with his committee and, therefore, impair his credibility, which is necessary in order to sell the package. This occurred in the Regis School Committee case and, with more severe consequences, in Sheridan Firefighters. In that case, an off-the-record deal was created and then strategically sold to the union committee. But because the committee had not fully participated in the creation, its commitment to the package was in doubt. According to the mediator after the case, when the union committee presented the tentative agreement to its membership, support was not unanimous and the constituency rejected it. It appears, therefore, that strategies have implications not only for the immediate resolution of the issues in dispute, but affect, as well, the process and outcomes of the ratification process. Further, just as the building and narrowing strategies have consequences for the relationship between spokesmen and their committees, so too, they may affect the mediator's ability to do his own job credibly.

6

Mistakes and the Evaluation of Strategic Approaches

The connection between the mediator's strategic activities and the outcomes of his efforts—a settlement, strike, or a continued state of impasse—is a matter subject to some debate. Some observers of the process allege that the outcomes reflect more the underlying political and economic circumstances of the dispute than they do the strategic efforts of the mediator. As far back as 1955, Clark Kerr argued that strikes appear to have their own logic and respond to forces other than the deliberate and rational actions of the mediators. More recently, others have suggested that the parties, particularly those who are skilled in negotiations, have more control over the process and the outcomes than does the mediator (Kochan and Jick, 1978).[1]

Practitioners seem to agree. They are reluctant to claim responsibility for either success or failure. As one mediator quoted by Kressel (1972) describes it, "It is very difficult to evaluate the role played by the mediator in terms of its utility in negotiations. He acts as a catalyst. He reorders the issues in order to reduce their pressures. He helps to diffuse the heat that's there by keeping them apart and acting as a go-between. But in the final analysis, the settlement is between the parties. You may help bring them there, but to what extent your wanderings back and forth did it, who knows?" (p. 31).

Douglas (1962) suggests that this public dissimulation is deliberate, that it discourages curiosity about what mediators do and insulates them from charges of irresponsible behavior. In this regard, she observes that mediators invoke a particular brand of determinism—

"the Strike is the disciplinarian and the Economy holds the purse strings"—that links the terms of settlement to sources outside the domain of mediation (p. 109).

This perspective may also be observed in the evaluation practices of mediation agencies. Like many another organization whose product is ambiguous, these agencies are reluctant to measure the output of their employees.[2] In a survey of mediation agencies, Parker (1970) found that few used any standards to evaluate mediator performance. In particular, the frequency of strike occurrences and impasses were perceived as unreliable measures of the mediator's contribution because they are thought to arise from circumstances outside the mediator's control. Those evaluation standards that are used, although their use is not widespread, tend to be based on informal feedback from the parties and the frequency with which mediators are requested by the parties (McClellan and Obermeyer, 1970).

The ambiguous connection between what mediators do and the results of their efforts is lent some support in the present study. Working toward a similar goal—a settlement—the state and federal mediators achieved this end using markedly different means. Yet in the sixteen cases observed, there were no strikes. All of the federal cases resulted in a ratified agreement. The state mediators were less consistent in their performance; three cases were not settled until the factfinding step. How much this reflects on the mediators' performance and how much this result was "determined" by other factors are difficult to assess, for the dealmaking behaviors observed in these three cases did not appear to differ markedly from those used in cases where settlements were reached. It may be that given the pattern of obscuring the relation between mediatorial means and ends, and given the nature of the structural interdependence of the parties, which inevitably results in a settlement, the standards by which mediators can be judged will always be problematic.

If the minor variance in outcomes in this study constrains evaluation, the variance in means used does not. Starting with similar goals, the state and federal mediators make use of different strategic means to reach them. These strategies seem to have implications for how credibly and competently the mediator can perform his role, and they have consequences for his longer-term relationship with the parties.[3] Further, if feedback and frequency of requests are to be the standards by which an agency judges its employees, these evaluations will be made by the parties on the basis of perceived performance during the process and not solely on the outcomes.

Mistakes are bound to happen in every occupation (Hughes, 1971). The more a doctor, lawyer, plumber does the work of his profession, the more likely it becomes that on occasion he will do it wrong. Some mistakes, as Hughes observes, are more serious than others for the person who makes the mistake, for his colleagues, and for the recipients or clients. Mediators make mistakes. Some that they make may jeopardize their own performance, while others may also harm the parties. A settlement may elude the parties because of a mediator's blunder, or more commonly, one of the parties may fail to gain all that it might have (Douglas, 1962).

The problem comes in defining a mistake. Without clear criteria to define a success, it is difficult objectively to define its opposite. For a settlement may be reached in spite of mistakes made by the mediator. Hughes suggests that in occupations where success and mistakes are hard to define, one can locate them by the "rationale whistled by members when events don't go according to plan" (p. 318). It is therefore in the historical reconstructions of the event, where occupational members justify and rationalize what they have done, that one's attention is called to the incidence of a mistake. These accounts of actions taken in the face of untoward events locate a mistake for the outside observer (Lyman and Scott, 1970). This is the primary criterion used here to identify mistakes. When the parties voiced displeasure at the mediator's actions and the mediator justified those actions either to the parties or to me or both, I inferred the possibility of a mistake.

This definition of a mistake represents a departure from the analyses described in the earlier chapters. There it was the *mediator's understanding* of his role, his use of meetings and tactics, and his relationship with the parties that constituted the basis for analysis. In this chapter the discussion of mistakes represents *my perspective* and in some ways my assessment of the implications and consequences of the contrasting mediator approaches—orchestrating and dealmaking. The mediators would not necessarily agree with all the assessments I make, for our definitions of mistakes will be based in part on different premises. To a mediator, a mistake is defined and judged primarily in the context of his immediate concerns in the case—that a confidence has been violated or a party's position misrepresented. I too am interested in the instances when such mistakes seem to occur, but emphasize not merely the immediate occurrence but what seem to be the short-range consequences and longer-range implications of common errors associated with dealmaking and orchestrating. This contextual evaluation suggests that despite high settlement rates, there are ways that a mediator's behavior may detract from his performance.

Mistakes Made by State Mediators

The role of dealmaker, with its attendant tactical attempts to control and to manipulate a strategic process whose outcome ultimately rests with the committees, seems particularly fraught with the potential for making mistakes. Consider some of the observed ways in which the building activities associated with dealmaking can give rise to mistakes.

Misreading the Role

Intent on building a package, state mediators sometimes misread the role the parties wished them to play. This occurred in two cases. The impasse petitions for mediation in these cases were initiated by the union committees, which alleged that their proposals were not getting a fair hearing from the management committees. They petitioned for mediation, or so they claimed, for the sole purpose of having the mediator convene a session with the full school committees (not just their negotiating subcommittees) present. In both of these cases, the full school committees did participate after the first sessions. But in the meetings that preceded the school committees' attendance, the two mediators tried in their usual way to build a package. Their suggestions for movement were greeted with hostile responses.

In the Scripps School Committee case, the mediator concluded his first meeting with the union by offering the following advice: "I'd advise you to look at their wage offer. It's a good offer compared to other settlements I've been getting." To this a union member replied, "You don't seem to understand. You say it's fair, but we want more. We want to talk directly to the school committee. We petitioned to get them here. We know we have the votes on the school committee to increase it." In the Ulster School Committee case, the mediator tried to assess the priority issues in an effort to start building a package: "The way I see it, there are only six really important issues separating you—it's the 8 percent on wages, the administrative ratio, the sick leave bank, RIF, and the coaches' and nurses' salary. It's not that much. We can start to move it." This brought the following response from the union attorney: "You're reading it all wrong. Get the whole committee here. We're not going to do anything until the school committee gets here."

In both cases, the mediators based their actions on the articulated premise that the unions had to make some moves before the school committees would be willing to attend. The union committees, however, seemed to view such preliminary sessions as occasions to brief the mediators on their requests and to review the issues. They did not see these sessions as the forums for discussing changes in their proposals. Movement would occur when the full school committees were present. The committees expressed some irritation at the mediators for failing to understand the reason they had petitioned for mediation. Indeed, in these two cases, the final agreements were reached, not in mediation, but after the parties returned to bilateral negotiations.

Gaps in the Facts

In their use of separate meetings to learn the facts of the cases, state mediators did not always learn all the issues in dispute. Their practice was to meet with the unions first, obtain their demands, and then meet with the management committees to review the unions' demands. Frequently, the presentation of the unions' positions led to a discussion of union issues with management, and there was no opportunity for management to present its demands. In a few cases, management demands were lost in the shuffle.

In the Ulster School Committee case, at the end of the first session, the management attorney, in the context of an off-the-record discussion with the mediator about the union's noneconomic issues, asked the mediator the status of the school committee's demands. The mediator responded, "What are they?" The attorney indicated that the maternity-leave change was the number-one priority. However, the mediator did not covey this to the union, or even mention maternity leave, because most of the union members had already departed for the day. In the second session, when the full school committee attended, it pressed for maternity leave, an issue the union assumed that management had dropped because the mediator had never mentioned it to them. The issue was resolved, but the parties refused to let the mediator meet with them to discuss it. Said the mediator, "Can I try to mediate it?" to which the union attorney replied, "No, just give us time."

In the Rutgers School Committee case, two union demands were "lost." During the off-the-record meetings to complete the agreement, the union negotiator noticed that two of the union's demands had never been discussed. This case settled as well, but required several more rounds of discussions on these issues at 4:00 a.m.

Demands are lost in part because learning the issues is coupled with learning priorities and encouraging the parties to make moves. In this process the wages are usually seen as the priority issue. If noneconomic demands are not explicitly emphasized, the mediators tend to consider them of low priority. Even if they are mentioned, the mediator may still interpret them as unimportant in the belief that they are part of the committee's strategy to "pad" their proposal and, hence, are not really priority demands at all. This process of assessing priorities is particularly fraught with the possibility for errors.

Misgauging Priorities

Accurately gauging priorities is crucial to a successful building process. Yet such information is hard to come by. The mediators relied on signals and certain rules of thumb about membership blocks and order of presentation to assess priorities. Sometimes they were wrong. Further, in their roles as "active message carriers," state mediators often conveyed their interpretations of committees' priorities only to find that they had misunderstood or misinterpreted them. This is not a problem per se, in that these errors can be corrected later in the case. However, when a mediator suggests areas for movement to the other committee, misidentified priorities can become the building blocks for a response which may address the wrong demands or omit the priority ones entirely.

In the Taft School Committee case, the union presented the mediator with seven demands, four of which were discussed in some detail. The final three were mentioned but not discussed. The mediator, in his meeting with the school committee, gave his assessment that only the first four demands were priorities and that the remaining three were off the table. The school committee, in turn, made a proposal that touched on the four priority demands. The union, in its response, emphasized the importance of one of the "dropped three," release time for teacher evaluations, and dropped one of the priority four, a change in the maternity-leave clause. The mediator believed that the union had changed its priorities and took this alteration as evidence that the union was "unstable and irrational." From the observer's perspective, there was no indication of this. The initial assessment of priorities was based on the mediator's (reasonable but by no means guaranteed) assumption that if three issues were not discussed, they were not priorities. On the basis of the mediator's advice to the school committee, the union received less in wages in the final settlement than the school committee had been willing to give. Management believed that conducting evaluations during release time was advantageous to it and therefore was willing to concede both issues. The mediator justified his actions with the claim that by saving the school committee money, he had improved his "rapport" with it.

In the Regis School Committee case, during the first meeting, the mediator asked the school committee for its priorities and obtained from it four issues that he transmitted to the union as the school committee's proposal. The union's response was altered in kind. In the second session, however, when the mediator made reference to the four priority issues during his meeting with the school committee, the spokesman claimed that they had six issues:

Mediator: You didn't tell me this was a key issue. Should I make my list six or seven? They're going to retrench. I misled them and told them you only had four.

Management Attorney: I gave you those four issues off the top of my head in the heat of that meeting. It's not fair to hold me to that.

In reporting to the union, the mediator described the situation.

Union Rep: Did you find out about the four issues?

Mediator: I didn't make much headway. In fact, maybe I went backwards. But I just finished telling the attorney that he deserves what he gets for reneging.

Deals disintegrate in part because they are based on erroneous information and optimistic projections. In Tulane Firefighters the mediator told the union committee that if it reformed its proposal in accordance with his suggestions on EMT, then management would concur. But he later found that the other side was not as fully convinced of the merit of his EMT plan. Examples such as these, of misunderstood or misinterpreted priorities, were observed in most of the state cases, and they appeared to compromise the mediator's credibility. In the Tulane case, when the mediator reported his assessment that the union would not settle without an EMT stipend, the management attorney belittled his assessment: "You read them that way? Last time, their offer was at 15 percent. Just go back to them and give them this offer."

In the Ulster School Committee case, the union attorney similarly deprecated the mediator's assessment of management's proposal.

Mediator: Here's what I can get for you—five and three and something on the fringes. That's my reading.
Union Attorney: I don't care. Your job is to bring everything [total management proposal] back to us.

Such perceptions on the part of the spokesmen seemed to detract from the mediator's efforts to build a package.

Misfired Moves and Excessive Pressure

The mediator's tactical efforts to get the parties to make moves on specific issues sometimes resulted in a direct challenge to the mediator's abilities. In the Rutgers case, the management attorney complained at the time pressure put on him: "You don't seem to understand that these people are committed to their position. I agree that it is unreasonable, but they need time to adjust to the change. Let's schedule another meeting." The mediator refused, and the attorney returned to his committee and apparently was able to change their minds, for a settlement was reached late that evening.

Two mediators were chastised for putting too much pressure on a committee to make a particular move. A member of the school committee in the Scripps case complained about the mediator's efforts to persuade them to make a concession on the longevity payments: "Let me say this. This has not been a satisfactory experience. I feel that you have used more than reasonable exertion here." In the Reed School Committee case, a member of the school committee also complained about the pressure: "I have a question about mediation. We're still where we were when we started. I am not pleased with this whole proceeding." It is perhaps suggestive that in these two cases where committee members were moved to complain, neither of these committees made any further concessions. The unions settled largely for the offers the school committees had made prior to mediation. Whether their entrenchment was solely a reaction to the mediator's actions is hard to gauge without reference to the committees' private deliberations. One of these mediators, however, suggested that further concessions might have been forthcoming if his relationship with the management attorney and school committee had been more cordial.

Perhaps less striking than the direct criticisms, but nevertheless "mistakes," were the instances in which early efforts to persuade and pressure the parties barred the mediators from direct participation in the later stages of the cases. In the Rutgers School Committee case, the mediator claimed that his overzealous and even strident efforts to persuade the school committee to drop its wage plan meant that during the final session, he could no longer meet with that committee: "I came on very strong last session and may have outstayed my welcome. Now I can't do any more." In the Ulster case, the mediator was completely barred from meeting with both committees.

Management Attorney: I don't want you to try to sell the proposal. I want you to let them work it out themselves.
Mediator: Do you want me to work on your people to see if they'll give more on money?
Attorney: No.

When a pro was expected to collaborate in making and selling a package, he sometimes balked as well: "If you don't stop telling me to whisper the number in your ear, I'm going to piss in it."

Long-Range Implications
The mistakes they made in trying to build a deal appeared to compromise the credibility of the mediators in the eyes of the parties during the cases. Though rebuked and deprecated at times, they still managed to build deals that were accepted by committees and ratified by constituencies. Indeed, the settlement rate for the agency is high; some 80 percent of cases are resolved in mediation. This is borne out in the present study as well; seven of the ten cases were resolved in mediation or shortly thereafter. The problem in this regard may be the longer-range implications of these mistakes and the kinds of reputations that result. Since state mediators may

encounter the same parties in subsequent negotiations and most certainly will meet many of the spokesmen on other cases, it is instructive to consider how damaged credibility carries over from case to case.

In the Taft School Committee case, the mediator was virtually attacked by the union committee for his behavior the last time it had been in mediation with him. He was accused of "selling out the union": "This is your fault. You threw this at us right at the end last time. Now we want to be paid for it." Although this particular case settled, for its duration the union requested that the mediator leave it to caucus while it prepared its responses to management's proposals. This amounts to expulsion, since Thomas's practice on other cases and, indeed, with the school committee in the Taft case was to remain with the committee and participate in its deliberations.

In the Scripps School Committee case, the mediator had worked previously with the management attorney, one whom the mediator had openly criticized for his passive behavior. At the start of the Scripps case, the attorney commented to me, "Joe is quite new at this game isn't he? He's got a lot to learn." Further into the case, the mediator expected this attorney to be an ally and help persuade the school committee to make a concession on longevity payments that would be more in line with the pattern of other units in the town. The spokesman sat silent throughout these meetings and never supported the mediator's arguments. It is of course difficult to be sure that the spokesman would have participated if their relationship had been different.

Finally, certain mediators in the state service seem to have developed a reputation that does not reflect well on their abilities. One of the pros commented on this: "The problem with some of the mediators from the state is that they push too hard and too soon. I wonder whether some of them have a brain. They come into these complex cases. They don't understand that they have to get a handle on it before they can go after the details." Perceptions like these probably do not enhance the spokesman's desire to ally himself with the mediator in building a package.

Mistakes Made by Federal Mediators
Mistakes of the sort routinely made by state mediators were rarely observed on the federal cases, perhaps because federal mediators

assiduously avoid the types of entanglements that might cause them to occur. The use of joint meetings to learn the issues and full proposals in order to keep track of moves are the safeguards they use to ensure that positions are not lost. Content to let priorities emerge, the federal mediators were rarely caught transmitting premature or erroneous information about priority issues. Since they are not trying to make a deal, they cannot be embarrassed when such a deal falls apart. One operational principle they adhere to is not to promise that they can get something from the other side. They prefer across-the-table transfers of proposals to ensure that positions are not misstated: "That's why I want them to tell each other directly; so I don't blow it in translation."

When forced to act as a "message carrier," federal mediators carefully recorded such mesages, whether proposals, questions, or requests for information. In one case, a final proposal was checked three times with the committee before the mediator carried it to the other side. This contrasts with the state mediator's more casual efforts to convey messages, sometimes without notes. This contrast is not merely one between sloppiness and punctiliousness, but reflects the different conceptions of who is responsible for the content of the messages—the mediator or the committee. Finally, federal mediators more often help a pro sell than do the actual persuading themselves. Challenges to their tactical moves were rare. Rather, the federal mediator's efforts were more likely to be praised than scorned. As one union rep put it, "You really do good work. See, boys, we got a good deal." At the end of another case, the union rep complimented the mediator by saying, "For the International, I feel we can recommend the contract. We extend our appreciation to you and the Service for a job well done."

Challenges to the federal mediator's credibility may come from other sources. The narrowing strategy requires, indeed demands, that pros play their role in the process. To the degree that pros, for whatever the reason, fail to conform to these expectations, the mediator may be placed in situations that are akin to those observed in the state cases. And when they are, they too make mistakes. A crucial distinction, however, is that the building strategy of the state mediators seems to place them in such positions more frequently. The federal mediators were observed in such positions only when they believed the situations required a departure from their accustomed role.

Taking the Spokesman's Role

When a novice spokesman represents a committee, the movement for which the pro is responsible may not occur. As a consequence, the opposing committee may lose its patience with the process and threaten to break off negotiations. More frequently it enlists the mediator to intervene. In the Duke Hospital case, the mediator was put in this position quite early in the case. He met with the union committee and started to work through its proposal, prodding, pushing, and suggesting modifications. The union committee was less than pleased with his actions and let its feelings be known. The mediator commented on the meeting: "They're really nasty in there. We had a real argument. Joe's [union pro] having trouble with his committee. He's new. He can't push them. They weren't ready to hear from me that they have to attach a dollar cost to each thing and that they won't get anything more on the wages." Though the outcome was successful in this situation, federal mediators report that when forced to play such an active role early in the case, their credibility sometimes becomes so damaged that they enlist the aid of another mediator—one to be a surrogate spokesman and the other a devil's advocate. One mediator described such a case. "I got into the case on Monday. On Tuesday, the union said there would be no additional proposals until management went back to its prestrike offer. I yelled and screamed to get some movement, but was careful not to promise anything in return. The union moved, but I figured I had shot my wad because the move wasn't enough. So I called Washington and they sent in another mediator and we worked together."

In the Alfred Corporation case, several interrelated circumstances converged to place the mediator in a difficult position. After a rejection by the membership, the parties were in mediation to resolve only the cost-of-living clause. Therefore narrowing was impossible. The management attorney had never been in mediation before and therefore had few suggestions to resolve this issue. He wanted the mediator to develop some alternatives and present them to the union. The mediator had his suggestions rebuffed and ridiculed by the union pro: "Didn't you hear what I said: This is really aggravating me. The answer is no. We've reached an impasse, and I'm going to take action against the company." At the end of the case, the mediator described his experience to the parties. "I learned something, but it was tough on me. One of my jobs is to keep probing both sides to see if there is any flexibility. There wasn't. I guess I had to take the heat here."

Miscues from Pros

Although it is difficult to assess the intentionality behind their moves, pros sometimes gave miscues to the federal mediators that entrapped them in embarrassing situations. In Albion Broadcasting, at the request of the pros the scheduling of broadcast time was detached from the rest of the proposal as a priority issue and negotiated off the record by a subcommittee. Although the chief negotiators proposed this forum to the mediator, the mediator was enlisted to present it as his suggestion. He did, the meeting took place, and the issue was resolved. But then the management pro seemed to assume that the case was settled despite the existence of six other union issues that had yet to be discussed. The mediator was attacked by a member of the management committee:

Member of Management Committee: This is impossible. When we made those concessions on the schedule, it was with the understanding that the other demands were off. I wouldn't have made them otherwise. You assured us this was it.

Mediator (rummaging through his notes): No, on the first day we agreed to isolate this issue. I'm not confused.

The mediator, to restore his own credibility, reviewed what had transpired during the first meeting and sought to justify the union's position that these other issues needed to be resolved. His failure to keep detailed notes on the proceedings, however, meant that management had to take his reconstruction on faith at a time when his credibility was at a low point. The mediator blamed the pro for placing him in this awkward position.

In the Carroll University case, a miscue from the pro appeared to cause a more serious error. Early in the case, the union pro told the mediator that despite the inclusion of other issues in the proposal, he wanted only to secure from the university administration its commitment to use only union subcontractors for the duration of the contract. At the time of this confidence, all the union's issues were on the table as well as a demand that management agree to keep XYZ contractor, the one they intended to hire, for the three years of the contract. Later in the case, the mediator was enlisted by the management pro to present a compromise on the table position when he knew the real one. The union pro exploded, "You don't seem to understand. I told you where we were going on this. How could you bring in something so far off?" The mediator blamed the union pro for misleading him and then apologized because he believed his actions had "muddied the waters:" "I may have hurt the situation. I heard that you wanted the three years with XYZ and I tried to knuckle them to get it. I tried to get a compromise and did—two years instead of three. I succeeded. Then you changed it to assurances about a union contractor in the future. Maybe going after two years muddied the waters." Despite Carr's admission that an error had been made, it is instructive to note that he placed the blame on the pro and then sought to justify his actions as serving the interests of a settlement: "I really knew that they wanted the assurances, not a commitment with XYZ. But by taking credit for the compromise, it gives the union the impression that I have been working hard to get concessions from the university. It builds their confidence in me for later when we reach the settling stage." The union did not appear to view this mistake in such strategic terms.

Impressions of Passivity

In their effort to avoid possible errors and entanglements, the federal mediators sometimes appear passive and withholding. This is particularly true in the later stages of the cases, when the parties, who may be at a stalemate, seem to be waiting for a new idea or suggestion from the mediator. The mediator, sometimes unwilling to risk making an unacceptable suggestion, expects the pro to "close" it. In a few situations, the pro made no move in that direction and an awkward and uncomfortable silence ensued. The discomfort was not necessarily a problem per se, but the lack of ideas, suggestions, or solutions ran counter to the official presentation the mediator had given of himself as a creative problem solver.

Like their state counterparts, the federal mediators have an impressive settlement rate. All the disputes in this study were settled and ratified. As noted, in part this is inevitable. Without further dispute resolution stages, all cases in the private sector ultimately settle in either mediation or direct negotiations. In the process, however, federal mediators took fewer risks and were less likely to make mistakes, particularly ones that jeopardized their relationships with the pros or the pros' positions with their committees.

Long-Range Implications

For the most part, federal mediators appeared to enjoy a cordial, if not intimate, relationship with the pros on their cases, particularly those whom they knew from other cases. Pros continually drifted into the mediator's office during lulls in the process and chatted informally with him about sports, mutual acquaintances, children, and politics. This kind of informality occurred only in selected state cases. Further, pros frequently complimented the mediator, not only at the case's conclusion but at the start as well: "I hear XYZ Broadcasting settled. Weren't you the yeoman on that? Good work. You know the best organization in the federal government is FMCS."

The relationship between the federal mediators and the pros they work with does not occur by chance. When the mediator employs tactics that help the pro, that give him time, assistance, and support with his committee in a given case, the mediator does so not solely out of a short-term interest in settlement. These tactics serve to cement future relations with pros whom the mediator continually encounters.

Mistakes made in the context of building and narrowing provide an interesting counterpoint to some of the current thinking about the changing character of mediation strategies. The findings from recent research suggest that the parties prefer aggressive mediators to ones who are more passive (Krislov, Mead, and Goodman, 1972) and that such aggressive behavior is more likely to result in concessions and settlements (Kochan and Jick, 1978; Gerhart and Drotning, 1980). Some argue that this behavior is particularly appropriate in the public sector (Liebowitz, 1972; Robins, 1972; Ross, 1976), that without the pressure from a strike, responsibility falls to the mediator to create this pressure through his own active and persuasive tactics. The state mediators consider themselves aggressive and emphasize, in their building strategy, persuasive and pressure tactics. Their strategy obviously yields settlements. But in the process, mistakes in timing and errors of judgment were frequent. What is compromised by such a strategy, therefore, may not necessarily be the outcomes, although some committees appeared to lose more than they gained. What seems to be compromised is the mediator's face, his claim to be a credible, competent, and trustworthy practitioner. This loss may have implications for the conduct of the current case and affect the longer-range reputation of the agency and its practitioners. These may be the risks of an active dealmaking stance, risks that seem to be avoided by the orchestrating posture of federal mediators.

7

Conclusions: The Roots of Orchestrating and Dealmaking and Their Implications

In practice the public face of work frequently differs from the private face. Mediation is no exception. Mediators characterize their work as art, a public posture that highlights the idiosyncratic character of their work and the creativity and flexibility of those who practice. Artistic rhetoric suggests that the competent practitioner is one who first diagnoses the situation peculiar to the dispute and then flexibly tailors his approach, one that is uniquely his own, to fit the dynamics of the case. Such perspicacity is not generally evident in the practice of the institutional mediators observed in this study. Indeed, the process appears to be more one of pattern and routine than it is of creativity and innovation.

Orchestrators and dealmakers exhibit remarkable conformity and consistency in their modes of practice. Mediators' preconceptions about their role limit the range of diagnostic information they seek about a case. Rather, they seem to rely on cultural categories of interpretation to convert what is peculiar and idiosyncratic about a case into features that are recognized and expected. These background assumptions lead to strategic repertoires that transcend the unique features of any given dispute and lend to the practice in each agency a distinctive form that differentiates it from the other. In the arrangement of meetings, the treatment of substantive issues in dispute, and the relationships with the parties, orchestrators and dealmakers seek to organize the process in ways that suit their own strategic objectives.

Sources of Role Differentiation

The roots of the differences between the roles of orchestrator and dealmaker are difficult to untangle. The mediators account for them with reference to the characteristics of the sector in which they most often work. Thus federal mediators emphasize those attributes of collective bargaining most commonly associated with the private industrial sector. In contrast, the state mediators highlight the ways in which collective bargaining in the public sector departs from the private ideal and so requires, they argue, a different mediator role. Although these accounts are in many ways incomplete and inconsistent, they do seem to touch on some basic differences between an institutionalized and culturally regulated framework, which is found in the private sector, and a system that is still developing and changing, which is the public sector. Structure and policy within the agency likewise reflect the differences in ideology and practice and tend, in contrasting ways, to reinforce the particular roles the mediators play.

Collective bargaining in the industrial sector dates back some 150 years and on a large and regulated scale since the 1930s. Its institutionalized set of rules—some of which are formally set, while others are more cultural in character—that have developed over time color collective bargaining with "ritual" that leads to some predictability and mutual expectations about the proceedings (Stevens, 1963). For example, union and management negotiators commence bargaining with demands that depart significantly from each other, the so-called law of large opening offers, and this is intentional. Through a process marked by stylized moves and behaviors, the parties under the tutelage of their expert negotiators gradually scale back their demands until an agreement is reached. The strike deadline purportedly propels this process to its conclusion. Indeed, another stylized feature is the last-minute flurry of moves as the strike becomes imminent. Against this general background, orchestrating occurs. Thus the federal mediators emphasize the ability of the pro to move his committee and the ever present strike threat to justify his role. Given these dynamics, they argue, the role of the mediator is to provide the forum for the pros to work with their committees and to highlight the pressure from the strike in order to encourage movement.

When the state mediators account for their dealmaking role, they dwell on how negotiations in the public sector differ from those in the private. In particular, the state mediators allude to the parties' inexperience, the lack of delegated authority to negotiators, and the bar on legally condoned strikes. They argue that negotiating committees more recently endowed with the right to bargain collectively have not yet developed an understanding of the dynamics of negotiations. Rather than seeing opening positions as a stylized gesture, for example, the committees adopt them tenaciously and are reluctant to make concessions. The political context in which public-sector bargaining occurs exacerbates this problem. The diversity of interests at the level of local government is reflected in the bargaining committees at this level and makes it difficult for management as well as labor to coordinate negotiations. Further, these committees often do not realize their own limitations and, therefore, fail to delegate bargaining authority to their spokesmen. Finally, the state mediators argue that the legal ban on strikes by unions in the public sector considerably weakens these unions' bargaining power and also removes the pressure toward accommodation created by strike deadlines.

But few of these state practitioners have any direct involvement with mediation in the private sector, so that these comparisons seem to be based more on onlookers' impressions than on substantive evidence or experience. One state mediator gave an interesting account of his impression of the differences between practice in the public and private sectors:

The public sector is going through what the private sector went through thirty–forty years ago. You would hear about the garment industry. The union and management negotiating committees would meet in the most expensive restaurant, where they would have cocktails, drink, lobsters and steaks. This was all before the proposals were ever submitted. It's a cultural thing. "Look how good we're living. There's no reason we can't come to a settlement." They'd break bread first, the Jews and the Italians. The general framework was food and drink versus the public sector, where it's the school committee and the taxpayer against the teachers and their families. Mediation isn't really needed in the private sector. In the public sector you're part of the process. You have to use recommendations because the parties aren't strong enough or don't know how to say it themselves.

A very dramatic and idealized picture. Now consider the reality. Lack of personal knowledge of bargaining committees is perhaps the most salient example. Union bargaining committees in the private sector (and the public as well) typically include officers of the locals and representatives who are elected solely for the purpose of negotiating an upcoming contract. Elections of these committees are part of the political process of the union, and as a result these bodies typically represent the diversity of interests within the membership. Turnover among local officers is frequent as leaders are voted in and out of office based on their negotiating performance and their willingness to undertake the duties of office with minimal compensation (Strauss, 1977). Precise data on officer turnover is scarce, and for bargaining committees nonexistent. Mills (1978) suggests, however, that the changing interests of members, the lack of compensation for service, and the almost inevitable dissatisfaction with new contracts lead to frequent changes in committee membership. In the four federal cases, where the mediator had worked with the parties previously in mediation, the union committee members, with the exception of one union president, were strangers to him. Although management committees in the federal cases tended to be more stable, turnover was apparent there as well. Thus it is not at all clear how the membership of bargaining committees comes to possess, except at the highest corporate or union level, its vaunted experience.

Similar inconsistencies can be identified with regard to pros and the role of the strike. In brief, pros in the private sector do not automatically possess bargaining authority. Rather, pros seem to seek mediation for the assistance it gives them in building their authority in the eyes of their committees so that their advice and expertise will be heeded. The strike also seems to operate in practice in ways that depart from the idealizations of both federal and state mediators. In each of the federal cases, at points significantly before the deadline, the mediators were assured by the parties that a strike would not occur (see especially Albion Broadcasting and Bard Manufacturing). Thus whatever pressure the strike might have exerted was dissipated well before the final hours of mediation.[1]

These images of the contrasts between the sectors are compelling to the mediators despite evidence that their view is incomplete and not totally accurate. This observation does not necessarily detract from the validity of their claims, for these images of sectoral dynamics do seem to underly the mediators' understanding of why their roles differ. As a theoretical explanation, however, the claims of the mediators cannot be taken as definitive, for they are not independent of the mediator's role and purpose in the proceedings. But it may be that what the mediators define, from their immediate experience, as differences between the sectors is a reflection of a broader issue that touches on the contrast between institutional development in the two spheres. In the private sector the institutional framework is well articulated, consistent with the dominant ideology of free collective bargaining. The translation of this institutional framework to the public sector results in certain inconsistencies for the emerging institutions and places the mediators, therefore, in a problematic and ambiguous situation that they are left on their own to resolve.

Ideology and the Institutionalization of Federal Practice

Collective bargaining in the private sector is based on a pluralistic conception of industrial society. In such a view the competing interests of capital, labor, and the public are reconciled, but not permanently resolved, through an institutional framework of rules that promote industrial peace. The state in this system is seen as the guarantor of the public interest but neutral with regard to the interests of labor and capital. Value is placed on the idea of free collective bargaining, which holds the interests of the parties in bilateral negotiations as paramount and minimizes the role of outsiders in setting the terms and conditions of the contract.[2]

Federally sponsored mediation services developed in the context of this framework. Although the FMCS was not formally established as an independent agency until 1947, the basic structure of the agency dates back to World War II, when it was under the aegis of the Department of Labor. Therefore during the decades that collective bargaining was developing its institutional identity in the industrial sector, the federal mediators were directly involved. Even before the agency was granted independent status, its recruits were required to have extensive negotiating backgrounds on either the management or union side. Consistent with its pluralist ideology, the agency, from its earliest days, sought to balance its hires, half from management and the other half from labor.[3] Thus first as principals and then as mediators, the federal practitioners were influenced by the ideology of free collective bargaining with its limited role for outsiders. Nowhere is this more apparent than in the espoused philosophy of the agency, one that is articulated by its former director, William Simkin: "There are few comments that can be made about the philosophy that should underlie the many value judgments that must be made. *One basic principle designed to promote the maximum of direct negotiations is that the mediator should do as little as is required"* (1971, p. 118, italics added).

The extensive training federal mediators receive only serves to reinforce these values. Formal training is brief, with apprenticeship in the field offices used as the primary means of socialization. One-on-one training of this type is often an intense value-laden process whose outcome depends upon the nature of the affective relationships formed (Van Maanen and Schein, 1978). In the FMCS the new recruit and the seasoned mediator often come from similar work backgrounds and, indeed, may know each other already from cases where one has mediated and the other has been an advocate. It is not uncommon for federal mediators to recommend that certain negotiators they encounter on a case consider application to FMCS.

Once initiated into the service, the philosophy is reinforced in several ways. Formally, the national headquarters continually remind the mediators of the officially sanctioned role they are to play. Changes in public policy frequently provide the occasion for these reminders. For example, when wage/price guidelines were issued by the federal government, a directive was sent to the field mediators that stated official policy with regard to the mediator's role. Testimony from their director instructed the mediators *not* to compel the parties to conform in any way: "If a mediator is seen as part of a government enforcement program, he will lose his credibility. There is always the danger that the mediator will be seen as part of a conspiracy between business and government to suppress wages." The memo went on to inform the mediators of the guidelines so that they would be able to answer questions when asked.

There is a certain amount of collegial control as well. Although the federal mediator works by himself on a case, for reasons of preference and sometimes strategy, these cases are typically convened in the agency field office. This encourages the mediators to interact frequently with each other before, during, and after their cases to share experiences and to seek support and advice from their peers. Discussions with mediators suggest that they are well informed about how their peers practice and that each is judged accordingly. This was borne out when one of the mediators left the service and several of his colleagues noted how ill suited his arbitratorlike style was to mediation.

Collegial control seems to occur outside the agency as well. The pros, particularly those on the union side, and the mediators appear to be linked to each other in ways that transcend the boundaries of the case. The mediators are, as mentioned, frequently recruited from the ranks of the pros and share, in many instances, a common ethnic and socioeconomic background. In the local industrial-relations community, pros and mediators are likely to encounter each other at meetings, seminars, awards dinners, and numerous other social occasions. They have many friends and acquaintances in common, and when they meet on a case they are more likely than not to exchange stories and gossip about these people. This community of pros is important in several respects.[4]

The mediators often have more in common with the pros than the pros have with the committees they represent. Pros and mediators seem to share a common framework about collective bargaining and mediation that yields a clear, though unstated, understanding about how each is supposed to do his job and work with the other. Although the data in this study are not definitive on this issue, it appears that the decision to seek mediation is made by the pros for the extra support they expect to get from the mediators in the work they have to do with their committees. This is what they seem to expect, and this is what they receive from the federal mediators.

In the mediators' eyes, the pros are invested with considerable knowledge, talent, and cunning, a perception that leads the mediators to be guided by the pros' desires and expectations. The cultural rules, shared values, and ideology of the pro/mediator community serve, in perhaps the strongest and most immediate ways, to constrain the behavior of each. Failure to conform to the broad outlines of these rules may bring rebukes, snubs, or "luke-warm support" and jeopardize their ability to work together in the future. Reputations ride on abiding by these standards. On the part of the mediators, they know and are wary of the pros who cannot be trusted—the "sewer rats" and "goldbrick salesmen"—whose reputations follow them from case to case (Kolb, 1977). Presumably, pros too avoid or treat with care those mediators who breach the cultural rules of interaction.

The orchestrating role, then, seems to be one that has emerged from the normative, cultural context of what has come to be seen as "mature" collective bargaining in the private sector.[5] The role is consistent with the ideology of free collective bargaining and seems to reflect the institutional accommodation of third-party involvement in that sector. The ideology is likewise apparent in the structure and policies of FMCS, which serve to perpetuate the values in formal and informal ways. Finally, the shared values of mediators and pros yield to a set of cultural rules that constrain and control the behavior of each. In this way federal practice is congruent with the environment of private-sector collective bargaining. If major changes in role or strategy are to occur, they will likely do so only in response to changes in that environment.

Discrepancies and Individual Adaptation in State Practice

The state context is different. The institutional framework that developed in the private sector has, with certain modifications, been imposed on the public sector, with the exception that in time it will mature like its counterpart.[6] The problem is that the ideology of free collective bargaining as exists in the private sector is anomalous in certain respects when translated to the public sector. First, management is not capital but government officials elected to represent the majority public interest. The framework is, therefore, multilateral, not bilateral (Kochan, 1975). Second, unions have options in addition to the negotiating table for voicing their stands on compensation and working conditions—electoral politics, lobbying activities, and civil-service protection.

These differences between the role of government in relation to management and labor as they exist in private- and public-sector institutions seem to underlie the images invoked by the state mediators when they describe the discrepancies in public-sector practice. Their accounts are not couched in terms of these broader institutional issues, however, but rather in terms of the immediate behavioral problems they encounter on a case. Thus the mediators emphasize the absence of decisionmaking authority on a management committee, for example, and not the underlying political structure that makes such behavior almost inevitable. The state mediators' definition that the problems in the public sector are behavioral and not structural allows them to mediate in a way that they believe compensates for the critical dynamics missing in public-sector collective bargaining and mediation. Another interpretation of the dealmaker's role may be, therefore, that it is an effort on the part of the mediators to create the dramatic impression that the ideology of free collective bargaining applies in the public sector and that the problems they face are ones primarily of development and maturity. This may explain why the state mediators frequently allude to the teaching function they perform.

The specific actions the state mediators take are consistent with this interpretation that dealmaking creates the impression that bargaining is bilateral and that the parties at the table possess the resources to reach their own accommodation. The mediators frequently try to deny or to minimize the influence of other governmental bodies. In the Reed School Committee case, for example, mediator Richards articulated this view when the school committee tried to argue that they were constrained by the town budget:

Town Negotiator: The money in the budget is finite.

Mediator: I know school committees can do whatever they want. You can make an agreement here and go back to your town meeting and get it.

In the Sheridan and Ulster School Committee cases, the mediators refused to bring the entire school committees to the session until the negotiating committees made concessions on their own. And in the Tulane Firefighters case, the mediator tried to convince the attorney to override the mayor's position on EMT. In each of these examples, the state mediators pressed the bargaining committees to act as if they had authority to settle, ignoring the multilateral context in which the parties operated.

The mediators also use their own behavior to compensate for the dynamics they believe are missing in the public sector—the pressure from a strike. This occurs in several ways. On occasion, they will actually encourage the parties to strike. In the Regis School Committee case, for example, mediator Richards made this suggestion and provided the union with numerous examples from his case experience where the union had done so to its advantage. More commonly, the mediators see themselves in a way as a substitute for a strike. As I noted in the Reed School Committee and Tulane Firefighters cases, they openly adopt an advocacy role to compensate for whatever power imbalance they perceive and do so to preserve the semblance that bargaining is bilateral between parties of equal strength.[7] They also adopt a frenetic, high-pressured building strategy that they seem to believe compels the parties to make concessions akin to their images of the way the strike works. Mediator

Richards's use of time to pressure the school committees in the Rutgers School Committee case provides an example of this. The management attorney wanted the mediator to adjourn the session so that his committee would have time to prepare its final offer. Richards responded, "You know I have to keep the pressure on. Tell them this is it. If they don't move, I'm going to certify an impasse and they'll have to go to factfinding."

The common thread in each of these examples is the way the various state mediators tried to preserve the semblance of bilateral bargaining under pluralistic assumptions consistent with their image of its application in the private sector. The outcomes of their efforts, however, suggest a different pattern—the parties did not strike, did not make concessions until the full school committee attended, and did not usurp authority from town executives. The divergence between their images and their experience seems to place the mediators in a role that is problematic for them. As they try to manage these impressions, they tend to minimize the political realities of the situation, and so risk damaging their own credibility and their relationships with the parties that they often undercut the agenda they set for themselves (see chapter 6).

The structure and policies of the state agency accommodate the problematic nature of public-sector bargaining. The agency has no formal recruiting and training policy—a reflection, perhaps, of the difficulty actors in the public sector have in defining what the characteristics of a mediator should be and what behaviors require reinforcement. The state mediators come from diverse occupational backgrounds. Most of the mediators entered the agency under the provisions of Civil Service and had no prior labor-relations experience. Of the more recently hired, two have union backgrounds and two were recruited directly from school.

The agency has no formal training program. Historically, new mediators were assigned cases upon hire and left to develop their own styles of practice by trial and error. Informal training now exists; the new recruit may choose to accompany a more experienced mediator on some of his cases before going out on his own. But the mode of learning is still primarily by direct experience on one's own cases.

Collegial interaction is also less frequent in the state agency. The space limitations in the office mean that the mediators are continually on the road and therefore have little opportunity to interact with their colleagues in order to gain their advice and support. The burden is placed on the individual mediator to fashion a role and then evaluate the efficacy of his approach. Feedback is hard to obtain and even more difficult to use. Parties will rarely comment on a mediator's approach unless they are moved to complain, and complaints rarely give rise to any systematic rethinking of role or the more general issue of mediation in the context of public practice.[8] Where the structure and policies of FMCS seem to emphasize ideological consistency in practice, those of the state seem to encourage individual accommodation. Indeed, the structure may be interpreted as a response to the question of how the government can be neutral in a government sector. For in the way state practice is organized, the mediators rarely have an occasion as a body to confront the dilemmas of practice they routinely encounter.

External collegial control is also less apparent in the state practice. Most of the pros are attorneys and come from different backgrounds than the mediators. Even those pros who do not have legal backgrounds have little in common with the state mediators.[9] Thus most of the state mediators do not feel themselves to be a part of the community of pros. As one mediator described it,

Most of the negotiators are lawyers. You've got to understand lawyers in this business. They fight across the table, but outside they talk to each other. They are one club. They'll meet together at the Bar Association meetings. They're a club I'm not privy to. They fight, but they're really like brothers. You also have to understand the teachers' union and the school committee. The officers and the school committee know each other. So you never really know in a case, where everybody knows each other, where you stand. You'll recommend something and you may not know it's been settled already.

There appears to be a labor-relations community in the public sector, but the mediators do not feel they are a part of it. Without participating in this community, the cultural rules of pro/mediator behavior observed in the federal practice cannot easily develop. Indeed, the rather cavalier treatment of pros by the state mediators and the deprecating remarks made by pros about the mediators are indicative of this situation (see chapters 5 and 6). Both internally within the agency and externally in the community, the behavioral controls are less stringent than in the federal practice.

Left on their own to create their role, the state mediators seem to model their behavior on popular and conventional myths of how mediators ply their craft. These accounts typically highlight the pivotal role the mediators have played in a highly visible case. One image is of the aggressive mediator who forcefuly kept the parties at the table all night and early into the morning; unkempt and unshaven, he emerges to report the results of his efforts to the press. Another image is of the mediator's recommendation that resulted in a settlement. Quite recently, a colleague described the efforts of the mediator in the national football strike in these terms: "I know Sam. He's an aggressive mediator. If I know him, he's in there banging heads" (radio broadcast, November 1982). The popular lexicon is filled with such metaphors—"head banging," "forcing the parties to stay at the table," "not letting them off the hook." These are the images from which the state mediators seem to construct, without guidance, their roles.[10]

In sum, the state approach to mediation seems to reflect a set of interwoven factors that push the mediators to play a role that is significantly different from the institutionalized and sanctioned part federal mediators play. The state mediator's images of practice in the private sector encourage him to play a role that compensates for the dynamics he believes are lacking in the public sector. In doing so, the mediator takes it upon himself to create the impression that free and bilateral collective bargaining is viable in his sector. The policies and practices of his agency place responsibility on the individual mediator to resolve any inconsistencies between role and environment that exist. Collegial interaction is low both within and outside the agency, so that these dilemmas are rarely confronted. This leaves the state mediator relatively free to adapt his style in the way he sees fit. In so doing, popular impressions of mediator style seem to be paramount. There are, however, some indications that state practice is changing. These changes come from two sources, one within the state agency and the other outside.

A new director with a background in negotiations on the union side has taken a more serious interest in the mediation practice of the state agency. Anxious to upgrade and professionalize the office, he has recruited new mediators with organizing, negotiating, and legal backgrounds. In addition, the salaries of state mediators have been upgraded and the facilities of the agency have been expanded so that meetings can be convened there, opening up the possibility for more collegial interaction. Seminars have been instituted in order for the mediators to talk about their cases and the problems they encounter as well as changes in local public policy. The director's plan is to involve outsiders in these discussions, including academicians, other mediators, and representatives from government and unions. To the degree that the dilemmas of mediation in a government sector are confronted and discussed, a philosophy of mediation that reinforces practice or alters it may begin to emerge from these and other interactions.

There is also some evidence that pros are becoming more forceful in constraining the behavior of state mediators. In several instances, the mediators alluded to the changing behavior of the pros:

It's getting more difficult to get pros away from their committees. They act less and less individualistic. They only want to do what's good for their troops and not what's right.

Now it's getting harder to get the negotiator away from his team. When you call him out, he says, "What are you doing: You'll ruin my rapport with my troops."

Some of the pros are becoming more rigid. They say this is our position. Take it in and bring back theirs. The only role you can play is a conciliator, and that's not mediation.

Although the state mediators deprecated this type of behavior, they usually complied with the request for the duration of the case. For this pressure to influence their strategic thinking, it will require (if federal practice is indicative) a better appreciation of the pro's role within his committee as well as a closer relationship with him. In this regard, the new recruiting policies of the agency and the opportunities to discuss with colleagues the import of this changing behavior enhance the possibilities that the strengths and weaknesses of the dealmaking role will be evaluated.

Implications: The Mobilization of Bias

Collective bargaining and the institutions that support it are intended to control the ever present conflict in the system of industrial relations (Slichter, 1949). Mediation is but one of these institutions. As Simkin (1971) notes, "The primary purpose prompting the establishment and operation of every governmental (mediation) agency is the public desire 1) to prevent strikes and 2) to terminate those that get started" (p. 34).

Does mediation achieve this goal? Practicing mediators overwhelmingly believe that without mediation the number of industrial strikes would increase considerably (Indik et al., 1966, p. 33). Evidence is scarce to judge whether these practitioners are correct. Strike activity has remained relatively constant over the last quarter-century, with variations attributed primarily to changes in the business cycle and the level of real wages (Kauffman, 1978). In the public sector, resort to other impasse procedures (factfinding and arbitration) are interpreted as an indicator of the degree to which mediation fulfills its mandate. Empirical research in this sector suggests that although certain mediator strategies are more likely to lead to mediated settlements, overall the ultimate outcomes are determined by political and economic forces over which the mediator has minimal control (Kochan and Jick, 1978; Gerhart and Drotning, 1980). These findings echo Kerr's (1955) assertion that mediation may avert strikes only when they are caused by misunderstandings and faulty communications. The mediator can correct these problems. But, Kerr suggests, strikes arise from these sources when the parties are inexperienced, a transient situation. For the vast majority, he concluded, "mediation is part of the game, but not an essential one" (p. 236).

My observations of mediators at work support this view. The contributions the mediators make to the achievement of industrial peace appear quite limited. In its most institutionalized form in federal practice, the assistance that the mediators seem to provide is primarily facilitative—they give support to chief negotiators. The federal mediators contribute "another voice." The state mediators, with fewer pros on their cases, attempt a more substantive contribution in the form of a deal. Yet in this sector the evidence is quite clear that the success of mediation rests more on the external forces in the dispute than on the strategic efforts of the individual mediator (Kochan and Jick, 1978). This is not to suggest that the mediators' contributions are unimportant, but rather that it may be wrong to assess a particular mediation approach primarily in terms of whether the institution serves its stated goals. For there are indications in the data that suggest that mediation may be important, not for the outcomes it achieves, but for the way the process serves to preserve and reinforce the institution of collective bargaining.

Mediation is in many ways a captive of the system of which it is a part. To the degree, therefore, that collective bargaining displays a normative bias implicitly granting power to one group of actors over another and emphasizing narrow concerns over more fundamental change, these traits will be reflected in mediation as well

(Hyman, 1982). But mediators are not passive actors within the system, and the more they share its ideology, the more likely it is that they will, sometimes unwittingly, mobilize or accentuate the biases that already exist in the system.[11] In their efforts to facilitate settlement, the federal mediators appear to mobilize bias in ways that make management's interests more prominent, while both groups of mediators seem to accentuate the institutional and professional interests of union leaders over rank-and-file members. The implications of these behaviors seem to be that economic issues, which already dominate collective-bargaining agendas, receive even more attention in mediation than those issues that touch on worker control over hours and conditions of employment.

Preparedness and Management's Interests

The pluralistic ideology of collective bargaining takes for granted the assumption that a balance of power exists among competing labor and management interests (Hyman, 1978; Hill, 1981). Indeed, the legal framework of collective bargaining is often interpreted as the effort by government to offset management's domination of the work place by granting collective-bargaining rights to workers (Taylor, 1948). Despite the existence of these institutional safeguards, critics argue that capital continues to wield considerable power at the bargaining table, that it is able to control the bargaining agenda in such a way that only a limited subset of rights and benefits are considered (Hyman and Brough, 1975; Hill, 1981). As Fox (1974) so eloquently describes it, "Capital can, as it were, fight with one hand behind its back and still achieve in most situations a verdict that it finds tolerable" (p. 279). If this structural bias exists in collective bargaining, then we shall probably find it in mediation; and we do. But the federal mediators, through the actions they take, also seem to accentuate it.

The narrowing strategy appears to result in a set of dynamics in which the union committees make the majority of the concessions while management is encouraged to implement a concession strategy that the mediator believes has been formulated prior to mediation.[12] This outcome stems from the way the federal mediators organize the process consistent with the contrasting assumptions they hold about the relative preparedness of the two bargaining committees. In the narrowing strategy, the first mediator-initiated move is a joint meeting, where the parties come together to "agree where to disagree" about the issues in dispute. During these meetings, the union as the "moving party" typically presents its demands. Management either signals its assent to these issues without offering a formal proposal of its own or highlights some areas in which it is willing to move. This ritual of "the union makes the demands and management responds," characteristic of collective bargaining, is continued in mediation. The ritual, however, appears to give management considerable control over the issue agenda.

Union committees frequently come to mediation with lengthy proposals. In the cases observed, they ranged from one issue to over fifty, with the average around twenty-five. Management, in contrast, adopts an early position that is often a continuation of the status quo or some marginal adjustment to it. This "law of large opening demands" (Stevens, 1963) is a common feature of collective bargaining, but it has a particular effect. It means that almost by definition, the union will have the most concessions to make. But this is only part of the picture. The mediators believe that extensive demands made by unions indicate that their priorities are unclear, or, to use mediator Baker's terminology, that their proposal is "not in focus." The mediators believe that the union will decipher its priorities only as management responds to their demands. Indeed, the use of joint meetings for the purpose of proposal exchange is preferred because the impact of a management response is stronger. This kind of thinking is also fostered through the mediator's tactical use of "strategic suggestions." For example, the mediator early in the Duke Hospital case instructed the union to prepare its proposal in a way that would facilitate and clarify management's response:

Mediator: I will tell you that before a settlement will take place, dramatic moves will have to be made. You have to address the issues. You want sick leave; put it in. You want shift preference; put it in.

Union: We want a lot.

Mediator: Well, put it all in so they can respond. Then we'll see where they are willing to go.

Afterwards, he commented to me, "They're [the union] not ready to make decisions about priorities. They're still thinking in terms of discrete issues. If they can put it all in a proposal, management can respond and it will start to come together." What seems to occur in a case like this, where the union's demands are extensive, is that the union sets the overall agenda for negotiations with its proposals, but management exerts considerable control through its responses. Mediators mobilize this bias in that they take what was implicit and unstated in the bilateral negotiation and make it an explicit element of strategy.

The federal mediators' perceptions of the management committee tend to mobilize bias even more. They consider management to be, in general, "well controlled," "prepared," "strategic," and "businesslike" in their thinking. As a result, the mediators tend to assume that management committees have planned their concessionary strategy beforehand as well as the staging of its implementation. When a management committee is represented by a pro, the mediator seems even more confident in this conviction. As a result, the mediators frequently take management's position as the basis for predicting the settlement range. In Bard Manufacturing, for example, mediator Baker described management in this way: "These people are disciplined and businesslike. They know how far they are willing to go. They'll stick at the 7 percent on wages, give the COLA and bonuses because they gave them last time, and after that I don't think there is much else." Baker was basically correct in this assessment. Although some marginal adjustments were made in management's contribution toward health insurance and the duration of sickness and accident coverage, the union dropped some eighteen issues when the final package emerged.

Because of this conviction that management is organized and clear about its concession strategy, the federal mediators spend considerably less time with management encouraging them to make concessions. This is borne out in the meeting arrangements. Of the separate meetings held with the parties (44 percent of the total), on average 35 percent of these were with management and 65 percent with the union. What seems to occur is that because of their assumptions about management strategy, federal mediators tend to take management's position as a boundary constraint on the settlement and seek to predict what future concessions they are likely to make (using information from the past contract and wage patterns) and orchestrate the process so that the union committee will narrow its demands and propose in the end what management had planned to concede all along. Although the federal mediators report that they often challenge management's strategy, such behavior seems to be more the exception than the rule. In two of the cases where management made significant concessions—Albion Broadcasting and Alfred Corporation—it was the union pros who took the initiative to press management with the threat of a strike. But even then, the mediator believed that the president of Alfred Corporation had planned to make the concession on COLA right from the start: "He understands more than he lets on. He was negotiating with me just like a businessman. He knew what he was going to do all along." In general then, particularly when the total contract has been reopened, the federal mediators provide a forum for management committees to implement their concessionary strategy, whereas they expect the union committees, under the tutelage of their pros, to narrow their proposals considerably. Indeed, tactics to help the pro were more often observed at union meetings than at management sessions.

The relative influence of competing interests in the public sector is more difficult to decipher. Given the political context within which collective bargaining occurs, the distinctions between power at the bargaining table to control the agenda and influence exerted through other political means overlap. While the legal ban on strikes, at least theoretically, handicaps public unions, there are multiple avenues these employees can pursue to supplement and to support their positions. Further, the diffusion of power on the management side makes them appear more like a democratically elected union committee than a disciplined arm of corporate management (Kochan, 1980). Finally, at the time this study was conducted, management committees frequently had substantial proposals of their own for regaining some of the rights they had conceded previously, ones that had proved costly or inconvenient to them.[13] As a result of these factors, it is more difficult to detect bias mobilization patterns in the state cases.

The dealmaking strategy and the assumptions on which it is based reflect this ambiguity. The state mediators describe both parties in similar terms—inexperienced, unclear about their priorities, and diffuse in their decisionmaking structure. In building a package, they do not clearly distinguish between movers (or demanders) and responders. Rather, they develop their own conviction about the elements of a "fair" settlement, one that includes elements from both sides and that conforms to patterns with which they are familiar. Then they press both sides to make concessions that conform to their visions. This balanced attention to union and management is reflected in the separate meeting patterns. Of the total meetings convened by state mediators, 75 percent were separate meetings, and of this an average of 47 percent were with management and 53 percent with the union.

There is a certain irony in the implications of these strategic approaches. The federal mediators, on many counts, seem to be the more professional of the two services. Respected by the negotiators with whom they work, they are loathe to embroil themselves in the substantive development of the package. In their orchestration of the process, they seek to continue negotiations in a new forum and so, unwittingly, seem to mobilize the management bias that may already exist in the bargaining relationship. The state mediators, with their images of bilateral bargaining in mind, try to balance the strengths of both parties. But without reputation and credibility to back up their strategies, they are limited in how much they can accomplish.

Economic Issues and Institutional Influence

The primacy given to economic matters, a distinctive feature of collective bargaining in the United States, is another source of bias that is mobilized in mediation.[14] The proposals unions bring to mediation are heavily weighted toward economic issues. FMCS data based on notification statements indicate that of the 46,734 issues identified in 1978, close to 50 percent concerned wages and fringe benefits; working conditions accounted for only 5 percent of the issues mentioned. Thus mediators tend to work from proposals that are overwhelmingly economic in nature. Noneconomic issues, however, were not uncommon in the observed cases. Yet in contrast to the monetary issues, few of these demands were realized in the final contract. In part this outcome may reflect, as polls suggest, the true preference of members (Gershenfeld and Schmidt, 1981; Olson, 1981). That is, these work-related demands may be of less concern to the rank and file than those that promise higher remuneration. Yet this explanation neglects the two important ways in which mediators appear to mobilize the bias toward certain economic matters. Their tactics are designed primarily to address these issues, and their relationships with the pros mean that any issues of concern to these leaders will receive more attention from the mediators than those that are not.

The mediator's skills are well suited to the consideration of monetary issues and are not as applicable to those demands that are more local and job related in character. Mediators know about wages, fringe benefits, vacations, longevity schedules, and personal leave. These are the issues they encounter again and again in their caseloads. Their knowledge of localized work practices is less complete because these are less often raised by unions. Likewise, the tactics both federal and state mediators use to encourage concessions are well suited to issues that can be translated into monetary terms and that have an applicability across cases—cost calculations and pattern identification (see chapter 4).

The mediators' limited knowledge of local work rules and conditions means that they believe they have a lesser role to play when these issues are discussed or when they are central. In the Albion broadcasting case, for example, in which the major issue was scheduling of broadcast staff, the mediator sat silently through the off-the-record meeting where the issue was discussed and resolved. Afterward the mediator commented, "I don't have much of a contribution to make on this issue. I'm just monitoring it to make sure they keep working on it." Similarly, in the Sheridan Firefighters case, where one of the major issues was manning levels, the mediator remained with the chief negotiators, but let them work it out themselves: "I don't really understand this issue. Apparently it concerns the construction of a new firehouse. It's pretty complicated." Nor are the mediators as interested in these working issues as they are in matters of money. In the Bates case, for example, a joint meeting was held at the urging of management to discuss the thirteen noneconomic issues the union proposed. The mediator was absent for part of it and commented to management afterward, "Let's sweep some of these noneconomic issues off the table. Where you've indicated movement, do it. I'm tired of them. I'm hoping he'll [union pro] get rid of some too so that then we can turn our attention to the money." "Real work" for the mediator appears, then, to be aiding the parties on economic issues. As mediator Carr noted in the Carrol University case, "I don't like this kind of case, Usually you have wages and fringes. Here it's a different kind of issue. I can't be that active."

There are some differences worth noting about how the strategies used by the federal and state mediators serve to highlight these economic issues. In narrowing the federal mediators leave it to the union committees, under the leadership of the pros, to make their own decisions about the substantive changes they will make in their proposals. But in assisting them to frame the problem, the mediators try to cast the decision primarily in terms of the financial aspects of the proposals. In the Bates case, for example, after the meeting on noneconomic issues, the mediator instructed the union in the following way: "All I'm trying to say is that you have a bunch of economic proposals, put some weights on them. You're asking for 62.5 percent on wages. On the basis of your standard average hourly rate, that would be 12 percent up front. Nobody's getting that. You haven't told us about COLA or Blue Cross-Blue Shield. You have to put it all in so we can see what it will cost." By helping the parties see the dollar value of their choices more clearly, the mediator feels he makes a significant contribution to their decision-making. He is not as sure when the issues are noneconomic. As Baker remarked about his contribution on the noneconomic issues, "I can ask questions and give them the benefit of my opinion. But really they know the situation best."

When the state mediators attempt to build a package, they look in both proposals for the building blocks that they believe should be priorities. These issues are often, but not always, of an economic nature—wages, salary schedules, holidays, vacations, medical insurance, and leave policies. Deals are built from such issues. Although noneconomic issues of general concern to the public sector, such as reduction in force, may receive their attention, local work issues do not. For example, in the Tulane Firefighters case, the union had a duty tour that was, according to the mediator, unique. The union initially proposed that this practice be put into the contract. Although the union presented this demand, the mediator never discussed it with management, except to suggest that management threaten to abandon the practice if the union did not concede EMT. In the Rutgers School Committee case, two noneconomic issues—expansion of the grievance procedure and seniority rights after maternity leaves—were almost omitted from the final package because the mediator forgot that they had been proposed.

Unless a committee actively presses for a particular work demand, that demand is unlikely to be given serious consideration. Even then the mediator may try to stifle discussions of such issues as performance evaluation, manning levels, and teacher responsibility for parent conferences as extraneous to the task at hand. In both the Sheridan Firefighters and Taft School Committee cases, the mediators tried to convince the union committees to drop issues of this sort or face a lower wage package as a consequence. It appears, therefore, that both the federal and state mediators tend to emphasize economic issues, in part because it is where their experience, skill, and knowledge lie. But this tendency is even more pronounced if the pros emphasize these types of issues as well.

In the federal cases, the pros oversee the narrowing process and will attempt to influence their committees, to the degree they are able, to focus on those issues of most concern to them and their institutions. Frequently, though not always, these concern monetary issues that invite easy comparison with other units. And in the discussions the mediator holds with a union committee, it is the pro's position that is supported and reinforced, not that of the committee or particular members.[15] For example, in the Carroll University case, the pro's goal, according to the mediator, was to make sure that the university commit itself to use only union subcontractors so that the union could retain the unit. In pursuing his objective, the mediator believed that the pro did not act in the best interests of the members: "He sold them out and wanted me to tell his people they had a good deal. But he didn't get them anything. I'm not a judge. I have to support him, but I tried to be pretty noncommittal." Similarly, the focal points for discussion in the Bates and Bard Manufacturing cases—the protection of the National Union's pension fund and the National Union's health insurance plan, respectively—were of most concern to the union pro. Whether members' goals were actually displaced by these efforts is difficult to tell without being privy to the committee decisionmaking. What does seem clear, however, is that tactics to help the pro move his committee may be read in part as efforts by the mediator to help the pro realize his own institutional objectives.

The relationship between pros and mediators in the state cases is different. Most of the pros were attorneys, not union representatives. Although these attorneys do not have any institutional affiliation with labor, they do have their own interests and careers to protect. They too need to have their settlements judged favorably by their clients. The mediators feel they help the pros realize this objective. As one mediator stated it, "I always ask the spokesman, how many meetings do you need. He has to justify his existence. If he settles too quickly, they'll think he could have done better.

The money is really important. You need to know what they have to get." In the Ulster School Committee case, the union pro was quite clear about this. He needed to improve the salary structure for the administrative staff. The attention given to economic issues by pros is based as well on the case experiences they have. Like the mediators, their practice covers negotiations in local communities. Thus according to the mediators, pros are their allies in persuading bargaining commmittees to follow patterns on economic issues. Patterns also cover certain noneconomic issues. Reduction-in-force clauses and maternity-leave policy, because they are so pervasive in the public sector, have patterns associated with them as well. Thus in the Ulster School Committee case, the reduction-in-force plan used in one town became the model for the one adopted by Ulster. Pro/mediator collaboration does not, therefore, always result in minimal attention to noneconomic issues. Rather, it is the local work practices and conventions, about which the pros and mediators have less knowledge, that tend to get downplayed in mediation.

These behavioral dynamics undoubtedly occur in bilateral negotiations in both caseloads. Pros, because of their experience and expertise, exert considerable influence on the thinking of committee members. But the pro's outsider status and the necessity for ratification limit the influence he can exert. Mediators, because they tend to view the dynamics of collective bargaining in much the same light as the pros, strengthen the position of the pro through their tactical interventions. As a result, whatever bias toward money or institutional or professional interests exists in the system is mobilized through the actions of the mediators. It may be that mediation is sought by pros because they anticipate this kind of assistance. But what seems clear is that the dominance of economic and other institutional interests already prominent in collective bargaining is further enhanced in mediation. Although mediators could become expert on matters of working conditions, safety, supervision, and quality of work life, they do not. In this way, they mobilize the bias inherent in the system in such a way that historical solutions to work problems go largely unreviewed and immediate concerns on the job are unlikely to be seriously considered, despite claims to the contrary.

One cannot fault the mediators for these outcomes. Collective bargaining has a structure and determinism built into it that makes these outcomes of mediation all but inevitable. The dispute domain is well defined and preformulated prior to mediation. The issues that will be negotiated tend to follow a more or less standard litany, with changes confined to the margins of the contract. And given the interdependent relationship between employers and employees, settlement of disputes is largely preordained. The labor mediator works in this highly structured context, and therefore his domain of discretion or influence over the issues negotiated and the substantive outcomes is circumscribed and limited.

Within this narrow domain of activity, mediators carve out their strategic roles. They are creative roles, in that they allow the mediators to perform in situations where their control and authority are minimal. Orchestrators and dealmakers each in their limited ways do seem to assist the parties to disputes to reach an agreement, either by providing a forum for the pros to work with their committees or highlighting the elements of a viable deal. This is certainly a contribution. Less often appreciated, however, are the contributions the mediators make to preserving the existing social order.[16] This is not only because their efforts may minimize the instances and duration of overt conflict but because their efforts serve to reinforce and maintain the ideology of the system. This may be the major institutional role played by mediators.

Appendix: Methodology

Spaced over a two-year period, I was participant observer in these two agencies. In that role I "hung around" the offices, met informally with mediators, trainees and parties to disputes, reviewed old cases (from the official record, pencilled notes and retrospective discussions), attended some training seminars and socialized over numerous luncheons and dinners. To study mediation practice *in situ*, I accompanied ten mediators on over 400 hours of actual cases. Although the mediators and parties knew of my research purpose, we agreed that I could best learn their approach to the practice of mediation if I were treated as a trainee. I reviewed the historical records, learned all the mediator knew about a case prior to its start, and discussed proposed strategy for the case with him. During the sessions I was present at all the meetings and caucuses, including many that took place "off the record." When lulls occurred, the mediator and I discussed his view of the case, the "readings" he made of the issues, position and people, his plans for the next move, and his analysis of the one just past.

Kolb (1981, p. 3)

As a method, ethnography is akin in many respects to a detailed diary of all the actions and activities that comprise a day, evening, and night spent in a particular setting. For ethnographers participate (albeit with varying degrees of distance and style) in the daily working and social lives of the groups whose special realities they seek to understand and to report. Ethnographers, either by their own choice or by spatial constraints, rarely expose all the prodigious activity, decisionmaking, and false starts that stand behind the production of their work. More typically, readers are left to fill in a glossed-over summary like the one in the quoted remarks opening this chapter in order to draw their own conclusions and lessons about the method of the work. My intention in this appendix is to expose the fitful character of the field work and analysis that underpin this study.[1]

Observing in the Field

Field researchers would probably agree that gaining access to a setting is a combination of strategic planning and dumb luck. This was true for me. Negotiating entry was a two-step process in this study—clearance from the agency directors and case clearance from the individual mediators.

My official clearance was accomplished largely through the efforts of two faculty members at the Sloan School of Management at MIT. One, the director of the industrial relations section, knew the senior mediator at the FMCS office. My entry into the FMCS was quite smooth. The section director wrote a letter of introduction to the field mediator, vouching for my credentials and the scientific worth of the proposed study. My initial phone call was greeted with rec-ognition and welcome. I later learned that some twenty-five years ago this mediator had been similarly involved in a doctoral dis-sertation at the Sloan School. My early meetings with this senior mediator were casual and friendly. He explained mediation to me, and I described my purpose to him—to get the mediators' perspective on their cases. During our first meeting, we set up the procedures for my participation in FMCS cases. He became my contact point. Each week I would call him to see whether there were any cases starting that I could attend. He suggested that I contact two of the mediators separately. The extent of our research contract was threefold: that I respect the wishes of the individual mediators, that my presence be cleared by the parties, and that certain cases might not be open to me. I considered the bargain a good one.

My entry into the state agency was not so smooth. The dean of the school knew the director of the state agency and had recently overseen a research project for him. The director expressed concern about all aspects of the study: problems of confidentiality, nuisance to the mediators, and harmful effects on the parties. On several occasions the dean called the director to vouch for me and his personal interest in the study. The director agreed to let me enter, he said, primarily because he owed the dean a favor. However, I was warned that if he heard any complaints about me from any of the mediators, I was out. Further, the ground rules he laid down were, it seemed at the time, considerably more confining than those at FMCS. I could not record the proceedings in any way, including taking notes; I was barred from attending off-the-record meetings; and any publication of my findings would require his clearance. After the weeks of trying to get an appointment with him, I willingly agreed to these rules. Due to the director's role in the agency, the rules proved to be quite malleable. His activities were confined primarily to the arbitration side of the agency, and he was therefore removed from day-to-day mediation activities. All the agreements about transcription and participation were negotiated with individual mediators. Most of the mediators had worked for the agency before the director's appointment and expected to be there after he left. It appeared at times that they were actually eager to thwart his authority in any way, even regarding the rules of my participation. At any rate, the director played no further role in the research and was gone from the office before its completion.

Beyond assisting my entry, the dean and section director continued to facilitate my research role. All the mediators and many of the parties knew these two personally or by reputation and used this information to introduce me to the parties and, I guess, to justify their collaboration in allowing me to be there. When introduced to an attorney or bargaining representative, the mediator would often say, "This is Debbie Kolb. She's doing a study on mediators over at MIT with Charlie Myers and Abe Siegel." Such an introduction would invariably provide the occasion for a greeting to be conveyed, or a story told about the last case they had or sometimes even a joke at Myers's or Siegel's expense. Awkward moments were filled by these conversations and occupied the time so that a description of my research often proved unnecessary. Myers and Siegel helped in other ways as well. Invitations to mediation events, the launching of a new FMCS office, were sent my way. Early in the study a conference was held at MIT, and I had occasion to interact with some of the mediators on academic turf. I attended the national FMCS training seminar at the invitation of William Simkin, former director of the agency, arranged by the section director.

There are two points worth mentioning about the process of gaining entry. There is an adage that a "wise researcher" seeks out intermediaries who can perform, advise, set up inside contacts, and run interference for the researcher attempting to break into the system. But not all intermediaries are equal. The fact that in the field of industrial relations practitioners and academics belong to the same "community" meant that the contacts were both professional and immediate. That is why I never mentioned to anybody in the field that my major area of study was organization behavior, not industrial relations, or that Myers was not, in fact, my primary thesis advisor.

Getting past the gatekeepers of the mediation agencies was only the first stage in securing access to the research sources. The loose structural link between the administration of the mediation agencies and the mediators, as well as the solo nature of mediation practice, meant that negotiations continued with each of the mediators. Clearance from the senior FMCS mediator and the state agency director merely secured permission to start these negotiations.

During the first few weeks of the project, I spent a good deal of time at the FMCS field office, talking to the mediators, reviewing official records and penciled notes on the cases. I had occasion to meet separately with each of the mediators which enabled me to introduce myself and to explain my research intent. I planned to attend two cases with each mediator, and each of the mediators, with one exception, gladly agreed. Their only proviso was that the parties give their assent. One mediator refused. Apparently he never lets anybody accompany him on a case, even trainees.

Despite their gestures of cooperation, actually attending a case proved to be more complex and time consuming than I had at first imagined. Two months elapsed before I saw my first case. Our arrangement was to have me call each mediator at the start of the week to see what cases he had scheduled. Because of the monitoring process they use, federal mediators often do not know which of the cases they follow will require a joint meeting until right before the meeting is held. Further, I started the study, so the mediators claimed, at a sluggish time of year and at the beginning of the month, while caseloads are heaviest at month's end. Some of the mediators were in "midstream" on health-care cases, and they felt, and I concurred, that it would be most desirable to observe cases from the start. Finally, and I think in retrospect this may have been overriding, they wanted to minimize the awkwardness that my participation presented. Thus they waited for cases where they knew the parties personally or where the spokesmen had worked with the service before. Although many of these requirements were relaxed as I became a more familiar fixture, negotiations with individual mediators continued to be a time-consuming process. With a new mediator, I waited a year before we went on a case together.

Arranging cases with the state agency proved less time consuming and detailed. The state caseload was more stable; cases started at regular intervals and then ran for long periods of time. After I was cleared by the agency director, I called each mediator, introduced myself and my purpose and asked that he let me accompany him on a case. Frequently, we would set a date at that time. Occasionally, I had to call back because his calendar was blank, but this occurred infrequently in comparison with the federal mediators. State mediators did not clear my presence before the start of a case.

Each mediator had his own ground rules for my participation. By and large, the federal mediators agreed that if cleared by the spokesmen, I could participate in all phases of the process. Note taking was also permissible. To respect the confidentiality of off-the-record meetings, I rarely wrote about them while they were in session, but scribbled furiously at their conclusions. The state mediators were somewhat more diverse. With some, I participated in all phases, including extrasession dinners with the spokesmen. Others barred me from off-the-record meetings and note taking because, they said, it would make the spokesmen nervous. As a case proceeded, these rules were relaxed, in large part, it appeared, because the mediator forgot that he had stipulated them.

Whether my access was cleared prior to the case or once it had started, the mediators needed to construct a plausible explanation for why I was in tow. These introductions often distorted my purpose, and maintaining the role that the mediators had erected for me proved troublesome at times. All the mediators seemed to need to "fill in" an interest in the practice of mediation on my part, although I had not expressed such an occupational concern. The federal mediators gave accounts to the parties, often invoking the section director and dean, that for the most part closely resembled my agenda, that is, research. The state mediators, however, tended to introduce me as a budding mediator and a trainee with their agency. I let the mediator's explanation for my presence pass, only to find myself caught backtracking later on. During a case, I often had occasion to chat with spokesmen while committees caucused. As a matter of courtesy or curiosity, they would inquire about my background, training, and aspirations. Concurrently writing a thesis and training to be a mediator seemed an implausible explanation.

I found myself therefore backtracking: "Of course, I want to be a mediator, but right now I am studying mediation." Such an admission never barred me from continued participation on a case, though several of the mediators had predicted that it might. Given my peripheral status, it is more than likely that only I recalled the introduction anyway.

With these minor exceptions, my allegiance was to the mediator. When the parties tried to involve me in any way, I demurred. Often a spokesman, not necessarily out to undermine the mediator, but as a matter of interest, tried to solicit opinions from me about positions, the other party, and the mediator. I was noncommital, claiming ignorance and inexperience. In one case, a management spokesman, as a condition for my participation, requested at the end an evaluation of the process and how the mediator performed. I agreed but hoped that in the glory of settlement the promise would be forgotten. At 4:00 A.M., it was. There were other times when spokesmen took me aside to discuss the mediator. Though curious, I resisted these overtures. One spokesman commented to me on a case, "Joe is quite new at this game, isn't he?" To which I replied, "Gee, I don't know."

Though I was meticulous with parties, I was not above gossiping with the mediators. Within each service, I listened as mediators flattered and criticized their colleagues. The federal mediators rarely depicted their peers in any but the most complimentary light. In contrast, state mediators pronounced definitively on the shortcomings of their colleagues. "Oh, you've been out with Jack. Everybody knows he never does anything. The parties know it; that's why they never request him."

Whereas I merely listened to the within-agency characterizations, I openly participated in discussions with mediators about their counterparts in the other agencies. The isolation of mediation makes mediators curious about their colleagues. On several occasions with select informants in both agencies, I openly gossiped about practice in the other agency. I was not altogether sanguine about sinking to this, but these few sessions were among the most valuable I had, not because I learned of their low esteem for the other mediators—I already knew that—but because in ridiculing each other they revealed much about their own practice. Much of what I observed was verified in these gossip sessions. Had I passed up these opportunities, valuable data might have been lost; but they did violate the bargain of confidentiality I had struck with the mediators. It is perhaps inevitable that these bargains lead to such conflicts. Needless to say, I walked a thin line here and could only hope that my deceptions would not be discovered.

My allegiance was tested in a rather concrete way early in the study. The parties in a particularly complex case found, after a mediated settlement had been reached, that they were unclear about the agreement. The mediator's notes on the case, bound by convictions of confidentiality, could not be used to clarify the situation. The parties, not the mediator, agreed that they would procure my notes and use them as proof, for one position or the other. I knew nothing of this at the time. Apparently, the attorneys attempted to contact me while I was on vacation. On my next case with the agency, I learned of their efforts. I immediately assured the mediator involved that I would destroy my notes rather than turn them over, thereby demonstrating that I too respected the confidentiality of the proceedings. The mediator accepted my assurances, and other mediators from the agency allowed me to accompany them. However, this particular mediator never took me again. Although he never directly alluded to the situation, he never seemed to have a case starting or going when I called him up or met him on other cases.

The nature of the relationships I formed with the mediators was colored in part by my motives for undertaking the study. I saw the research as instrumental to my career in two ways. From the theoretical perspective, I surely believed that such an *in situ* study was warranted; but I had a more practical, instrumental agenda as well. I hoped to use the knowledge gained and the contacts made to facilitate my own entry into the part-time practice of arbitration and factfinding. In this regard, I saw the mediators and the spokesmen as potential future allies in my professional career. I was most anxious to remain acceptable for the duration of the study (a goal of all field researchers)—and afterward as well.

I sought an insider's status by couching the object of my study in flattering terms—to portray mediation from the practitioner's standpoint. Once into the field, however, I found that the well-articulated fronts of neutrality, rationality, and problem-solving expertise contained some chinks. In practice, mediators favored passivity as a guard against mistakes, overtly pushed one committee's interests over another's, and punished committees for lack of cooperation. Exposing this underside of mediation potentially jeopardized my future with people I wanted as allies. As it turns out, my revelations about mistakes and misinterpretations have disturbed other practitioners far more than they disturbed those I studied.

As the study progressed, my notions of what it is to have an insider's status underwent some changes. I came to view the federal mediators as more professional, competent, and effective. I seemed to observe more *faux pas*, errors in judgment, favoritism, and duplicity in state than in federal practice. Reviewers of my work have noticed and demonstrated to me the subtle and sometimes overt ways I flatter the federal mediators and expose the state mediators. In retrospect, my desire to be accepted by those I came to see as more professional blinded me to some of their foibles.

The roles I came to play in the field also underwent changes. The structure of mediation constrained my options in several ways. My position could not be hidden from the mediators or the chief spokesmen. Furthermore, with parts clearly assigned, I could not participate in a meaningful way, but was placed in an observer role. Beyond that, I admit I gave little thought to my position vis-à-vis the mediators and the parties. I came to consider myself a learner of the process and found that acting as a trainee enabled mediators to adopt a seemingly natural posture toward me. This decision emerged as a result of a fortuitous and jarring experience.

One day early in the study, before I had occasion to witness a case, I had a chance encounter with three FMCS trainees assigned to the field office as apprentices to the mediators there. We spent several hours discussing their training and the experience they had with the same mediators I was observing. I learned that the "side bar"—time and space to review strategy—was the major vehicle by which the trainees felt they came to understand the practice of these mediators. I too wanted the mediators to discuss their strategies with me but found that I was having some difficulty in these conversations.

This was clearly brought home to me in an early case that I blush to recall. The mediator seemed to have difficulty answering my questions about the role he was playing. He recounted to me an experience he had had with other researchers. Apparently, the FMCS "brass" had sent two academics who were writing a book on mediation to see him. They questioned him about his theory of group dynamics and how he used peer pressure. He told them that he was not sure, that all he could do was give his reading on the case. When I asked him to give me a reading on what he had just done, as if I were Jim Jackson (a trainee), he talked for twenty minutes about the meeting we had just left. Until that point, I had not realized that without casting myself into some culturally meaningful role, the mediators were unclear about what I wanted from them. Perhaps that is why they filled in my interest in mediation. From that point on, I described myself as akin to a trainee with a research interest in the process as well.

During the time spent with the parties, I tried to be as unobtrusive as possible. I attired myself in a suit or dress, that is, in the equivalent of the jackets and ties worn by the mediators and spokesmen. Management committees were similarly attired, whereas union committees were typically more casually dressed. Like the mediators, I carried pen and paper; mine was loose, and theirs attached to clipboards or notebooks. While the mediators noted only positions on the issues and addenda to them, I took more copious notes. During the meetings I sat next to the mediator at the head of the table, with the parties on the sides, silently observed, and wrote.

What to put in these notes was a complicated matter. I had an advantage other field workers rarely have: to be in a setting where note taking is a practice of the group under study. Thus note taking per se was not generally a problem. The problem was to select from all that I heard what to put in the notes. Using shorthand skills acquired early in my career, I tried to transcribe the proceedings as best I could. Obviously, I was not totally successful at capturing all the byplay of the case. But I tried my best to note as precisely as possible all the mediators' comments and interventions.

A few mediators barred me from note taking during the formal meetings. I obliged in a way. I did not transcribe, but kept small folded pieces of paper in my lap to jot down key words or phrases. In these cases I made frequent trips to the ladies' room to embellish these notes after what seemed to me at the time to be crucial incidents. These were of two types: if the mediator had just lectured a committee and/or if the mediator had experienced some problems and the committee gave him a lecture. The notes from these cases clearly, upon further reading, do emphasize more of the dramatic than the mundane when compared to the fully transcribed cases.

In off-the-record meetings I was usually invited to observe, but out of choice limited my participation to watching and not recording.

When alone with the mediator, during lulls in the case, we easily slipped into a teacher/trainee role. The mediator would usually ask if I had any questions about what happened and I would ask some. Like a student, I was often tested: What would I do in a given situation? Why was the spokesman acting that way? My responses to these questions changed as I learned more about the mediators I was studying. I was always somewhat torn on these occasions between demonstrating my worth and blundering badly in the response. At the beginning, I had only my textbook knowledge to go on. In response to questions about how I would have handled a particular circumstance, I tried to be noncommittal. This was true even as I came to develop an understanding of how the mediator might respond and a sense of how I might have managed better. I was somewhat uncomfortable with this stance, particularly when events proved that the mediator might have been spared some unhappy and uncomfortable moments had I been more direct.

Questions about why people acted as they did were somewhat easier to field. At first I answered with a stock, textbook answer: The spokesman doesn't want to leave time between settlement and ratification because it might give the opposition time to coalesce. Later, I responded to the same question by saying the agreement would burn a hole in the pro's pocket. I tried to show that I was educable, but not too smart or expert.

Though I considered myself a trainee in the proceedings, the mediators perceived me in different ways. I was benignly accepted by most, a helper to others, and a more active participant with a select few. At times mediation can be very lonely. With no colleagues on a case with him, excluded from committee caucuses, the mediator frequently spends a great deal of time by himself in his office or roaming around the halls in a strange public building. For that reason, any kind of companionship is welcome. I think that for most of the mediators, I was a *student companion* who helped them pass the time. There were many occasions, however, where I gave some assistance, not to the process per se but to the provision of amenities, which lightened the burden on the mediator. In this role, I was like a *good secretary*. For a select one or two, I was sort of an *objective consultant*, there to listen to strategic plans and expected to make some contribution.

I spent most of my time as a student companion, by the mediator's side, avidly soaking up his perspective, wisdom, and commentary. I listened to his renditions of the case, the agency, the state of mediation in general, his gossip about other mediators, his vacation plans, how the local ball teams were doing, the standing of his children's Little League teams; on one case, I picked some horses. My notes are filled with these discussions. I think the state mediators welcomed a companion on their long, late-night commutes. Many mediators remarked to me how pleasant it was to have a companion. But apart from this, I was totally dispensable to the proceedings. Just how dispensable became clear when I was sent home from two cases because the mediators judged that it was unsafe for me to be out so late. Early in the study, I was a dispensable student.

As time wore on and I volunteered for certain tasks, I became more of a good secretary, able to fill some of the peripheral functions that a secretary, were one present, might. I got coffee and other refreshments for the parties and the mediators. I xeroxed proposals or copied them from the board at the mediator's request. Many of my activities were like those of a dispensable student, but they were perceived differently by the mediators. My notes are a good example. I had been taking notes all along, gleaned from official records and petitions, the mediator's abbreviated notations about positions, and my own partial transcriptions. When questions arose about a meeting, often the mediator had not recorded it or could not read what he had written, so he would have me consult my notes to report their contents. In the extreme, there was the case of the threatened subpoena of my notes. As the good secretary, I reconvened meetings when the mediator was on the phone or otherwise engaged. On cases other than the one I was observing, I was often sent to fetch a spokesman with the pretense of a phone call.

Probably the major difference between the dispensable student and the good secretary was the degree to which the mediators looked to me, as they might to a secretary, for support. I was the person to whom they could recite their tales of woe, a noncritical ear for their version of an untoward event. There were several occasions when the mediator said or did something that brought forth some condemnation from the parties. The mediators, at the nearest opportunity, would take me aside to explain what happened. These were situations where the mediator felt he had been used or intentionally misled, and I was the only person available to listen to such confidences. There are some complicating features about these occasions. The mediators had typically made an error of some sort—too hasty an action, shoddy communication, untested assumptions. These were the data for mistakes lent validity by the mediators' accounts to me of their causes. It may be that my presence on the scene, an audience to the mistake, called forth these account-giving sessions. I do know that in certain situations the mediator was visibly troubled by what had occurred. For whatever reason, I gave them a forum to present their unopposed views, a common secretarial function.

The solo practice of mediation fostered not only a desire for companionship on the part of the mediators but also curiosity about the performance of their peers. For some mediators I became a source of information, insight, and assistance about inter- and intra-agency practice. Based, I assume, on my performance in these sessions, two mediators came to see me more as a resource, an objective consultant. They would, on occasion, solicit my advice on how I would handle a situation that seemed to be turning thorny. In one case a mediator was berated by one committee for failing to understand their demands and by the other for exerting undue pressure. These accusations were couched in rather strong language, and when, in private, the mediator asked for my assistance, I first lapsed into the part of the good secretary and listened but then suggested some general things he might consider. I could have been more direct and regretted afterward that I had not given more guidance to help this mediator, who had become by the time of the case a good friend as well.

My input was solicited at times on issues of labor law and public policy. I guess that because of my participation on a variety of cases as well as my official student status, some mediators looked to me to provide information they did not have. The mediators seemed to assume that I was more informed than in reality I was. But even when I knew an answer, I soon learned to reply to such queries with care. In one case, an attorney argued that fringe benefits were not exempted from the wage/price guidelines. The mediator disagreed and turned to me, his "expert." I supported the attorney's position for it was basically correct. After the session, the mediator in private chided me for "queering his pitch." He claimed to know full well that the attorney was correct but was hoping to intimidate the committee. I became, as a result, more circumspect in contributing my meager advice. When asked publicly in meetings, I would nod agreement with the mediator and, if asked later, reveal my information in private. Although the mediators solicited my advice as they might a consultant, I came to read such requests more as overtures for support than real advice. I was more comfortable as the good secretary than the objective consultant.

The balance among these roles differed between the two agencies. In line with my perceptions of the professional status of the federal mediators, I was the dispensable student to them, and on occasion the good secretary. I did exchange information with them, but was never in the position of providing advice or expert information. I was not asked, nor did I feel competent to give, it. Some of the state mediators seemed less sure of their expertise and drew on me on occasion in a more consultive role.

Frames and Analytic Evolution

I started the study with a rather vague and ill-defined conception of what I wanted to study—strategies from the mediator's perspective. With grounding in the mediation literature, I planned at the start to look for indicators of the mediator at work gaining the trust and confidence of the parties and then getting them to face reality. Not surprisingly, after the fact these categories were of little use as a guide to what I was supposed to be observing. My sense of strategic practice and its thematic correlates evolved during the first two months of the study as I observed my first round of cases.

Before describing this evolution, the use of cases as the primary analytic unit bears some mention. Prior to the observational stage of the study, I interviewed and conversed with each of the mediators about himself, his agency, and, most specifically, about his cases and how he mediated them. In these discussions, the mediators seemed to agree about the conduct of the process even across the agencies. For example, the state mediators described the use of joint meetings as the way to learn the facts of a case, and the federal mediators talked of how pros tell the mediator their real positions off the record—in both cases descriptions that deviated from what I later observed. In part, my antennae were not attuned to the nuances of mediation conversation, but also the interview format gave the mediators virtually free rein to discuss the elements of practice in glib and rather general terms. The concept of the pro is a good example. Both the state and federal mediators seemed to define the attributes of a pro in similar terms. Further, the interviews suggested that pros are distinguished from other spokesmen by their understanding of priorities and their willingness to share information and flexibly to discuss alternatives and compromises to the degree that they are delegated authority by their committees (Kolb, 1977). These idealized versions were realized only occasionally in practice. This I learned from observing the cases.

Mediation occurs in case contexts, and each case has its own unique culture. With only intermittent collegial interaction, mediators do not seem to partake of an embellished and shared culture noted in other domains of organizational life. Though the strategies used in the agencies had much in common, the individual mediator's lexicon and tactics of mediation were uniquely his own. Thus mediators agree that certain spokesmen who fail to compromise when a settlement is within reach are troublesome, but some mediators will call him a "ragpicker," some a "slow turtle," and still others will call him "irrational." The bases for shared experiences and communications are created anew on each case. On one case the mediator adopted the dancing metaphor used by the spokesmen to discuss progress, while in another the same mediator employed a sports analogy, again led by the spokesmen. Thus cases are not only different because the issues and people are unique but also because each situation creates its own fleeting culture for the duration. To learn of the broader culture of mediation, then, I needed to study its situational expression.

From a methodological point of view, a case provided the concrete material from which observational and talk-based operational data could be drawn. A focus on cases lessened two of the major dilemmas faced by field workers. First, responses to questions posed are only as good as the questions themselves. The conviction runs deep with mediators that each case is sufficiently unique that to generalize about parties and strategies would misrepresent the process.[2] My presence on a case with a mediator gave us a common and particularized basis upon which to build discussions of practice. Rather than discuss how a mediator handles management's claim that they are financially unable to meet the union's demands, I could observe the mediator's behavior in that situation and in our recapitulation discuss why he did not, for example, believe the claim. From similar discussions of other cases, I came to see that claims of inability to pay are generally never believed, and when they are, only certain types of people can make the claim and expect to be credible.

Field workers perenially run the risk that primarily talk-based, presentational data will overwhelm the observational, operational data (Van Maanen, 1979). The line between the two is difficult, if not impossible, to maintain consistently. Cases certainly provided the occasions for gathering operational data, but because the play of the cases was never totally under the control of the mediators, I was frequently able to glimpse behind the front of smooth mediation practice. However, the mediators could control my participation in cases where they expected all would not be as planned, a practice used by the federal mediators.

Midway into the study, a strike occurred against a major employer. I was at the FMCS office when they learned of it. Amidst a flurry of phone calls between the regional and field offices and the spokesmen, plans were made for mediator involvement. I was excluded from these conferences and from observing the case when it came to mediation. The grounds for my exclusion were the visibility of the case and the antagonistic relationship between the parties as a result of the strike. I learned later that my participation was vetoed largely because of the expected role the mediator would play. Historically, the mediator in disputes between company and union is something of a shill, passing the time until someone from national headquarters enters to settle the dispute.

The state mediators, either because they were unaware of this means of control or because they felt they had less to hide, exercised no case control and were left open to more instances of exposure. This kind of foreknowledge was never complete, and once into a case, mediators were able to exercise far less control over what I could observe. Once into the case with both agencies, I was able to observe rebuffs of the mediator's efforts, promises denied, miscued communications, all aspects of practice that the mediators would have preferred, I assume, to keep hidden from view.

Finally, the cases bracketed the setting for me. Faced with cognitive overload in the first few weeks in the field, I used the transcription process and the commentaries around the cases to guide my note taking. But within the case contexts, I continually cast my net to find categories of analysis that were relevant both conceptually and empirically. The process of analysis was an evolving one.

Serendipitously, the first two cases I observed could not have been more different. In the first case, one with a federal mediator, my textbook expectations were upended. The mediator appeared inactive, almost timid in his overtures to the committees and spokesmen, anxious not to make a move that might be misinterpreted. In contrast, on the second case, the state mediator was frenetic, actively engaging a school committee in vehement arguments and debates over the issues. My observations were reflected in the discussions I had with these two mediators about their objectives in the two cases and in the formal presentations of their roles that they gave to the parties. Roles and perspectives on mediation were, therefore, themes that struck me right from the start and that I continued to embellish in subsequent cases. Of course I was interested in strategies, and these I listed as strategic categories one through ten at the end of the analytic notes for these cases.

Another set of thematic categories emerged from the case situations I witnessed next. In case number three I again saw a federal mediator provide a "forum," but this mediator elaborated on why, in the current case, such a role was preferred. He believed that the pros had a "scenario" worked out between them, one to which, he claimed, he was not privy. The mediator worked with care, he said, not to alter the script. However, the mediator was given a more substantial part to play than he had anticipated, and he made a mistake in its execution, a mistake he defined. Thus mistakes, how they are made and their implications for practice, became another category of relevance. And in the fourth case, one with a state mediator, I saw many mistakes. Certainly I was now attuned to them, but in this case, the mediator was barred from further participation in the case because he had overdone "hammering" in the early stages.

I started to understand the role of the other players in the fifth case, one with a state mediator. People, I knew, were important to the mediator, and I had made some initial stabs at creating typologies of the players. But after observing this case, I shifted from the notion of static typology to looking at people from the role perspective of the mediator. The presence of two spokesmen who openly collaborated with the mediator on a deal that was then sold to the committees was described by the mediator as a near-ideal case. My emerging sense of dealmaking was given form in this case— particularly my sense of the parts pros are expected to play.

The next federal case, also a case with pros, was in marked contrast to the state case. In the federal case the mediator emphasized the relationship between the pro and his committee and the strategies used to aid the pro in this endeavor. The final case of the first round, a state case, was with a mediator who seemed more able than most to discuss his underlying principles of mediation. By this point in the study, I was quite sure that I had witnessed two rather differing brands of mediation based on contrasting expectations about the parties and resulting in strategies that differed in shape and timing. I still had difficulty defining what I meant by strategies, however, and found myself confused when I tried to detail them. I left the field at this juncture to analyze my notes and to try to link my empirical observations with theoretical concepts.

The research endeavor is a constant movement between the level of theory and the groundings of the data (Bailyn, 1977). On considering what I had learned in light of theory, I was at once clearer about the themes of the study and overwhelmed by the data. My practice had been to group old and new insights into broad analytic categories on a case-specific basis, with some mention of comparisons. My reexplorations of the symbolic-interaction literature, in particular, the dramaturgical works, helped me to frame the disjointed data-based categories. For example, in the early stages I had focused on a typology of people and issues, led by the mediation literature and my early interviews to think that defining the situation, the diagnostic stance, was essential to understanding strategies; in this framework, the fit of role was ambiguous. But when I examined my data in light of interaction theory, I saw that directionality was often in the other direction. That is, any definition of the situation clearly depended upon how the mediator saw himself in the proceedings, and moreover, his definitions were limited, biased, and intimately tied to his own purpose.

Armed with my increased understanding of the conceptual underpinnings of the study, as well as its general direction, I sought in the next round of cases to test the variance in practice. I did this by going out again on a second round of cases with all but one of the mediators I had observed in the first round. With few exceptions, I found that the mediator's strategic behavior in the second round was remarkably and surprisingly similar in form, though not always in substance, to what I had observed in the first round. The agency distinctions were validated with each successive observation.

The second round of negotiations presented a wholly new set of problems. I became overwhelmed with what I knew and what I could make out of a given piece of transcript. After my first case, 100 pages of field notes, I was able to extract 2 pages of analysis. By case number eight, the first one in the second round, I produced 75 pages of analysis on 50 pages of case transcript and commentary. At this stage of the analysis I faced three problems with the data—my understanding, the categories of relevance, and the lack of a comparative framework.

At the level of particulars, I was coming at long last to "grasp the native's point of view." In the analyses of the first round, I took what the mediators said and did and grouped these data into loose categories: roles, types of people, lists of strategies, mistakes. By the second round, I was able to fill in the contextual motivations and the rationale behind the actions and accounts I recorded. But like the mediators, my understanding became highly specific and situational. I could follow and reproduce why in a specific case a mediator was unsure of the union's position but less clear about management's, why he took on the union at one point in the case and why he postponed the next meeting; but these renditions were so specific and intimately tied to each case that I was puzzled, to say the least, as to how I could compare the mediators and the agencies, not to mention the cases.

The problem with my early analytic strategy was that it was both too specific and too general. It was too specific in that I considered each case in virtual isolation. The slant of my analysis reflected each new piece of understanding I acquired. It was too general in that the categories I used were an amalgamation of conceptual and empirical themes. Though my appreciation for the mediation cultures was advanced, the validation of my theories lay buried in the field notes. When I sought to array the data into these rather vague categories, I had trouble distinguishing between elements. Where, for example, would I put observations about time? Time was a definitional element in theory, but in practice it was a strategic variable used by the mediator to manipulate and manage movement.

I was rescued from premature burial under my notes by two fortuitous events. Peter Manning came to the Sloan School of Management for a seminar, and I was recruited to entertain him while the faculty attended a departmental meeting. I discussed my analytic problem with him, and he made some suggestions, the precise content of which I cannot recall, but whose thrust was that I might consider arraying my data according to the mediator's "map" while at work on a case.[3] Although the framework underwent several revisions as I pieced together the comparative case data, this approach proved a workable one after some time-consuming effort. It took me six months to map and to index the sixteen cases. The framework's outline took the following form:

Roles
1. Official statements to the parties about mediation
2. Requests the parties made of the mediator
3. Off-the-record accounts of their roles to me
4. How the mediator handled the request

People
1. Generalized presentational accounts of committees
2. Specific descriptions of the parties in the case
3. Pros in general—attributes and expectations
4. Pros in the case—attributes, expectations, and actions

The issues
1. Learning the issues: forum; how the mediator learned; topics covered
2. Where the parties are going: how the mediator learned this information; types of information sought
3. Gauging movement: criteria for reasonable positions; criteria for positions without merit; changing perceptions of the issues; calling the case (accuracy of calls at different points in the case)

Getting movement
1. Tactics used
2. Accounts of tactics
3. Timing
4. Aiding the pro

I worked through each case and culled the observational and verbal data according to these categories. As the data were transformed into writing, the chapters on roles and people came to reflect primarily the verbal accounts mediators gave of themselves and others, whereas the strategies came to reflect my own observations. In this way, I made some progress in distinguishing between presentational elements of mediation and the operational, observable dimensions.

In the midst of reformulating and indexing my notes, I was asked to give a seminar on my findings to an audience unfamiliar with field work of this type. Clear that my restructured analysis could not be completed in time, I cast about for a way to present my comparative findings in form that would be compelling for this audience. In a flash of insight, I latched onto meeting arrangements as an element that could be crudely but empirically measured and would lend validity to my qualitative findings. Right from the start, I was struck by the different practices regarding meetings. I had noted this on several occasions, but had never explicitly compared the mediators along this dimension. By working through each transcript, I was able to construct tables of meeting arrangements and was surprised to see the amount of contrast between the agencies. I might add that in a sea of qualitative observations, it was comforting to find the more or less objective rock of meetings to convince myself that I had indeed found contrasts in practice.

Qualitative research manuals tend to be rather cursory in their treatment of field-data analyses. Guidelines tend to emphasize microtechniques that enable the researcher to test the validity, reliability, and variance of the data (Barton and Lazarsfeld, 1951; Becker, 1958; Filstead, 1970). Assistance in the management of field data is rare. These remarks are meant to illustrate how overwhelming, frustrating, and fitful the analysis of field data can be. I was a neophyte who had never undertaken an in-depth field study of this magnitude before. Since I was new to the theory and the research methods, it was easy for me to lose sight of what I was studying. Also, the distance between theoretical concepts and the concrete situational elaboration of behavior fluctuated during the study and, at least for me, was confusing. In part, I misunderstood the use of theory. Symbolic interaction is a loosely formulated lens through which to view behavior, not a tight model of hypotheses suitable for prescribing the indicators for a field study. As such, the theory is more a stance than a set of categories relevant to analysis. Within the perspective afforded by theory, the latitude for choice is enormous. But the need to find categories of relevance, a framework, is compelling for the novice faced with voluminous field data. And the frames from the field are slow to come.

But frameworks may limit as much as they elaborate. The metaphor of the two roles—dealmaker and orchestrator—was as much a function of chance as plan. Though satisfied with the distinctions they yielded, I still wonder at the other directions the study might have taken if the first two cases had been different. The potency of a framework was made clear when, in the process of writing, I reread some interviews done early in the study before I had made any case observations. I found that some of the differences in roles, strategies, and perceptions of pros were articulated in those interviews, but that because I was looking for common themes, I did not pick up the contrasts.

The findings a study yields are not merely random or attributable to the luck of a framework; they must pass certain standards of validity. For a field worker membership tests are perhaps the most stringent. The responses of the mediators who have read a paper based on the present study were unexpected. Although I attempted to keep my assessment of the relative merits of orchestrating and dealmaking under wraps, the bias in favor of the federal mediators does come through. Yet the state mediators enthusiastically vouched for the version of practice I presented. Orchestrating, however, was read by some of the federal mediators as passivity, a stance that runs counter to the active presentation mediators give of their work. Other elements of the present study have come in for criticism by mediators. Some have dismissed my findings as atypical and incomplete, drawn from a sample that is not representative. Some also suggested to me that any appearance I give that mediators are less than forthright, neutral, and effective at their job might do irreparable harm to future proceedings. These reactions contribute to certain lingering doubts I inevitably have about the accuracy and fairness of the work, but convince me as well that I may have stumbled upon some tender areas of mediation practice. Of more personal concern, however, are the pangs of betrayal I feel toward the mediators who so graciously permitted my presence.

Under the scrutiny of the field worker's observing lens, much of what usually passes without comment is recorded and then reproduced for others to view. I have honored my pledge of confidentiality—the agencies, mediators, and cases are disguised—but with a modicum of detective work, identities can quite easily be unmasked. In a small and tightly knit industrial-relations community, where practitioners and academics glide from one milieu to the other, mediators and readers of this work have had, and will have in the future, many occasions to meet and even to work together. The transparency of my confidentiality pledge was revealed in a conference paper I presented, one that was sprinkled with direct quotations from the mediators. After the session, a professor from a local university came up to me and said, "Wasn't that Joe Smith from the state whose comments you read?" I demurred, but he formed his conclusions anyway, and he was correct. Perhaps in field work, as in mediation, confidentiality and neutrality are fictions, impossible to maintain.

Notes

Chapter 1

1. Anthropologists have shown a keen interest in the societal mechanisms by which order and structure are maintained in a culture. Mediators are viewed as a kind of complement to the formal structural fabric of the society, and, indeed, their actions are essential to its maintenance (Evans-Pritchard, 1940; Barton, 1949; Freeman, 1957; Gulliver, 1977, 1979).

2. The reference in this work to mediators by masculine gender is an editorial convenience, but reflects as well the reality of the occupation. Although there are some female mediators, the occupation is dominated by men. In the Federal Mediation and Conciliation Service, for example, there are currently 27 females, compared with 273 males (FMCS Annual Report, 1978).

3. The belief that mediation is an art permeates the writings of practitioners and analysts alike (Meyer, 1960; Maggiolo, 1971; Simkin, 1971; Robins and Denenberg, 1976; Kheel, 1979). This perception is apparently shared by rank-and-file mediators as well. In their survey of government mediators, Indik et al. (1966) found that 96 percent of federal mediators and 99 percent of those employed by state agencies concurred with the statement that "mediation is an art that can only be learned by experience." Indeed, the persistence of this perception has led some to conclude that the process is ill-suited to systematic analysis (Shister, 1958; Rehmus, 1965; Kockan and Jick, 1978).

4. Surveys of mediator attributes and attitudes conducted by Weschler (1950), Landsberger (1960), and Indik et al. (1966) reveal that mediators with high IQs, command of technical knowledge, and from labor or management backgrounds are seen as more effective by their peers and representatives of the parties. Kressel (1972) conducted in-depth interviews with twelve noted mediators and produced a monograph that captures these mediators' beliefs about various topics that touch on mediation, particularly the timely use of strategies. Lovell (1950), Douglas (1962), and Frees (1976) undertook extensive observational studies of mediators, and each amplified slightly different aspects of the process. Lovell emphasized how mediators use pressure to encourage the parties to settle, whereas

Douglas and Frees emphasized the mediators' sense of timing and use of time.

5. Mediation has been a favorite topic for laboratory study. Among the facets of the process simulated in the lab are the conditions under which mediator suggestions have the most impact (Pruitt and Johnson, 1970), the implications of the timing of entry into a dispute (Pilisiuk and Rappoport, 1964; Hornstein, 1965), the influence of the mediation site on perceptions of neutrality (Martindale, 1971), the effects of communication tutoring (Wichman, 1970; Druckman, 1975), and the effect of single-issue consideration versus packaging (Frohman and Cohen, 1970). Stevens (1954, 1963) developed a model of the process the prescriptively links tactical practice with particular types of bargaining situations. Kockan and Jick (1978) postulate and test a multidimensional model that relates characteristics of the dispute to mediator efficacy.

6. A theme that connects many of the different types of studies that have been undertaken of mediation is a concern with the conditions under which mediators employ (or should employ) particular tactics and strategies. For example, Kressel (1972) and Douglas (1962) argue that stage in the case is paramount, that is, that certain tactics are more appropriate early in the dispute, while others fit better in the final phases. Stevens (1954, 1963) postulates that the effective mediator chooses his tactics in such a way that they are appropriately linked to the kind of agreement obstacles that exist in a dispute. Pruitt and Johnson (1970) argue that mediator suggestions have their maximal impact when negotiators have a high need to "save face." Kochan and Jick (1978) and Gerhart and Drotning (1980) suggest that aggressive strategies are needed when disputes are difficult or intense. Differences in how individual mediators or groups of mediators would respond to these situational contingencies are not addressed.

7. What I have labeled an interpretive approach is really an amalgamation of several strains in sociological thought and inquiry. These include symbolic interaction (Mead, 1934; Blumer, 1969; Becker, 1973; Denzin, 1973) dramaturgic analysis (Goffman, 1959, 1961, 1967; Manning, 1977) and ethnomethodology (Garfinkel, 1967; Douglas, 1971; Cicourel, 1974). The feature common to these schools is a concern with the interpretive assumptions taken for granted that underlie social processes.

8. The concept "social construction of reality" best captures the essence of interpretive social theory. Social constructionists argue that societies' structures and institutions have no inherent existence apart from the members who create them and must be seen and studied as ongoing accomplishments of these members (Berger and Luckman, 1966; Lyman and Scott, 1970). It is this character of the social world that distinguishes it from the natural and that requires a theoretical and methodological orientation wholly different from that in the natural sciences (Cicourel, 1964).

9. Within the social sciences, there exists a major difference of opinion about the goals of empirical research, differences rooted in certain core ontological assumptions about the nature of social reality (Morgan and

Smircich, 1980). For those (and indeed their voices are many) who view social structure as more or less objective and concrete, in the nature of social facts, the empirical task is to investigate and to model causal relations among these objective facts across time and space. To those who view reality as a social construct, such model building is fraught with problems of interpretation and facticity. These "context builders," as Van Maanen (1981) calls them, have an almost "obsessive concern" with meaning and the "situational particulars" upon which social behavior is built. For context buiders, the social-science enterprise is one of discovering grounded theory rather than verifying it (Glaser and Strauss, 1967). Discovering grounded theory means that the social scientist comes to see the work context from the perspective of its participants and makes visible the cultural bases upon which such interpretations are built (Rabinow and Sullivan, 1979). Accumulated knowledge in this view comes from the close, careful, descriptive and comparative work of ethnographers or participant observers by means of which a sense of conceptual clarity and understanding may be achieved. Some examples of this research agenda that inspired the form and structure of this work are Dalton (1959), Becker et al. (1961), Sudnow (1965), and Manning (1977, 1980), among others.

10. The term "role" has a variety of meanings in the fields of sociology and social psychology (Biddle and Thomas, 1966). The difference in meaning concerns such issues as fixedness, fluidity, specificity, and relationship to social status, among others. Functional role theory (Merton, 1957; Katz and Kahn, 1978) assumes a regularity and patternedness in roles that derive from formal and informal forces toward conformity and the overriding importance of expectations. An alternative approach, rooted in symbolic interaction, emphasizes the creative and negotiated processes involved in role creation and maintenance (Mead, 1934; Turner, 1966; Blumer, 1969). It is this latter conception that informs the usage here.

11. Assessment of other interactants in social contexts is one of the ways people render experiences meaningful and coherent. Schutz (1962) identifies three kinds of relevancies that are used to map the social space in situations. Topical relevancies structure the setting in terms of what are taken to be the issues at hand, the content of the interaction. Topical relevancies are transformed, in light of the person's purposes and intents, into interpretational relevancies that allow the person to plan his own line of action. Motivational relevancies are the commonsense heuristics that people use to understand why people act as they do and the implications of these actions. One of the major functions of these interpretive spatial categories is that they provide the criteria for recognizing a true fellow worker (Hughes, 1971). One particular type of fellow worker is the teammate, whose dramaturgical cooperation is needed if a role is to be enacted successfully (Goffman, 1959).

12. Role enactment may be observed in occupations and professions that are characterized by uncertain and equivocal work environments (Weick, 1979; Manning, 1980). To make predictable and routine those features of

work that are inherently indeterminate and unstructured, lawyers (Sudnow, 1965), welfare workers (Zimmerman, 1970), doctors (Becker et al., 1961), and police (Manning, 1980) have been observed enacting their environment. In doing so, role encumbents rely on rules that order in some way certain problematic features of their work (Zimmerman and Weider, 1970; Douglas, 1971; Mehan and Wood, 1975); these rules are constitutive in the sense that they emerge from experience and have no meaning apart from the practices they tacitly govern (Taylor, 1979). Constitutive rules cover both instrumental and expressive domains of interaction (Goffman, 1959). Instrumental rules serve to simplify and make routine much of the everyday decisionmaking encountered in a work context (Garfinkel, 1967; Mehan and Wood, 1975). Relational rules are the cooperative practices of all interactants that serve to maintain the integrity of the situation and protect the "face" of the actor and the other performers (Goffman, 1967). These relational rules are not usually the ostensible reasons for an interaction, but they are a necessary condition for its success.

13. Retrospective justifications for actions taken are known as accounts (Lyman and Scott, 1970). In enacting their environment, actors act and then assess the meaning of the situation in light of their actions. In accounting for these actions, people attempt to demonstrate that they have acted plausibly, practically, and rationally (Garfinkel, 1967; Lyman and Scott, 1970; Cicourel, 1974).

14. Although mediation is the primary function of these agencies, they do provide other dispute resolution services. The FMCS, for example, maintains lists of registered arbitrators that parties can obtain for grievance settlements. Some state agencies retain their own panel of arbitrators. In addition, FMCS provides technical services and relationship-development programs, services that are provided by field mediators.

15. Two other federal agencies provide mediation services to particular industries. The National Mediation Board employs twenty mediators who mediate some 300 cases annually in the rail and airline industries. The Atomic Energy Panel, established in 1949, retains a small panel of mediators, active in disputes that occur in atomic-energy installations.

16. FMCS has recently reorganized its field structure in order to trim its budget. There are now four regions instead of seven. Two of the old regional offices and twelve of the field offices are now designated district offices, staffed by an assistant regional director who is located in the district. The other field offices remained the same.

17. At the time of reorganization, FMCS staffing practices and procedures were changed as well. The regional offices have only a regional director and no longer have staff charged with overseeing administration. Special assistants and assistant regional directors are now located in the district offices. Thirty-day notices are now sent directly to the national office, where they are checked to determine whether FMCS has jurisdiction and if so are routed directly to the district offices, where case assignments are made by regional staff located there. With less staff at all levels and with

a more decentralized structure at the level of district, reporting requirements have been decreased.

18. There are exceptions to this. Occasions may arise where the field mediator is joined by another mediator from his office or from the region or even the national office. This so-called "escalation within the agency" (Simkin, 1971) occurs in cases with national impact, or where such escalation is normally the practice, or when the mediator is unable to resolve the dispute on his own and asks for more "senior" assistance.

19. In its move to cut its operating budget, the administration of FMCS attempted to retain as many of the line mediators as possible. As a result, cutbacks were made in the physical plant and nonmediation staff. The mediators in the FMCS field office studied (now a district office) have moved to a different building with less commodious offices and minimal conference space. These mediators now share their offices with each other and cannot convene meetings on a regular basis in their offices. As a result, their cases are now convened on the parties' grounds, a change that affects the strategic resources they have to work with. In addition, the mediators no longer have a secretary, but use answering machines for their calls, and are responsible for their own reporting and coffee.

20. The cases and mediators have been disguised to the best of my ability. Federal mediators have been given fictitious names, alphabetically from A to D, and the state mediators from S to V. The cases are named for colleges, according to the same alphabetical scheme. For example, mediator Shaw on the Sheridan School Committee case is a state mediator on a state case.

Chapter 2

1. Roles of mediators have typically been equated in the empirical literature with their functions. The notion is that for the parties to settle, a set of dynamics must occur that either pressures them to make concessions or eases certain aspects of the bargaining dilemma—the negotiator's need to make a move yet to appear to keep his resolve at the same time. Different researchers have highlighted specific aspects of these mediation functions. Lovell (1952) and Warren (1954) emphasize the mediator's role in accentuating the pressure the parties feel from a strike threat. Landsberger (1955) and Douglas (1962) are more concerned with the ways mediators aid the interpersonal dynamics at the bargaining table so that overt hostility between the negotiators is contained. Stevens (1954) and Pruitt and Johnson (1970) emphasize the face-saving role that mediators play, allowing negotiators to make concessions under the guise of mediator recommendations without appearing weak. Each of these treatments of role is tied to the dynamics of the process and not to the perspective of the mediators. In this sense, they are based on a functionalist view of role, as opposed to the interpretive and interactionist one that informs this work (Biddle and Thomas, 1966).

2. Apparently the view that parties can most creatively develop their own solutions to the issues when they directly confront each other in joint

meeting is a perception that is shared by at least one "celebrity" mediator. Theodore Kheel alleges that he prefers to have the parties meet jointly because "I find that I get closest to the truth when both parties are present" and because "the best insights come when the parties are in the presence of each other" (Kheel, 1979, pp. 30–31).

3. Indirect evidence from other empirical studies lends support to some of the findings presented here. In a survey of 82 state mediators from 20 states and 222 federal mediators, Indik et al. (1966) found that 85 percent of the federal mediators and 79 percent of the state mediators endorsed an active role for the mediator. However, the two groups differed somewhat on the amount of persuasion the mediator should employ when meeting separately with the parties. Forty-three percent of the state mediators felt they should exert the same degree of pressure that the parties would exert themselves if they were meeting face to face. By contrast, only 27 percent of the federal mediators concurred with this statement. This finding is interesting in light of mediator Allen's claim that he refused to act as an advocate and conveyed only minimal information in order to pressure the parties to return to a joint forum.

Frees (1976) observed the practice of state and federal mediators in Minnesota. Although he did not explicitly contrast their practices, he did describe some of the roles they played, and in the case examples he used to illustrate his conceptual categories, one can detect certain patterns that seem to support some of the distinctions in role noted in this chapter. For example, when he described mediators playing a ceremonial role (just convening meetings) or a role he called stage managing (a role akin to mediator Allen's staging of the joint off-the-record meeting) or a monitor role, the case examples were drawn from FMCS cases. In contrast, when he discussed the mediator's persuasive efforts to get the parties to "face up to the hard facts" or his use of suggestions, all the examples were from the state mediators' cases (which were a mix of public- and private-sector ones). In discussions with Frees, he alleges that the label "orchestrator" fits well his observation of federal mediators. This is not surprising, given that the federal mediators in both studies work for FMCS and have thus been recruited and trained according to the agency's organizational principles and ideology, into which an orchestrating stance neatly fits. As a former director of FMCS states it, "One basic principle designed to promote the maximum of direct negotiations is that the mediator should do as little as is required" (Simkin, 1971, p. 118).

The fit between the state dealmakers in this study and those in Minnesota is more ambiguous. According to Frees, the state mediators are less uniform in their approach. Some of the state mediators he observed learned their craft from the federal mediators and continue to work with them. These state mediators display more of an orchestrating style, while their colleagues are often more like dealmakers. Given the differing structures, policies, and environments of the state agency in this study and in Minnesota, one would not expect mediator roles to be as uniform in the two state agencies as in two branches of the FMCS.

Chapter 3

1. Casework is a common feature of work in other occupations, most notably law and medicine. In these domains, the boundaries of a case are ambiguous and much of professional work (and the evalution of it) involves making a case out of raw facts and taken for granted working assumptions and conventions (See Weaver, 1977; Manning, 1980). The features of casework in these settings is somewhat different than that in mediation, where the social construction of the case is less apparent. Mediators are given cases whose features are predefined by the assignment procedures. These procedures are an interpretive topic worthy of study, but one that is tangential to the domain of study here. For the practicing mediator, discretion over the decision to mediate a case appears quite minimal. This is more true of the state agency than the federal. Since state mediators chose not to investigate the existence of an impasse, their major area of discretion, cases once assigned tend to move directly to the meeting stage. The federal mediators, through their monitoring procedure, have somewhat more discretion over whether to meet. But most often this decision is made by the parties who agree to let the mediator meet with them. There were some occasions, particularly when disputes of public import were assigned, when the federal mediator more actively tried to move the parties into the meeting stage. These were examples of case making, but they were not frequently observed. For the most part, mediators in both agencies have minimal control over their caseload and do not appear to devote much effort to making a case. Their concern is, rather, to manage the case, once the parties meet, in such a way that an agreement can be reached.

2. The term "joint meeting" may be somewhat confusing. In official FMCS parlance, when the federal mediator actually meets with the parties, whether they face each other across the table or sit in separate rooms, for the record they are in joint meeting. Thus FMCS in its reports distinguishes between cases that have been monitored over the telephone (nonjoint meeting cases) from those in which the parties actually met (joint meeting cases). The term as used in this work, however, refers to the practice of convening a meeting at which the parties are physically present in the same room. The federal mediators similarly refer to this forum as a joint meeting. The reader may be confused, but the federal mediators are not.

3. Counting caucuses is somewhat problematic. Whenever a bargaining committee is left alone in its separate room, it is in caucus. Its discussions may well include the contract under consideration, or it may talk about the weather or the performance of a local ball team. Since I was always with the mediator, I had no way of knowing whether the parties were indeed caucusing or merely passing the time. Therefore, I define a caucus as one explicitly convened either by the parties or the mediator.

4. A portion of this case was omitted as it touched on issues that might make this case recognizable. The additional off-the-record meeting, present in the frequency distributions but unmentioned in the case, concerned this matter.

5. The patterns in meeting arrangements observed in this study receive some support from data reported in other published and unpublished works. Ann Douglas in *Industrial Peacemaking* (1962) appended to her analysis a transcript of the entire Atlas case (pp. 205–668), one that was mediated by an FMCS mediator. Douglas's precise timing of the start and conclusion of each meeting permits an analysis, not only of meeting frequencies, but also of the time spent in each forum.

	Frequency distribution (%) of meeting types (N=109)	Frequency distribution (%) of time spent in meetings (N=2,840 minutes)
Joint meetings	26	27
Separate meetings	63	60
Caucuses	9	11
Off-the-record meetings	2	2

The frequency distributions of meetings in the Atlas do not appear to replicate the negotiating arrangements for the federal mediators in this study. The Atlas mediator spent more time meeting separately with the parties and used caucuses with less frequency. These distributions mask, however, other similarities in meeting arrangements. For example, the first session of the Atlas case was convened in joint meeting, a meeting that lasted for four hours, at which the parties presented and discussed their proposals. Succeeding proposals and counteroffers were likewise presented and briefly discussed in joint meeting, and the final agreement was consummated in that forum. Indeed, the use of joint meetings for these purposes make the federal Atlas case appear more similar to the federal negotiating pattern in this study than it does to the state intervention approach.

These observations are lent further support in another work on mediation that includes cases conducted by federal and state mediators in another locale. In his unpublished dissertation, "Dispute Management in Labor Relations: The Mediation Process," Joseph Frees (1976) provides some selected data on meeting patterns for six of the cases he observed. As part of his discussion on opening moves in a mediation, he reproduces the meeting arrangements for the first session of three cases conducted by FMCS mediators and three by mediators employed by the state agency in Minnesota. These data and the supporting explanations provided by the mediators suggest some similarities and differences with the patterns in this study.

Frequency distribution (%) of time spent in meetings: the first session of the case

	Joint meetings	Separate meetings	Caucuses	Off-the-record meetings	Total
FMCS					
Services Co.	65	35	—	—	(N = 175 minutes)
Ogan Co.	57	43	—	—	(N = 140)
Titco Co.	21	58	21	—	(N = 70 minutes)
State agency					
Kamphor Co.	25	75	—	—	(N = 40 minutes)
School District XYZ	22	78	—	—	(N = 45 minutes)
Church Co.	67	7	13	13	(N = 75 minutes)

With the possible exception of the Titco case, the other federal cases appear quite consistent with the federal pattern and the practice of using the joint meeting to learn the issues in dispute. Frees reports that the Titco case was a departure from practice. Apparently the union and management committees arrived at the mediator's office simultaneously, and he was prepared to convene a joint meeting when the chief negotiator for management requested a separate meeting first:

He told the mediator that he was not quite ready to meet with the union. He was still assembling some comparative wage and benefit scales to support the company's proposal. When he finished, he asked the mediator to bring the figures to the union committee and then leave them alone to look over the material. The mediator did as requested, then returned to his office to do some paperwork. When he finished, he rejoined the management committee, discussed strategy, then brought them in for a joint conference with the union committee. [P. 210]

Like the practice of the federal mediators in this study, the mediator in the Titco case was willing to depart from the usual approach when requested to do so by the parties. The similarities in federal meeting arrangements in this study and Free's is not surprising. Both groups of mediators are members of the same federal agency and were trained in like fashion. The Minnesota state agency has no affiliations with the state agency in this study, and therefore it is not surprising that some differences in meeting arrangement seem to exist. In the Kamphor and School District XYZ cases, joint meetings were convened early in the case, but their short duration suggests that they were used not to discuss proposals, but rather as a forum in which the mediator could introduce himself and the process (p. 229). In this sense the arrangements in the Kamphor and XYZ cases were more like the state cases in this study. The Church case was somewhat different, but like the Titco case, the pattern suggests that it was of the parties', not the mediator's design. The session started in an off-the-record meeting with the management negotiator, then a short separate meeting with the union followed by a caucus without the mediator present. After these events, a lengthy joint meeting was held. In light of this pattern, it is interesting to note that the management negotiator had worked extensively with federal mediators; but Church was the first case he had with a state mediator.

In sum, the data from these other studies suggest that certain features of meeting arrangements are not unique to the mediators in this study. In particular, the federal mediators do seem to favor extensive joint meetings as the forum to learn issues and discuss proposals and as the place for proposals to be exchanged. The state mediators in Minnesota also make use of early joint meetings, but more as introductory forums than as working sessions. The use of the joint meetings for this purpose is in marked contrast to the infrequent use of joint meetings for even this reason by the state mediators in this study.

6. What may be happening here is a complex example of bracketing, or the use of scheme theory (Weick, 1979). The certification of impasse serves to bracket negotiations that were held before mediation from the mediation process itself. Ignorant of what transpired before mediation, the certification serves to select for the mediator only one salient element of the negotiation process—that it broke down. Bracketing may be amplified as group members reinforce one scheme over another and restrict the exploration for alternatives (Asch, 1952; Janis, 1972). This may be why state mediators, although empowered to investigate, rarely do so.

Chapter 4

1. The strategic behavior of mediators lies at the root of the reputation of the process as an art. For in their individualized and varied use of strategies and tactics, mediators give the process a personalized touch that makes such behavior difficult to analyze systematically. The depth of this perception is attested to by its persistence (Shister, 1958; Rehmus, 1965; Kochan and Jick, 1978; Gulliver, 1979).

2. The term "narrowing" is somewhat ambiguous. The federal mediators do not actually do the narrowing themselves. Rather, they use tactics that allow the parties to narrow the differences between them. However, getting the parties to narrow is the strategy. In shorthand, and in the interests of comparability, I have shortened this to "narrowing."

3. My presence on the cases affects this discussion of strategy in interesting ways. Mediators take many actions in the context of a case, only some of which may be considered strategic. As they work on cases, they may be observed acting in ways that one would be hard pressed to call strategic— for example, getting angry, laughing. These are merely reactions. However, when mediators talked to me about why they were angry or why they laughed, they couched their descriptions in deliberate, strategic terms. Thus when analyzing a mediator's strategy, it is important to bear in mind that much of what passes for strategy is a figment of retrospective constructions and not of preplanned method (Weick, 1979). Basically, mediators act and then account for their actions in language that signifies intentionality. Because of my presence on the cases, I try in this chapter to describe

and to analyze what the mediators actually did and not to rely solely on retrospective constructions.

4. In most of the recent research on mediator strategies, presentational strategies (Manning, 1977), which refer to the abstract and general statements mediators make about what they do to get a settlement, have been the primary focus of interest. Kressel's interview study of twelve practitioners presents an inventory of such strategies. The problem is that these abstract generalizations do not neatly map to the actions the mediator actually takes in a particular case. For example, an often reported presentational strategy is for mediators to "get the parties to face reality" (Kressel, 1972; Kochan and Jick, 1978). Mediators would probably agree that such an objective is indeed an important element of a mediator's strategy. Where they might disagree is on how operationally or tactically they can accomplish such an objective. In recent cross-sectional studies, strategies and tactics are lumped together. As a result, it becomes difficult to separate what the mediator is trying to accomplish, for example, "educate the parties to the bargaining process," from the tactics he uses to accomplish this end, for example, "by pressing the parties hard to make compromises" (Kochan and Jick, 1978, p. 240).

5. Stage models of mediation suggest that the parties pass through distinct transitions in their progress toward settlement (Douglas, 1962; Gulliver, 1979). In the early stages of the dispute, parties seek "to establish the range," "reconnoiter that range" during the midphases, and "precipitate the decisionmaking crisis" as the final stage (Douglas, 1962). Analogously, mediators use different strategies during these phases. Mediators use "reflexive strategies" early in the case—for example, gaining the trust and confidence of the parties, discovering the real issues and leaders—and use "nondirective" strategies during the midphase—producing a favorable negotiating climate, pacing negotiations and establishing priorities (Kressel, 1972; Kochan and Jick, 1978). Finally, in the later stages, more "directive" or "contingent" strategies would be brought into play—for example, changing expectations, getting the parties to face reality, making suggestions for compromise. Based on observations of cases in this study, this conception of chronological action is ambiguous. It fits in some respects, but not in others. Certain tactics that presumably characterize the later stages were observed at the beginning and vice versa—mediators made suggestions at the first meeting and were still trying to gain trust and confidence at the end.

6. Categories of relevance are the means by which raw information about issues, people, and bargaining environments are made meaningful. Categories allow the mediator to identify the people and their behavior as recognizable features of the situation and to gauge his own behavior accordingly (McHugh, 1968; Spradley, 1980).

7. By the end of the Tulane case, Thomas no longer considered the management attorney to be a reneger. Rather, he blamed the mayor for his intransigent attitude. These altered perceptions of the competence and

expertise of the management attorney are an example of a "status-maintaining account" (Garfinkel, 1967). Because spokesmen and mediators stand in a certain relationship to each other that transcends individual cases, even if a spokesman has acted unprofessionally, and hence jeopardized the mediator's performance, such feelings frequently change by the end of the case. By shifting the blame for reneging to the mayor, the management attorney was absolved. Accounts such as these help the mediator maintain his relationship with valued allies (Goffman, 1959; Lyman and Scott, 1970).

8. The shift from considering issues in light of pattern deviations to more contextual factors follows Schutz's (1962) depiction of situational definitions. In the interpretation of social space, topical relevancies—the issues and their objective merit—tend to be transformed into interpretational relevancies that help the mediator decipher the interactional properties of the process. Since the mediator is interested in the potential for settlement, how the parties act with regard to these issues becomes more salient. Finally, to understand why the parties act as they do, mediators supply motivational relevancies—for example, the relative bargaining power between the parties.

9. An earlier version of this section appeared in Kolb (1983).

10. Mather and Yngvesson (1979) note the tendency for third parties in diverse cultural settings to transform disputes by rephrasing, narrowing, and expanding the issues. The overarching use of patterns by state mediators may have the effect of narrowing the dispute, in that those issues that can be made to fit patterns become prominent, while those that cannot may be minimized or ignored. In contrast, federal mediators transform disputes by rephrasing, by finding a common framework—the proposals—within which resolution can be undertaken.

11. In practice, it is difficult to assess which of these two modes—full proposal or discrete consideration of the issues—is more effective. In laboratory studies of bargaining, however, the findings consistently show that consideration of the entire contract resulted in more effective processes and outcomes and was less likely than discrete consideration of issues to freeze the concession process prematurely (Kelly, 1966; Frohman and Cohen, 1970).

Chapter 5

1. In recent studies that attempt to gauge the sources of impasse and the difficulties that they present to the mediator, attributes of the parties figure prominently (Kressel, 1972; Kochan and Jick, 1978; Gerhart and Drotning, 1980). In these studies, indicators measure the bargaining experience of a committee, the degrees of conflict that mark intracommittee relationships and that between the parties, as well as the expertise of the chief negotiator and the amount of authority delegated to him. Cases characterized by inexperience, conflict, and poor use of negotiators tend to make mediation more difficult.

2. Constituencies are involved in the ratification process in different ways. After a tentative agreement has been reached in mediation, the union bargaining committee typically presents the package to its members and, if all goes well, recommends its ratification, which the members vote to accept. Ratification on the management side tends to be more of an ongoing process. Key decisionmakers may actually be in attendance at the mediation sessions, or the management committee may communicate with them over the telephone. In the public sector, there is an additional ratification step: approval by the legislative body charged with budgetary authority over the locale. This ratification may occur after the mediation, or quite commonly, the budget is set beforehand and negotiations are resolved within its confines.

3. The mediators may gather information about constituent blocs, but make use of such data only if it becomes necessary. When issues concern small blocs of members like nurses or athletic coaches and these issues become priorities, the mediator may try to learn more about the numbers of people affected and the associated costs of the provision. Similarly, if bargaining committees allege that the mayor or the full executive body is the advocate of a particular bargaining position, the mediator may include that member in the proceedings. But as Douglas (1962) observes, constituencies that are absent from the conference table relinquish their capacity to influence its outcomes significantly.

4. There were some exceptions to this. In industrial cases, bosses had considerable interaction with the mediators. In public-sector cases, school superintendents and fire chiefs were singled out because they were often actively involved in discussion of demands that affected working conditions. Finally, some bargaining committees made their presence known to the mediator through their active participation or obstreperous behavior.

5. The differences between how federal and state mediators view the generalized characteristics of management committees bear some mention. Management committees in the federal cases were composed of company or organizational employees whose hierarchical places on the committee were analogous, in most situations, to the positions they occupied in their organizations. This hierarchical structure signifies to the federal mediator that the management bargaining committee is well prepared and knows its priorities well. The potential problem with this preparation is that final positions may surface early in the case and constrain the search for a viable settlement. Management committees in the public sector are composed of elected officials and political appointees, with fire chiefs, police chiefs, and school superintendents usually there also in an advisory capacity. As a result, the decisionmaking structure is not as readily apparent. Further, these bodies tend to lack expertise in labor negotiations and fail, according to the state mediators, to use their attorneys to good advantage. Like their union counterparts, these management committees adopt "unrealistic" positions and appear to be quite inflexible once into the process.

6. There were two cases where management represented itself and did not employ an outside spokesman. In Taft School Committee, the super-

intendent of schools managed his committee, whereas in Urbana Housing Authority, the director and his assistant comprised the management team.

7. In dramaturgical terms, pros and mediators are a team (Goffman, 1959). As outsiders to the local relationship, their ends are similar: to achieve a settlement and to maintain their credibility with the committees so that they will be hired (or requested) again. Through their collaborative and cooperative practices, these teams manage the process of mediation. However, the parts each is to play differ, depending on whether the mediator is state or federal.

8. It is an accepted rule of field work that meanings of linguistical terms in a culture are often best understood in the situations that are exceptions to the rule. Goffman (1974) calls these negatively eventful occasions, while others refer to deviant occurrences (Emerson, 1970; Douglas, 1976). The point is that when mediators compared a given spokesperson's behavior to how they might expect a pro to act, I came to learn about the expectations for pros. However, these kinds of presentations needed to be balanced with observable instances of interactions with pros.

9. An interesting facet is demonstrated in the Sheridan Firefighters case. The union attorney was clearly not a pro—he had minimal experience in negotiations and had mediated only once before. But because he was present on a case with another pro, the mediator involved the union attorney as he might a pro. In essence, with a willing team member, prolike behavior is modeled by the mediator. By the end of the case, the mediator judged the union attorney to have "behaved like a pro."

10. In the Duke Hospital case, the federal mediator tried to shape the behavior of the novice union negotiator so that he would learn to act more like a pro. He suggested that the spokesman meet with the management pro to discuss areas of agreement and emphasized the need for him to "work with his committee" in the interim between sessions. This suggestion was made after the mediator, at the request of the management attorney, attempted to encourage the union committee to drop some of its demands. He suffered some verbal abuse in this endeavor.

11. The union pro's actions placed the mediator in an awkward situation, one that compromised his credibility before both the management and the union committees. In dramaturgical terms, the rules of facework that govern mediators were violated by the pro and, therefore, not easily repaired (Goffman, 1967). Although mediators claim that they do not mind being used this way, that it is part of their job, my observation was that when this occurred, the guilty party was punished by the mediator. In this case, he did not support the pro, and in one state case, on the advice of the mediator the union received less in wages than management was willing to concede.

12. Northrup (1962) suggests that the mark of the professional mediator is that he realizes that the bulk of mediation is carried out by representatives with their own people: in essence, that spokesmen are the mediators be-

tween the opposing side and their committee. In negotiations without a mediator, this practice of spokesmen is called intraorganizational bargaining (Walton and McKersie, 1965).

Chapter 6

1. The ambiguity of the link between mediation activities and dispute outcomes is lent credence by two recent empirical studies of public sector disputes. Kochan and Jick (1978) found that when mediators used aggressive strategies, they were able to bring about changes in the parties' positions, but that these tactics did not necessarily increase the probability of settlement. The data from another study (Gerhart and Drotning, 1980) imply just the opposite. They argue that when disputes are "difficult," an "intensive mediator style" (a measure that appears to approximate aggressive strategies) is more likely to result in settlement at an earlier stage in the impasse procedures.

2. Organizations that process people and seek to change their behavior (for example, colleges, police forces) typically have difficulty evaluating their product (Manning, 1977). What constitutes an educated person, a crime-free environment? Mediation agencies are no different; it is difficult to conceive of a measure that approximates the achievement of the goal of reducing the level of aggressive industrial conflict, particularly when practitioners believe it is determined by forces outside the mediator's control. Further, these types of organizations typically lack a consensus about the value of the product. For mediators, there is a continual debate whether mediators represent the public good or merely serve the parties. If they represent the public good, then they must be held accountable for the shape of the end product. Mediators are reluctant to adopt this position and argue that if they represent the public, their neutrality and hence their efficacy would be compromised (Douglas, 1962; Simkin, 1971).

3. To play a given social role successfully, a player must perform the functions normally associated with that role, but do so in a way that fits the audience's conception of the kind of person who is suitable and believable in that role. Potentially problematic in this regard is the ambiguous and fluid character of social interaction. Information is always available to interactants from which impressions about an actor and his performance may be judged. Some impressions support a particular claim, while others may discredit it. For a mediator, the management of impressions is particularly important. Since he lacks formal authority to induce settlement, his efficacy is directly related to the perceptions the parties have of him and of how reliable, competent, and credible he is. Mistakes, therefore, challenge the mediator's performance and always threaten to jeopardize his ability to enact his role (Goffman, 1959).

Chapter 7

1. Ann Douglas (1962) is quite eloquent on this "strike fiction": "Comments of a strike may crop up throughout very nearly all of the proceedings of

a case and an undiscriminating observer may deduce from this that it is the shadow of the strike, kept dangling like Damocles' sword, which takes over the situation, after all. But this does not seem to be knowledgeable observing. Somewhere in the course of negotiations the possibility of a strike will have to be assigned a weight in the calculations taking shape around the question: what price agreement? In this form, it can take its place alongside all the other verbal pressures which the parties exert at one time or another, presenting no more frightening prospects than any other given" (p. 112).

2. Dunlop (1958) argues that a shared ideology is a necessary feature of systems of industrial relations: "The ideology of the industrial relations system is a body of common ideas that defines the role and place of each actor and that defines the ideas which each actor holds toward the place and functions of others in the system" (p. 16). Sociologists suggest that ideologies may be seen to serve vested interests in society. Espousers of the ideology seek to present a justification and legitimation of a particular definition of reality, so that what is advantageous for them is deemed a value for society at large (Berger, 1963; Salaman and Thompson, 1980). Critics suggest that the ideology of free collective bargaining camouflages certain basic economic and political inequities in the industrial sphere and so serves to justify the interests of capital and institutions over those of workers (Hyman and Brough, 1975; Hill, 1981).

3. Personal communication from Dan Hurley, FMCS.

4. The relationships pros have with mediators and, it appears, among themselves, challenge certain assumptions about industrial pluralism. Pros seem to share a conception of how interests between the parties can be accommodated. In this regard, it appears that competing interests on the labor side between members and pros are potentially as great as that between the parties (Walton and McKersie, 1965; Hyman, 1982).

5. It would be erroneous to suggest that federal mediators handle only private-sector cases. Their jurisdiction includes the federal sector as well. These cases account for less than 5 percent of the total FMCS caseload. Unfortunately, I did not observe any of these cases. I would, based on discussions with the mediators, expect some differences. These cases apparently take longer and are described by the mediators as "endless and tedious" because they involve detailed work issues and regulations. Although the federal mediators work in this sector, their basic mode of practice is shaped primarily by their private-sector experience.

6. The studies of the "chilling" and "narcotic" effects of interest arbitration suggest how strong the tendency is to evaluate behavior in the public sector according to the ideology of the private sector. In assessing the performance of interest arbitration, the problem is defined as one of determining whether this procedure functions like a strike to compel bargaining. The findings that the parties become dependent or addicted to arbitration may derive more from the way the problem has been framed and is not as deleterious a policy outcome as some have claimed (Long and Feuille, 1974; Anderson,

1981). Specifically, one can hypothesize that the private-sector framework has blinded these observers to the ways that actors in the public sector have developed their own unique accommodation to the problems they face. Reanalysis points to the possibility that the use of procedures is selective and strategic and that the outcomes may be simply lengthened bargaining timetables and additional forums for mediation and not the erosion of bilateral bargaining (Kolb and Van Maanen, forthcoming).

7. Hyman (1978) suggests that the balance of power is a crucial assumption underlying the pluralistic conception of industrial society: "The argument has been repeatedly rehearsed that a combination of full employment and (perhaps excessive) legislative support for collective organization among workers permitted union power to equal or even exceed that of employers" (p. 21). Given this assumption that power is balanced, the conflict between interest groups in industry has been largely confined to narrow issues and details of the work place and the rules for regulating the relationship. Other critics suggest that this pluralistic ideology may be seen as basically a legitimation of social and political relations in the postwar United States that has served to channel industrial conflict, but has masked the imbalance of power that exists between labor and capital (Hill, 1981).

8. It is misleading to suggest that only the state mediators suffer from this shortsightedness. Neither group of mediators appeared to learn much from the mistakes it made. The pattern was unmistakable. When all goes well, the mediator shares the credit with the parties, reserving a considerable portion for himself. Failures of any sort are blamed solely on the parties or accounted for in strategic terms. Attributions and accounting are important face-saving maneuvers in mediation (Bem, 1970; Lyman and Scott, 1970).

9. Union representatives in the public sector appear to have a different career path than their counterparts in the private sector. In the latter context, leaders typically rise through the ranks, so that early in their careers they have performed the work of the unit they represent. As national unions have moved to expand their membership into other domains, for example, teamsters into hospitals, this is becoming less true. But the point still holds that most of the union pros had at one time been unionized workers. In the public sector, this is not typically the case. Representatives may be hired by the state union directly from school or from other occupational backgrounds. In the cases observed, chief negotiators for the teachers' union for example, had never taught or been members of any union before their tenure with the teachers' organizations.

10. The effects of training on the stance of a professional in other settings may offer another explanation for why state mediators act as dealmakers and federal mediators favor orchestration. In his study of psychiatric residents, Light (1980) reports that new residents adopted a "curative" stance with their patients, a stance they had learned in medical school and one that is consistent with popular views of the healing physician. They found, however, that such a stance did not appear to cure their patients. Exposed

during their first year to the tenets of psychoanalytic thought and coached through a supervisor/learner mode of socialization, the residents came to play a more passive role, transferring responsibility to the patients for their own cure. As one resident noted, "This has been a year of learning how to be passive, after having been active for so many years" (p. 123). Indeed, this is the lesson the federal mediators learn through a socialization process that is quite similar. Perhaps a facilitative role is one that requires patient teaching in a cultural context and can only be learned with difficulty on one's own.

11. Bachrach and Baratz (1962) criticize the pluralist tradition in political science for ignoring the ways that community structure "mobilizes bias" in decisionmaking. In particular, they suggest that students of community decisionmaking wrongly begin their analyses with key decisions and neglect the ways that interest groups control the setting of agendas in the first place. This criticism applies equally well to industrial relations, where the issues attending agenda formulation have been all but ignored in recent research (Hyman, 1982).

12. This type of behavior was more apparent in those cases where the total contract was reopened and the union's demands were extensive. In these cases the parties really did most of their negotiating in mediation. In three of the cases the issues to be discussed were more focused and the dispute revolved around one major issue—work scheduling in Albion Broadcasting, subcontracting in Carroll University, and COLA in Alfred Corporation. In these cases the major issue was isolated for discussion and management appeared to make compromises they had not originally planned for. To study this bias further would require a comparative analysis of a broader spectrum of cases in order to detect variations of this sort.

13. In the face of taxpayer revolts, local governments have taken a harder bargaining position. Yet it is not only on monetary issues that these revolts have had their impact. Black (1982) reports that management has used its increased bargaining strength to regain control of management prerogatives that it had conceded when times were flush.

14. It is often suggested that the dominance of economic issues in collective-bargaining agendas reflects the political realities of union leadership, that is, leaders pursue those issues they deem are most readily obtainable (Herding, 1972; Hill, 1981) and that can be comparatively judged by members (Hyman and Brough, 1975; Katz and Sabel, 1979). Evidence suggests that although union leaders do seem to place more emphasis on economic issues than their members (Lawler and Levin, 1968), these are issues the rank and file also support (Gershenfeld and Schmidt, 1981; Olson, 1981). It is important to note, however, that members are also concerned about safety, supervision, and quality of work life, matters they believe have not been adequately addressed in collective bargaining by their leaders (Kochan, 1980).

15. It is interesting to note in this regard that the mediator's definition of a well-disciplined committee is one in which only the pro speaks. Thus

committee members who were moved to state their own positions were viewed by the mediator as being out of line (see, for example, the Albion Broadcasting case).

16. In other cultures the institution of mediation, whether formally designated or not, is seen by students of these cultures to complement their societies' structural frameworks (Firth, 1965). Overt forms of conflict contain the seeds of destruction or disruption of a set of relationships upon which society is based. Mediation, by fostering the direct and immediate resolution of disputes, serves to limit the forms and occasions of unrestricted conflict. But mediators do more. Through their tactics, they enunciate and reinforce rules, norms, and cultural values that are the bases for society's kinship relationships. In this way, mediators serve to preserve and maintain the existing social order (Gulliver, 1979). The implications of this perspective and its relationship to bias mobilization in the industrial sector needs to be more systematically explored. Indeed, a research agenda might start with a challenge to the dominant ideology of industrial pluralism and investigate the ways in which the edifice of collective bargaining and associated institutions, for example, the grievance process, serve to maintain the social order and who gains and who loses by such an order.

Appendix

1. The first part of this appendix on field strategies appears in slightly different form in Van Maanen and Kolb (1983).

2. In order to avoid distorting the process of summarizing practices, I chose to present the findings in terms of specific cases with general observations on the entire sample. Each mediation case is in a very real sense unique, and to suggest otherwise would be to misrepresent not only the mediator's understanding but the reality as well.

3. It is quite easy to identify assistance at a crucial time in the analytic venture and ignore the patient assistance, insight, and support of those who saw the project through from its start to its conclusion. My bouts with the data and reports were aided throughout particularly by John Van Maanen and Lotte Bailyn. I hope they learned as much about mediation from me as I learned about the research adventure from them.

Bibliography

Anderson, J., 1981. "Evaluating the Impact of Compulsory Arbitration: A Methodological Assessment." *Industrial Relations* 20:128–137.

Asch, S. E., 1952. *Social Psychology*. Englewood Cliffs, NJ: Prentice-Hall.

Bachrach, P., and M. S. Baratz, 1962. "The Two Faces of Power." *American Political Science Review* 56:947–952.

Bailyn, L., 1977. " Research as a Cognitive Process: Implications for Data Analysis." *Quality and Quantity* 11:97–117.

Barton, A. H., and P. F. Lazarsfeld, 1951. "Qualitative Measurement in the Social Sciences: Classification, Typologies and Indices." In D. Lerner and H. Lasswell, eds., *The Policy Sciences: Recent Developments in Scope and Method*. Stanford: Stanford University Press, pp. 155–192.

Barton, R. F., 1949. *The Kalingas: Their Institutions and Custom Law*. Chicago: University of Chicago Press.

Becker, H. S., 1958. "Problems of Inference and Proof in Participant Observation." *American Sociological Review* 23:652–660.

Becker, H. S., 1973. *Outsiders*. New York: The Free Press.

Becker, H. S., B. Geer, E. Hughes, and A. L. Strauss, 1961. *Boys in White*. Chicago: University of Chicago Press.

Bem, D. J., 1970. *Beliefs, Attitudes and Human Affairs*. Belmont, CA: Brooks/Cole.

Berger, P. L., 1963. *Invitation to Sociology*. Garden City, NY: Doubleday.

Berger, P. L., and T. Luckman, 1966. *The Social Construction of Reality: A Treatise in the Sociology of Knowledge*. New York: Doubleday.

Biddle, B. J., and E. J. Thomas, 1966. *Role Theory*. New York: Wiley.

Black, R., 1982. "Proposition 21/2 and Public Sector Labor Relations: The Issue of Layoffs." Impact 21/2 Working Paper, Massachusetts Institute of Technology, Cambridge, MA.

Blumer, H., 1969. *Symbolic Interaction*. Englewood Cliffs, NJ: Prentice-Hall.

Bourdon, C., 1979. "Pattern Bargaining, Wage Determination and Inflation: Some Preliminary Observations on the 1976–78 Wage Round." In M. Piore, ed., *Unemployment and Inflation*. White Plains, NY: M. E. Sharpe.

Cicourel, A., 1964. *Method and Measurement in Sociology*. New York: The Free Press.

Cicourel, A., 1974. *Cognitive Sociology*. New York: The Free Press.

Coser, L., 1956. *The Functions of Social Conflict*. Glencoe, IL: The Free Press.

Dalton, M., 1959. *Men Who Manage*. New York: Wiley.

Denzin, N. K., 1973. "Self and Society." In J. D. Douglas, ed., *Introduction to Sociology*. New York: Macmillan.

Douglas, Ann, 1962. *Industrial Peacemaking*. New York: Columbia University Press.

Douglas, J. D., 1971. *American Social Order*. New York: The Free Press.

Douglas, J. D., 1973. *Introduction to Sociology*. New York: MacMillan.

Douglas, J. D., 1976. *Investigative Social Research*. Beverly Hills, CA: Sage.

Druckman, D., 1975. "The Influence of Situation in Interparty Conflict." *Journal of Conflict Resolution* 1:69–82.

Dunlop, J., 1957. "Wage Contours." In G. W. Taylor and F. C. Pierson, eds., *New Concepts of Wage Determination*. New York: McGraw-Hill.

Dunlop, J., 1958. *Industrial Relations Systems*. Carbondale: Southern Illinois University Press.

Emerson, J., 1970. "Nothing Unusual Is Happening." In T. Shibutani, ed., *Human Nature and Collective Behavior*. New Brunswick, NJ: Transaction Books.

Evans-Pritchard, E. E., 1940. *The Nuer*. Oxford: Clarendon Press.

Federal Mediation and Conciliation Service, 1975–1978. *Annual Reports*.

Filmer, P., M. Phillipson, D. Silverman, and D. Walsh, 1972. *New Directions in Sociological Theory*. Cambridge, MA: MIT Press.

Filstead, W. J., 1970. *Qualitative Methodology: Firsthand Involvement in the Social World*. Chicago: Markham Press.

Firth, R., 1965. "A Note on Mediators." *Ethnology* 5:386–388.

Fox, A., 1974. *Beyond Contract: Work, Power and Trust Relations*. London: Faber and Faber.

Freeman, M., 1957. *Chinese Family and Marriage in Singapore*. London: HMSO.

Frees, J., 1976. "Dispute Management in Labor Relations: The Mediation Process." Unpublished dissertation, University of Minnesota.

Frohman, L. A., and M. D. Cohen, 1970. "Compromise and Loyalty: Comparing the Efficiency." *Behavioral Science* 15:180–183.

Garfinkel, H., 1967. *Studies in Ethnomethodology*. Englewood Cliffs, NJ: Prentice-Hall.

Gerhart, P., and J. Drotning, 1980. "Dispute Settlement and the Intensity of Mediation." *Industrial Relations* 19:352–359.

Gershenfeld, W., and S. Schmidt, 1981. "Officer, Member, and Steward Priorities for Local Unions: Congruities, Differences." *Proceedings: Industrial Relations Research Association*, 227–236.

Glaser, B. G., and A. J. Strauss, 1967. *The Discovery of Grounded Theory: Strategies for Qualitative Research*. Chicago: Aldine.

Goffman, E., 1959. *The Presentation of Self in Everyday Life*. New York: Doubleday.

Goffman, E., 1961. *Encounters: Two Studies in the Sociology of Interaction*. Indianapolis: Bobbs-Merrill.

Goffman, E., 1963. *Behavior in Public Places*. New York: The Free Press.

Goffman, E., 1967. *Interaction Ritual*. New York: Doubleday.

Goffman, E., 1971. *Relations in Public*. New York: Harper and Row.

Goffman, E., 1974. *Frame Analysis*. New York: Harper and Row.

Gulliver, P. H., 1977. "On Mediators." In J. Hammett, ed., *Social Anthropology and Law*. New York: Academic Press.

Gulliver, P. H., 1979. *Disputes and Negotiations: A Cross Cultural Perspective*. New York: Academic Press.

Herding, R., 1972. *Job Control and Union Structure*. Rotterdam: Rotterdam University Press.

Hill, S., 1981. *Competition and Control at Work*. Cambridge, MA: MIT Press.

Hornstein, H. S., 1965. "The Effects of Different Magnitudes of Threat upon Interpersonal Bargaining." *Journal of Experimental Social Psychology* 1:282–293.

Hughes, E. C., 1958. *Men and Their Work*. Glencoe, IL: The Free Press.

Hughes, E. C., 1971. *The Sociological Eye*. Chicago: Aldine.

Hyman, R., 1978. "Pluralism, Procedural Consensus and Collective Bargaining." *British Journal of Industrial Relations* 16:16–40.

Hyman, R., 1982. "Review of Thomas Kochan's Collective Bargaining and Industrial Relations." *Industrial Relations* 21:100–113.

Hyman, R., and I. Brough, 1975. *Social Values and Industrial Relations*. Oxford: Blackwell.

Indik, B., B. Goldstein, J. Chernick, and M. Berkowitz, 1966. *The Mediator: Background Self Image and Attitudes*. Rutgers, NJ: Institute of Management and Labor Relations.

International Labor Office (ILO), 1973. *Conciliation in Industrial Disputes*. Geneva: International Labor Office.

Janis, I. R., 1972. *Victims of Groupthink*. Boston: Houghton Mifflin.

Katz, D., and R. Kahn, 1978. *The Social Psychology of Organizations*. New York: Wiley.

Katz, H., and C. Sabel, 1979. "Wage Rules: A Theory of Wage Determination." Paper presented at the American Economic Association Meetings.

Kauffman, B. E., 1978. "The Propensity to Strike in American Manufacturing." *Proceedings: Industrial Relations Research Association*, 419–426.

Kelly, H. H., 1966. "A Classroom Study of the Dilemmas in Interpersonal Negotiations." In K. Archibald, ed., *Strategic Interaction and Conflict*. Berkeley, CA: Institute of International Studies.

Kerr, C., 1955. "Industrial Conflict and Its Mediation." *American Journal of Sociology* 60:230–245.

Kerr, C., J. Dunlop, F. Harbison, and C. Myers, 1960. *Industrialism and Industrial Man*. Cambridge, MA: Harvard University Press.

Kheel, T., 1979. "Conflict Resolution—Or Agreement Making? . . . An Interview with Theodore Kheel." *Personnel* 56:28–37.

Kochan, T., 1975. "City Government Bargaining: A Path Analysis." *Industrial Relations* 14:90–101.

Kochan, T., 1980. *Collective Bargaining and Industrial Relations*. Homewood, IL: Richard D. Irwin.

Kochan, T., and T. Jick, 1978. "The Public Sector Mediation Process." *Journal of Conflict Resolution* 22:209–241.

Kolb, D., 1977. "The Mediator's Taxonomy of People in Mediation." Working Paper WP 929-77, Sloan School of Management, Cambridge, MA.

Kolb, D., 1981. "Roles Mediators Play." *Industrial Relations* 20:1–17.

Kolb, D., 1983. "Strategy and the Tactics of Mediation." *Human Relations* 36:247–268.

Kolb, D., and J. Van Maanen, forthcoming. "Problem Definition and Policy Research: Reflections on the Meaning and Use of Collective Bargaining Procedures in the Public Sector." *Administration and Society*.

Kressel, K., 1972. *Labor Mediation: An Exploratory Survey*. Albany, NY: Association of Labor Mediation Agencies.

Krislov, J., J. F. Mead, and J. F. B. Goodman, 1972. "Attitudes toward Mediation: U.S., Great Britain, and Ireland." *Monthly Labor Review* 98:55–59.

Landsberger, H., 1955. "Interaction Process Analysis of Professional Behavior: A Study of Labor Mediation in 12 Labor Management Disputes." *American Journal of Sociology* 57:566–575.

Landsberger, H., 1960. "The Behavior and Personality of the Labor Mediator." *Personnel Psychology* 13:329–347.

Lawler, E., and E. Levin, 1968. "Union Officers' Perceptions of Members' Pay Preferences." *Industrial and Labor Relations Review* 21:509–517.

Lester, R., 1958. *As Unions Mature* Princeton: Princeton University Press.

Liebowitz, J., 1972. "Public Sector Mediation: Some Observations on Techniques." *Journal of Collective Negotiations in the Public Sector* 1:91–96.

Light, D., 1980. *Becoming Psychiatrists: The Professional Transformation of Self*. New York: W. W. Norton.

Lipset, S. M., M. A. Trow, and J. S. Coleman, 1956. *Union Democracy*. Glencoe, IL: The Free Press.

Long, G., and P. Feuille, 1974. "Final Offer Arbitration: 'Sudden Death' in Eugene." *Industrial and Labor Relations Review* 27:186–203.

Lovell, H., 1950. "The Mediation Process." Unpublished doctoral dissertation, Massachusetts Institute of Technology.

Lovell, H., 1952. "The Pressure Lever in Mediation." *Industrial and Labor Relations Review* 6:20–30.

Lyman, S., and M. Scott, 1970. *A Sociology of the Absurd*. New York: Meredith.

Maggiolo, W., 1971. *Techniques of Mediation in Labor Disputes*. Dobbs Ferry, NY: Oceana.

Manning, P., 1977. *Police Work: The Social Organization of Policing*. Cambridge, MA: MIT Press.

Manning, P., 1980. *The Narc's Game*. Cambridge, MA: MIT Press.

Martindale, D. A., 1971. "Territorial Dominance Behavior in Dyadic Verbal Interactions." *Proceedings of the 79th Annual Convention of the APA* 6:305–306.

Mather, L., and B. Yngvesson, 1979. "Triads and the Transformation of Conflict." Paper presented at the Law and Society Association.

McClellan, L., and P. Obermeyer, 1970. "Science or Art: Performance Standards for Mediators." *Labor Law Journal* 21:591–597.

McHugh, P., 1968. *Defining the Situation: The Organization of Meaning in Social Interaction*. New York: Bobbs-Merrill.

Mead, G. H., 1934. *Mind, Self and Society*. Chicago: University of Chicago Press.

Mehan, H., and H. Wood, 1975. *The Reality of Ethnomethodology*. New York: Wiley.

Merton, R., 1957. *Social Theory and Social Structure*. New York: The Free Press.

Meyer, A., 1960. "Functions of the Mediator in Collective Bargaining." *Industrial and Labor Relations Review* 13:159–165.

Michels, R., 1915. *Political Parties*. New York: Dover Press (1959 reprint).

Mills, D. Q., 1978. *Labor Management Relations*. New York: McGraw-Hill.

Moran, R., 1968. "State Subsidized Arbitration." *Labor Law Journal* 19:628–639.

Morgan, G., and L. Smircich, 1980. "The Case for Qualitative Research." *Academy of Management Review* 5:491–501.

Northrup, H. R., 1962. "Mediation: The Viewpoint of the Mediated." *Labor Law Journal* 13:832–841.

Olson, C. A., 1981. "The Relationships between Union Member Preferences for Bargaining Outcomes, Union and Job Satisfaction," *Proceedings: Industrial Relations Research Association*, 236–244.

Parker, H., 1970. "Performance Standards for Mediators." *Labor Law Journal* 21:738–744.

Peters, E., 1958. "The Mediator: A Neutral Catalyst or Leader." *Labor Law Journal* 9:767–769.

Pilisiuk, M., and A. Rappoport, 1964. "Stepwide Disarmament and Sudden Destruction in a Two Person Game." *Journal of Conflict Resolution* 8:36–49.

Pruitt, D. G., and D. F. Johnson, 1970. "Mediation as an Aid to Face Saving in Negotiations." *Journal of Personal and Social Psychology* 14:239–246.

Rabinow, P., and W. M. Sullivan, eds., 1979. *Interpretive Social Science.* Berkeley, CA: University of California Press.

Rehmus, C., 1965. "The Mediation of Industrial Conflict: Note on the Literature." *Journal of Conflict Resolution* 9:118–123.

Robins, E., 1972. "Some Comparisons of Mediation in the Public and Private Sector." In J. J. Lowenberg and M. H. Moskow, eds., *Collective Bargaining.* Englewood Cliffs, NJ: Prentice-Hall.

Robins, E., with T. Denenberg, 1976. *A Guide for Labor Mediators.* Honolulu: University of Hawaii Industrial Relations Center.

Ross, A., 1948. *Trade Union Wage Policy.* Berkeley, CA: University of California Press.

Ross, J., 1976. "Federal Mediation in the Public Sector." *Monthly Labor Review* 99:41–45.

Salaman, G., and K. Thompson, 1980. *Control and Ideology in Organizations.* Cambridge, MA: MIT Press.

Schutz, A., 1962. *Collected Papers, Vol. I.* The Hague: Nijhoff.

Shaw, S., 1969. "The Federal Mediation and Conciliation Service." Unpublished paper, Harvard University.

Shapiro, F., 1970. "Profile: Mediator". *The New Yorker* August 10: 36–58.

Shister, J., 1958. "Collective Bargaining." In N. Chamberlain, F. C. Pierson, and T. Wolfson, eds., *A Decade of Industrial Relations Research 1946–1956.* New York: Harper and Row.

Silverman, D., 1971. *The Theory of Organizations.* New York: Basic Books.

Simkin, William, 1971. *Mediation and the Dynamics of Collective Bargaining.* Washington, DC: Bureau of National Affairs.

Slichter, S., 1949. "The Social Control of Industrial Relations," *Proceedings of the Second Annual Meeting of the Industrial Relations Research Association,* pp. 2–12.

Spradley, J., 1980. *Participant Observation.* New York: Holt, Rinehart and Winston.

Stevens, C., 1954. "Mediation and the Role of the Neutral." In J. Dunlop and N. Chamberlain, eds., *Frontiers of Collective Bargaining.* New York: Harper and Row.

Stevens, C., 1963. *Strategy and Collective Bargaining Negotiations*. New York: McGraw-Hill.

Strauss, A., 1978. *Negotiations*. San Francisco: Jossey-Bass.

Strauss, G., 1977. "Union Government in the U.S.: Research Past and Future." *Industrial Relations* 16:421–475.

Sudnow, D., 1965. "Normal Crimes: Sociological Features of the Penal Code in a Public Defender's Office." *Social Problems* 12:255.

Taylor, C., 1979. "Interpretation and the Sciences of Man." In P. Rabinow and W. M. Sullivan, eds., *Interpretive Social Science*. Berkeley, CA: University of California Press.

Taylor, G., 1948. *Governmental Regulation of Industrial Relations*. Englewood Cliffs, NJ: Prentice-Hall.

Turner, R., 1966. "Role Taking, Role Standpoint and Reference Group Behavior." In B. J. Biddle and E. J. Thomas, eds., *Role Theory*. New York: Wiley.

Van Maanen, J., 1977. "Experiencing Organizations." In J. Van Maanen, ed., *Organizational Careers: Some New Perspectives*. New York: Wiley.

Van Maanen, J., 1979. "The Fact of Fiction in Organizational Ethnography." *Administrative Science Quarterly* 24:539–551.

Van Maanen, J., 1981. "Some Thoughts (and Afterthoughts) on Context, Interpretation, and Organization Theory." Paper presented at the Annual Meeting of the Academy of Management.

Van Maanen, J., and D. Kolb, 1983. "The Professional Apprentice: A Comparative Treatment of Ethnographic Roles." In S. Bacharach, ed., *New Perspectives in Organizational Sociology*. Greenwich, CT: JAI Press.

Van Maanen, J., and E. Schein, 1978. "Toward a Theory of Organizational Socialization." In B. Staw, ed., *Annual Review of Research in Organizational Behavior*, Vol. 1. New York: JIP.

Walton, R., and R. McKersie, 1965. *A Behaviorial Theory of Labor Negotiations*. New York: McGraw-Hill.

Warren, E., 1954. "Mediation and Factfinding." In R. Kornhauser, R. Dubin, and A. Ross, eds., *Industrial Conflict*. New York: McGraw-Hill.

Weaver, S., 1977. *Decision to Prosecute*. Cambridge, MA: MIT Press.

Weick, K., 1979. *The Social Psychology of Organizing*. Reading, MA: Addison-Wesley.

Weschler, I., 1950. "The Personal Factor in Labor Mediation." *Personnel Psychology* 3:114–125.

Wichman, H., 1970. "Effects of Isolation and Communication on Cooperation in a Two-Person Game." *Journal of Personality and Social Psychology* 16:114–120.

Wilensky, H., 1964. "The Professionalization of Everyone." *American Journal of Sociology* 52:137–158.

Zimmerman, D., 1970. "The Practicalities of Rule Use." In J. D. Douglas, ed., *Understanding Everyday Life*. Chicago: Aldine.

Zimmerman, D., and D. L. Weider, 1970. "Ethnomethodology and the Problems of Order." In J. D. Douglas, ed., *Understanding Everyday Life*. Chicago: Aldine.

Index

Accounts (justifications)
of meeting arrangements, 64–65, 67–69
of role, 34–35
"status maintaining," 127, 207–208, 210
of strategy, 80, 86, 102, 111
Aggressiveness
consequences of, 148–149
myth of, 161
Albion Broadcasting (mediator Allen), 17, 18, 20, 29–32, 33–40, 42, 55, 67, 69, 125, 133, 146, 169, 214
Alfred Corporation (mediator Allen), 17, 18, 20, 40, 69, 110, 145, 167, 214
Anderson, J., 212
Art of mediation
basis for claim, 3–4
and enactment, 6–7, 150
and images of practice, 160–161
and role, 5–6, 23
Asch, S., 206

Bachrach, P., 214
Bailyn, L., 191
Baratz, M., 214
Bard Manufacturing (mediator Baker), 18, 42, 69, 80–102, 124, 129, 131, 133, 171
Bargaining committees
in federal practice, 23, 68, 114, 122–124, 165–166, 209
in state practice, 23–24, 34, 64, 65, 70–71, 93–95, 102, 114, 152–153, 167–168, 206, 209
Bargaining power

assessment of, 34, 91–92
balanced assumption of, 164
defined, 91
efforts to equalize, 167–168, 213
Barton, A., 194
Barton, R., 197
Bates, Inc. (mediator Baker), 18, 43, 51–58, 67, 69, 104, 123, 124, 169, 170, 171
Becker, H., 6, 194, 198, 199, 200
Bem, D., 213
Berger, P., 198, 212
Berkowitz, M., 162, 197, 202
Biddle, B., 199, 201
Bilateral bargaining, impressions of, 158–160
Black, R., 214
Blumer, H., 198–199
"Bottom line," 87–88, 117. See also Priorities
Bourdon, C., 92
Brough, I., 164, 212, 214
Building momentum, 111
Building strategy. See also Dealmakers
case examples, 74–79
defined, 79–80
and economic issues, 170–171
and mistakes, 137–142
and negotiators, 117–122, 127–128
on other state cases, 102–104, 105–112
tactics of, 86–89, 91–94, 98–99, 101–102

Calculating costs, 100–101, 169, 170

Carroll University (mediator Carr),
18, 20, 42, 124, 125, 146, 169,
171, 214
Case diagnosis. *See also* Bargaining
power; Chief negotiators;
Patterns
artistic conception of, 3, 6, 150
interpretive categories of, 91–96,
199, 207, 208
and movement tactics, 73–74,
95–96
Caucuses
defined, 48, 56, 203
justification, 64, 68
uses, 58–62
Chernick, J., 162, 197, 202
Chief negotiators. *See also* "Pros"
background, 115–116
defined, 114
interpretations of, 90, 93–95
Cicourel, A., 198, 200
"Closer," 126–127
Cohen, M., 198, 208
Collective bargaining
ideology of, 154–155
and mediation, 2–3, 162–164,
172–173
rituals of, 151, 165
Collegial control
federal mediators, 155–156
state mediators, 159–160, 162
Communications functions, 36–37,
39
Communication tactics
defined, 97
purpose, 98
timing, 98, 110–111
uses, 98, 108–109
Credibility. *See also* Mistakes
of mediators, 135–137, 142–144,
155, 159, 211
of pros, 148
Cultural rules, 156, 160, 199–200

Dalton, M., 199
Dealmakers (dealmaking)
accounts of, 41–42
as bilateral bargaining, 157–159
case description, 25–29
definition, 33–38
and power equalization, 167–168
rationale for, 151–152

risks of, 148–149
Denenberg, T., 46, 197
Denzin, N., 198
Difficult cases, 20, 43–44
Douglas, A., 4, 37, 134, 136, 197,
198, 201, 204, 207, 209, 211
Douglas, J., 198, 200, 210
Drotning, J., 148, 163, 198, 208, 211
Druckman, D., 198
Duke Hospital (mediator Dixon),
18, 20, 42, 69, 123, 124, 145, 165,
210
Dunlop, J., 92, 212

Easy cases, 43–44
Economic issues, dominance of,
158–171, 214
Emerson, J., 210
Enactment, 6–7, 70–71, 199–200
Evaluation of practice, 134–136,
160, 162, 211
Evans-Pritchard, E., 197

Factfinding, 14, 17, 64, 77, 159, 163
Federal Mediation and Concilia-
tion Service (FMCS)
caseload characteristics, 10, 212
field office site, 10–11
jurisdiction, 7–8
philosophy, 154–155
policies and structure, 8–10,
200–201
training, 155
Federal cases. *See* Albion Broad-
casting; Alfred Corporation;
Bard Manufacturing; Bates, Inc.;
Carroll University; Duke
Hospital
Federal mediators. *See*
Orchestrators
Feuille, P., 212
Filstead, W., 194
Firth, R., 215
Fox, A., 164
Freeman, M., 197
Frees, J., 197, 202, 204
Frohman, L., 198, 208

Garfinkel, H., 7, 198, 200, 208
Geer, B., 6, 199, 200
Gerhart, P., 148, 163, 198, 208, 211
Gershenfeld, W., 168, 214

Glaser, B., 199
Goffman, E., 198, 199, 200, 208, 210
Goldstein, B., 162, 197, 202
Goodman, J., 148
Gulliver, P., 73, 197, 206, 207, 215

Helping the pro
and dealmaking, 131–132
defined, 128–129
implications of, 167, 171–172
and orchestrating, 68, 128, 131
tactics, 129–131
Herding, R., 214
Hill, S., 164, 212, 213, 214
Hornstein, H., 198
Hughes, E., 4, 6, 136, 199
Hyman, R., 164, 212, 213, 214

Ideology
in federal practice, 154–157
in industrial relations systems, 212
in state practice, 157–158
Indik, B., 162, 197, 202
Industrial relations community, 156, 160. See also Collegial control
Interagency perceptions, 44, 152–153
Interpretive framework, 5–7, 198–199
and roles, 23–24
and strategies, 90–96, 199, 207
Intervention meeting arrangement
case example, 48–51
correlates of, 54–58
and dealmaking, 70–71
defined, 57
exceptions, 65–67
justifications, 64–65
in state cases, 58–63

Janis, I., 206
Jick, T., 73, 134, 148, 163, 197, 198, 206, 207, 208, 211
Johnson, D., 198, 201
Joint meetings
defined, 48, 203
justification, 67–68, 129, 144, 165
uses, 56–62

Kahn, R., 199

Katz, D., 199
Katz, H., 214
Kauffman, B., 163
Kelly, H., 208
Kerr, C., 134, 163
Kheel, T., 197, 202
Kochan, T., 73, 134, 148, 157, 163, 167, 197, 198, 206, 207, 208, 211, 214
Kolb, D., 17, 156, 208, 213, 215
Kressel, K., 37, 73, 134, 197, 198, 207, 208
Krislov, J., 148

Landsberger, H., 197, 201
Lawler, E., 214
Lazarsfeld, P., 194
Learning issues in dispute
during case, 56, 58, 60, 86–87
prior to case, 47
problems in, 138–139
as separate activity, 105–106
Levin, E., 214
Liebowitz, J., 16, 148
Light, D., 213
Long, G., 212
Lovell, H., 197, 201
Luckman, T., 198
Lyman, S., 136, 198, 200, 208, 213

McClellan, L., 135
McHugh, P., 207
McKersie, R., 211, 212
Maggiolo, W., 46, 47, 197
Manning, P., 198, 199, 200, 203, 207, 211
Martindale, D., 198
Mather, L., 208
Mead, G. H., 148, 198, 199
Mediation
agencies, 200 (see also FMCS; State agency)
as continuation of negotiations, 34, 39, 71
contribution to industrial peace, 34, 43, 162–163, 211
definition, 2–3
guides, 46–47, 197
history, 1–2, 7–8, 11–12
institutional role of, 2–3, 161–173, 197, 215
stages of, 37, 73

Mediation (continued)
study of, 4, 197–198, 201, 208
Meeting arrangements. See also Intervention meeting arrangement;
Negotiating meeting arrangement
in other studies, 204–206
and role enactment, 70–71
Meetings
strategic use of, 46–47, 70–71
types (see Caucuses; Joint meetings; Off-the-record meetings;
Separate meetings)
Mehan, H., 200
Merton, R., 199
Message carrying, 35, 38
care in, 144
mistakes made in, 139
Methodology, 17–22, 176–196
Meyer, A., 3, 197
Mills, D., 153
Mistakes
defined, 136–137, 211
and evaluation, 135–136, 211
in federal practice, 143–147
implications, 142–143, 148–149,
213
in state practice, 137–142
Mobilization of bias
and collective bargaining,
172–173
defined, 163–164, 214
economic bias, 168–171
institutional bias, 171–172
management bias, 164–168
and mediation, 172–173
Moran, R., 11
Morgan, G., 199
Movement by issue, 101, 103,
106–107, 109–110
Movement by proposal, 100, 104,
107, 129, 208
Movement tactics. See also Communication tactics; Helping the
pro; Procedural tactics; Substantive tactics
cycle of, 73–74
defined, 96
patterns of use, 100–104, 106–109
on single-issue cases, 109–111
timing of, 101, 110–111
types, 96–100

Multilateral bargaining, 157–158

Narrowing strategy. See also
Orchestrators
case example, 80–85
defined, 85–86, 206
and economic issues, 169–170
on federal cases, 104–112
and management interests,
164–165
and mistakes, 143–147
and negotiators, 122–129
Needs of the parties and role,
34–35
Negotiating meeting arrangement
case example, 51–54
correlates of, 54–58
defined, 57
exceptions, 69–70
on federal cases, 58–63
and helping the pro, 129–130
justifications, 67–68
and orchestrating role, 70–71
Northrup, H., 210

Obermeyer, P., 135
Observor's role, 20, 184–187
Off-the-record meetings
defined, 48
justifications, 56, 65, 68
and pros, 117, 118–120, 124, 133
uses, 56–57, 62–63
Olson, C., 168, 214
Orchestrators (orchestrating)
accounts of, 40, 42–43
case description, 29–32
definition, 33–38
institutionalized practice,
154–157
and management interests,
166–167
risks of, 147–149
Organizational contexts, 15–16

Parker, H., 135
Passive role, 24, 41, 44, 147
Patterns
assessment of, 92–93, 106–109,
169
defined, 90–91
and economic issues, 171–172
as movement tactic, 97–101

objectivity of, 92, 118
and pros, 118, 120, 125, 171–172
Pilisiuk, M., 198
Pressure tactics, 201
risks of, 141–142
as strike substitute, 158
Priorities
defined, 87
misgauged, 139–141
need to know, 87–88, 103
and pros, 117–118, 123–125
tactics to learn, 88–90, 104,
106–107
Procedural tactics
defined, 97, 100
purpose, 98–99
timing, 98–99, 110–111
uses, 98–99, 108–109
Professional work, 3–4, 134–136,
199–200
"Pros." See also "Closer"; Unprofessional behavior;
in building strategy, 117–122
and committees (see Trust)
defined, 115–117, 118, 122
evaluations of mediators, 143,
144, 148
incidence, 116
and mediatiors, 115–117, 155–156,
159–160, 162, 210, 212
in narrowing strategy, 34, 94–95,
122–128 (see also Helping the
pro)
Pruitt, D., 198, 201
Public sector-private sector
competing interests in, 167
contrasts between, 16, 43, 148,
152–154, 157, 159, 213

Rabinow, P., 199
Rappoport, A., 198
"Real work," 169
Reed School Committee (mediator
Richards), 19, 20, 25–29, 33–40,
141, 158
Regis School Committee (mediator
Richards), 19, 38–40, 106, 118,
120, 121, 133, 140, 158
Rehmus, C., 197, 206
Robins, E., 16, 46, 148, 197
Roles. See also Dealmakers;
Orchestrators

behavioral indicators, 35–38
cognitive perspectives, 34–35
definition, 5–6, 24–25
development during case, 37–38
and interpretive theory, 5–7, 199
and meeting arrangements, 54–
56, 70–71
misreading, 137–138
taking spokesman's role, 145–146
Ross, A., 92, 148
Ross, J., 148
Rutgers School Committee (mediator Richards), 19, 20, 38, 40, 58,
64, 66, 117, 118, 120, 139, 141,
142, 170

Sabel, C., 214
Salaman, G., 212
Sample characteristics, 17–20
Schein, E., 155
Schmidt, S., 168, 214
Schutz, A., 199, 208
Scott, M., 136, 198, 200, 208, 213
Scripps School Committee (media-
tor Shaw), 19, 64, 66, 106, 107,
121, 137, 141, 143, 159
Scripts, 50, 124–125, 127
Separate meetings
defined, 48, 56
justification, 56, 64, 67–68
mistakes arising from, 138–139
uses, 57–59, 166
Settlement rates, 135, 142–143, 147
Shaw, S., 8
Sheridan Firefighters (mediator
Shaw), 17, 19, 41, 48–51, 54–58,
65, 117, 120, 131, 133, 158, 169,
171, 210
Shister, J., 197, 206
Simkin, W., 36, 46, 96, 154, 162,
197, 201, 202, 211
Single-issue case, 40, 107, 110
risks in, 145–146
Slichter, S., 162
Smircich, L., 199
Socialization, 155, 213–214
Spradley, J., 207
State agency
caseload characteristics, 13–15,
142
jurisdiction, 11–12, 14
office site, 14–15

State agency (continued)
  policy and structure, 12–15,
    161–162
  training, 159, 161
State cases. See Reed School Com-
    mittee; Regis School Committee;
    Rutgers School Committee;
    Scripps School Committee; Sher-
    idan Firefighters; Taft School
    Committee; Tulane Firefighters;
    Ulster School Committee; Ur-
    bana Housing Authority; Van-
    derbilt School Committee
State mediators. See Dealmakers
Stevens, C., 47, 73, 165, 198, 201
Strategic cycle, 73–74
Strategies. See also Building strat-
    egy; Narrowing strategy
  defined, 72–73 (see also Tactics)
  and mistakes, 135–136
  and role, 72–73
Strauss, A., 6, 199, 200
Strauss, G., 153
Strikes
  and bargaining power, 91–92
  mediation as compensations for,
    64, 157–158
  pressure from threat, 145,
    151–152, 153, 167
  prevention by narrowing, 129
Substantive tactics. See also Calcu-
    lating costs
  defined, 97
  purpose, 98
  timing, 98–99, 110–111
  uses, 98–100, 106–109
Sudnow, D., 199
Sullivan, W., 199

Tactics
  defined, 72–73
  to help pro, 128–131
  to learn priorities, 88–90, 104,
    106–107
  and monetary issues, 166–171
  to move parties, 96–102, 106–109
Taft School Committee (mediator
    Thomas), 19, 20, 41, 64, 102–104,
    139, 143, 171, 209
Taylor, C., 200
Taylor, G., 164
Thomas, E., 199, 201

Thompson, K., 212
Timing, 34–35, 102, 125
  and helping the pro, 129
  and lowering aspirations, 110–111
Trust
  help with trust, 130–132
  between mediator and pro, 125,
    127, 156
  between pro and committee, 68,
    121, 124–125, 129–131, 133
Tulane Firefighters (mediator
    Thomas), 19, 20, 66, 74–79,
    86–102, 121, 140, 141, 158, 170,
    207
Turner, R., 199, 200

Ulster School Committee (media-
    tor Unger), 19, 20, 41, 64, 66,
    106, 117, 118, 121, 132, 137, 138,
    141, 142, 158, 172
Unprofessional behavior, 120–121,
    126–127, 146–147. See also Ac-
    counts, "status maintaining"
Urbana Housing Authority (media-
    tor Unger), 19, 20, 120–121, 210

Vanderbilt School Committee (me-
    diator Vance), 19, 20, 42, 106,
    132
Van Maanen, J., 155, 199, 213, 215

Walton, R., 211, 212
Warren, E., 201
Weaver, S., 203
Weick, K., 6, 199, 206
Weider, L., 200
Weschler, I., 197
Wichman, H., 198
Wilensky, H., 4
Wood, H., 200
Work rules, 169–171

Yngvesson, B., 208

Zimmerman, D., 200